THE
CANCER
REFERENCE
BOOK

THE CANCER REFERENCE BOOK

Direct and Clear Answers to Everyone's Questions

Paul M. Levitt
Elissa S. Guralnick
with

Dr. A. Robert Kagan
Dr. Harvey Gilbert

A DELTA BOOK

A DELTA BOOK
Published by
Dell Publishing Co., Inc.
1 Dag Hammarskjold Plaza
New York, New York 10017

Reprinted by arrangement with Paddington Press
Printed in the United States of America
First Delta printing—June 1980

And he shall be like a tree planted by the rivers of water,
that bringeth forth his fruit in his season.

Psalm 1.3

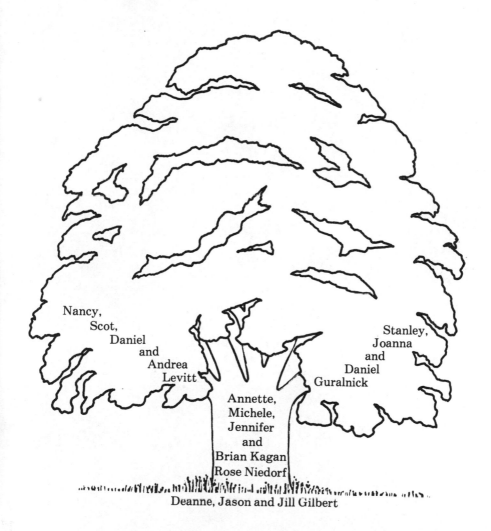

Nancy,
Scot,
Daniel
and
Andrea
Levitt

Stanley,
Joanna
and
Daniel
Guralnick

Annette,
Michele,
Jennifer
and
Brian Kagan
Rose Niedorf

Deanne, Jason and Jill Gilbert

Contents

ACKNOWLEDGMENTS

To produce this book, the authors, like stage directors, have had to ask numerous people to play various parts. Our cast, then, is as follows:

BEHIND THE SCENES

The following doctors from the Southern California Permanente Medical Group (SCPMG): T. Hart Baker, Paul Y. M. Chan, Jack Cooper, Richard Dorazio, Charles Sadoff, Sam Sapin, Philip Schulman, Randy Sharpsteen, James Warden, John Winkley, and Sheldon Wolf.

SCPMG Staff: Lilian Fox, Shirley Gach, Dolores Groseclose, Addi Moore, and Helen Reeves.

UCLA Cancer Center: Dr. Leo Lagasse and Dr. Richard J. Steckel.

University of Southern California Cancer Center: Rod Cramer, Dr. Denman Hammond, Patricia Heidelberger, Dr. John Hisserick, and Dr. Robert McKenna.

Dr. Jerome Block, Harbor General Hospital; Dr. Philip Di Saia, University of California, Irvine; Dr. David Plotkin, Brotman Memorial Hospital; The Rossi Fund.

Prof. Michael Bell, University of Colorado; Vice-Chancellor Robert Borchers, University of Colorado; Dr. Ernest Borek, American Cancer Research Center; Dr. Louis Fink, University of Colorado School of Medicine; Elsi Frederiksen, teacher; Harry C. Froede, pharmacist; Prof. Arnold J. Hennig, University of Colorado; Dr. F. G. Irwin, surgeon (retired); Benjamin and Jeanette Levitt; Sandra Levitt, social worker; Dr. Brian Lieberman, St. Mary's Hospital, Manchester, England; Prof. Siegfried Mandel, University of Colorado; Dr. William A. Robinson, University of Colorado School of Medicine; Bud and Dell Rockoff; Eva Schagrin; Dr. Stuart Schneck, University of Colorado School of Medicine; Prof. William Segal, University of Colorado.

American Cancer Society; Science Reference Library, Bayswater, London; St. Christopher's Hospice, London; University of Colorado Council on Research and Creative Work.

STROLLING PLAYERS

Wellcome Library, Euston Road, London
  With thanks for enabling the authors to conduct research in what must surely be the most comfortable and comprehensive medical library in the world.
Southern California Permanente Medical Group (SCPMG) Cancer Committee
  for insisting that to be valuable a treatment must improve the patient's quality of life.
Herman Nussbaum, M.D. at SCPMG
  for asking the right questions at the right times.
Aroor Rao, M.D. at SCPMG
  for practicing medicine with perception and meticulousness.
George Sleight, M.D. at SCPMG
  for bringing sympathy and love to the care of children.
Maurice Yettra, M.D. at SCPMG
  for maintaining that quality of life must be the measure of all treatment.
Christine Bernard, agent
  for serving not only as agent, but also as friend.
W. E. Briggs, Dean, University of Colorado
  for supporting the authors both morally and financially.
Douglas Burger, Professor, University of Colorado, and
Charles Evans, Professor, University of Colorado
  for lending a helping hand.
Stanley M. Guralnick, Professor, Colorado School of Mines
  for collecting valuable materials and keeping the home fires burning.
Don Mullins, supervisor, Colorado Regional Cancer Information Service
  for making available to the authors a storehouse of information.
Robert Rosefsky, author
  for introducing the authors to Paddington Press and to the ways of commercial publishing.

Ruth Schrock, friend and colleague
   for proofreading with care and completeness.
Arnold Wesker, playwright
   for encouraging and helping at all times.

LEADING ROLES

Theodora Arnold, Supervisor of Radiation Therapy at SCPMG, and
Barbara Coleman, Radiation Therapy Technician at SCPMG
   With thanks for administering with love and understanding to the
   psychological needs of patients.
Helene Brown, Executive Director, Community Cancer Control, Los
Angeles
   for crusading against worthless cancer therapies.
Emma Dally, Editor, Paddington Press
   for editing this book with sense and sensitivity.
Michael B. Van Scoy-Mosher, M.D., University of Southern California
Cancer Center
   for sharing the results of his important work on chemotherapy.
Juan A. del Regato, M.D., University of Southern Florida College of
Medicine
   for being matchless friend and counselor to Dr. Kagan over the years.
Aladeen Smith, University of Colorado
   for laboring days and nights to help the authors prepare the manu-
   script.
David Prescott, Professor, University of Colorado
   for teaching the authors what it means to be a learned scientist and a
   great gentleman.

WHAT THIS BOOK IS NOT

It is not:

1 A medical textbook

2 A dictionary of cancer terms

3 A history of cancer and cancer treatment

4 A collection of case histories

5 A battle plan for ridding the body of cancer

6 An argument for treating cancer one way and not another

7 A list of miracle cures

8 A formula for coping with a stricken member of the family

9 A recipe for keeping the body free of cancer

10 A forecast of the brave new world to come

WHAT THIS BOOK IS

It is:

1 Questions of importance for anyone interested in cancer

2 Answers of unusual clarity and simplicity

3 Descriptions of cell biology

4 Reports of vital statistics about cancer

5 Particulars of proven cancer treatments

6 Accounts of individual cancers

7 Facts about widespread cancer, hospices, and death

8 Summaries of unproven cancer treatments

9 Surveys of current cancer research

10 Concepts of a technical nature made readable

Introduction

At some point in our lives, all of us are deeply affected by the terrible disease known as cancer. Those who are fortunate enough to escape it themselves will almost certainly face cancer when it strikes a family member or friend. One out of every four people in the United States will ultimately suffer from cancer and one out of every five people will be killed by it. But these grim figures say little about the personal misery, the suffering, and the tragedy of premature death that are all too often the consequences of cancer. We cannot begin to calculate the great cultural, social, and economic losses wrought by this disease.

What is being done to control cancer? Through scientific research over the last twenty-five years we have increased our understanding of the disease – the initial step toward a cure. Through medical research we have achieved improved methods of diagnosis and treatment. But we obviously need to know more. If we are to solve the problem, research is our only hope. How soon the necessary knowledge will be found cannot be said. Research into the unknown is, by the very nature of the enterprise, unpredictable.

Prevention may come sooner than a cure. But prevention will be possible only after the causes of the disease have been identified. Research is steadily discovering these causes. For example, tobacco smoke has been identified as the primary cause of lung cancer. In the United States in 1978, 390,000 people died of cancer. Of these, 92,000 (about 24 percent) died of lung cancer. As a conservative estimate 85,000 of the 92,000 deaths were caused by cigarette smoke. Thus, *one-fifth of all cancer deaths in the United States in 1978 were preventable.* In addition to lung cancer, we can prevent other cancers that are also caused by cigarette smoke – for example, a great many cancers of the mouth, throat, esophagus, and some cancers of the bladder.

The solution to the cancer problem may lie in identifying the causes of cancer and removing them from our environment. After all, it would be far better never to be stricken by the disease than to be stricken and cured – if, indeed, a cure is ever found.

Until cancer can be prevented or cured, people can help themselves by avoiding carcinogens, like cigarette smoke, and by becoming as informed as possible about the disease. People should ask: What is the nature of the disease? What are its causes? What are the methods of treatment now available to cancer patients? Why is cancer difficult to treat and why does a given treatment work one time and not another? What course does the disease take, and how does it cause death?

The answers to these and other questions about cancer have not been readily available to the general public. Many books have been written about the disease, but most are highly technical discussions directed at specialists in biomedical fields. Those few books comprehensible to people with little or no biomedical background do not treat the questions for which they want answers.

This book is different: it asks the most important questions about cancer and answers them as accurately as our current knowledge will permit. Moreover, it does so in direct and simple terms that will be understandable to everyone. Understanding cancer may not prevent the disease, but it may lessen the anxiety and fear that infect cancer patients and their families when they are faced with the unknown.

The writers of this book, professors of English at the University of Colorado, have frequently criticized technical writing as being un-readable. It was their intention, for personal and intellectual reasons, to translate the difficult subject of cancer into language accessible to every-one. In my opinion, they have accomplished their intention admirably.

DAVID M. PRESCOTT
Professor of Molecular, Cellular, and
Developmental Biology
University of Colorado at Boulder
September 1978

1 Cancer

When the Academy of Lyons, France, advertised in 1773 that it was offering a prize for the best answer to the question "What is cancer?" the Academy was expressing the bewilderment of doctors since at least the time of Hippocrates (*c*.460–*c*.370 B.C.), and probably even before the rise of Greek medicine. In the *Ebers Papyrus*, for example, written approximately 3,500 years ago, there is to be found a warning against treating a tumor that "is loathsome and suffers many pustules to come forth." The presumption was that treatment was often fatal. Ancient doctors, in fact, had little success in treating cancer. As Celsus, the first century Roman doctor, observed in his famous *Encyclopaedia*:

> Some physicians used caustic remedies. Some cauterized, and others operated with the knife. The remedies, however, never did any good to anybody. On the contrary, by cauterization the tumors were activated, and grew the faster, until the patient died. When they were cut out they came back after the scar had been formed, and brought death also. To distinguish a benignant tumor that can be cured from a cancer that cannot is hardly possible. All we can do is to watch and see what will happen.

To treat a disease without first understanding its nature almost always produces poor results. It was not until the Greek doctor Galen (*c*.130–200 A.D.) introduced the idea of humors that the treatment of cancer was based on a theory of cancer. But alas, the theory was wrong.

Galen, influenced by Hippocrates, proposed that the body contained four fluids or humors that were responsible for a person's health and behavior: blood, phlegm, choler (yellow bile), and melancholy (black bile). When these humors were well balanced, the person was healthy; when they were out of balance, the person suffered from sickness and disease. According to Galen, melancholy people were inclined to have an excess of black bile, which collected in certain places in the body, thickened, and formed tumors, particularly in the lips, the breast, and the tongue. Since Galen regarded cancer as a disease that originated from inside the body, he advised that it be treated internally, with drugs, diets, and bleeding. Although not without its critics, Galen's idea prevailed into the nineteenth century.

Another theory, proposed in the seventeenth century, corresponded with the discovery of the lymphatic vessels. According to this theory, cancerous material was carried by the lymph; if the lymph thickened or coagulated, a tumor resulted. A tumor was therefore coagulated lymph. In the nineteenth century, the introduction of cell theory brought with it the hypothesis that cancer originated in the cells of the connective tissue; if the cells were injured or irritated they grew out of control.

The twentieth century has been no less inventive than previous centuries in proposing unworkable theories. As the distinguished Berlin surgeon August Bier remarked, "If a great scientist at the end of a brilliant career wants to make a fool of himself, he takes up the problem of cancer."

THE NATURE OF CANCER

What is cancer?

A misguided cell or cells. Cancer is the growing process gone berserk.

The body is composed of cells. All human life, in fact, begins with the fertilization of a female egg cell by a sperm cell. In nine months, the fertilized egg cell divides billions of times to form a baby. Think of a chess board. If one cell, placed in the first square, were doubled in the second square, and the doubling continued in each succeeding square, for the length and width of the board, the number of cells in the last square would be astronomical. In similar fashion, human cells divide from infancy through adolescence to form an adult. But once adulthood is reached, the cells divide at a much slower rate, reproducing only to maintain the status quo: that is, only to heal wounds and replace cells that have died. In other words, at maturity the body produces cells not in order to grow, but in order to maintain a steady state.

All reproduction, growth, and healing occur through cell division. But it is a mystery how cells know when to stop dividing, know when to stop forming the baby or the adult. Why, for example, does an arm or a finger not keep on growing – endlessly? The answer to that question is unclear because scientists do not know what turns cell division on and off. Similarly, they do not know why the body automatically stops mending itself once an injury is healed. Apparently, cells communicate with one another. They send out messages to stop the body from forming a finger, or mending a broken bone. But for reasons that no one can explain, a cancerous cell will, like Jack's beanstalk, keep on growing; it will divide endlessly, at the expense of its neighbors, until the entire area is overrun with runaway (cancerous) cells.

Does cancer occur only in humans?

No. Plants and animals, including insects, fish, and birds, also develop cancer. In fact, much of what we know about cancer comes from animal research, since research on human beings is often not allowed.

Is cancer one disease or many?

Many. There are more than 100 different types of cancer: some originate in the muscle and bone (sarcomas), some in the skin or in the linings of organs (carcinomas), some in the blood (leukemias), some in the lymphatic system (lymphomas); some develop slowly, some quickly; some grow like a balloon, some spread like a lava flow; some respond to treatment, some do not; some are mushy, some fibrous; some are common in the young, some in the old; some appear more often in one country or occupation, some in another.

What are the similarities among the different cancers?

(i) All cancerous cells are descended from a normal cell; (ii) cancerous cells divide more often than the normal cells from which they are descended; (iii) cancerous cells, unlike normal cells, do not serve a useful function; (iv) cancerous cells live longer than normal cells; (v) cancerous cells when observed under a microscope tend to have a disordered appearance; (vi) cancerous cells – unlike normal cells, which stay in their own territory – invade neighboring tissue; (vii) cancerous cells tend to leave the original site of the cancer and spread to distant parts of the body.

Is all uncontrolled growth cancer?

No. To some degree, hair grows out of control, as well as nails and men's beards. But hair and nail cells, unlike cancerous cells, have a specific function and do not spread to other parts of the body.

Why doesn't cancer, like a bad cold, eventually go away?

Because cancerous cells by some unknown process can immobilize the body's immune system, which is the system that fights disease; and because cancerous cells, if they die at all, die at a much slower rate than normal cells.

The body is always manufacturing cells: approximately $2\frac{1}{2}$ million cell divisions per second just to provide red blood cells, and approximately 25 million cell divisions per second to keep us alive. These divisions occur because cells are always dying, and the death of one cell requires the birth of another. But imagine how clogged the body would become if new cells were born before old cells died. This is what happens when a person has cancer. The cancerous cells, because they live much longer than normal cells and divide recklessly, keep on multiplying and spreading without end, crowding normal cells, until the organs of the body are choked to death.

Cancerous cells, scientists have found, are immortal. For example, the descendants of the HeLa cell – a cancerous cell that was removed in 1952 for research purposes from the uterus of a dying woman – are still alive in laboratories today.

How does cancer kill a person?

Cancer kills: (i) by causing a general weakening of the body (cachexia) until the body fails; or (ii) by crippling particular organs – for example, the kidneys – so that they cannot function; or (iii) by exerting pressure on the skull and brain; or (iv) by obstructing an air passage or a major blood vessel; or (v) by destroying the blood coagulants so that any cut or injury is subject to hemorrhage; or (vi) by blocking the immune system so that the body cannot fight disease – for example, pneumonia.

There are other less frequent causes of death not included here. As a rule, though, most cancer victims die from cachexia or from the inability of their cancer-weakened bodies to fight other diseases.

What is a tumor?

Any swelling or enlargement that does not serve a useful purpose in the body is called a tumor. The swelling can be caused by inflammation, hemorrhage, excess fluid (edema), or abnormal growths – for example, a cyst.

Are all cancers tumorous? What about leukemia?

Although not tumorous, leukemia is a form of cancer. In leukemia, the white blood cells grow out of control and lose their ability to fight disease.

Leukemia, which affects males more often than females, accounts for approximately 8 percent of all cancers. Acute leukemia is the most common cancer in children and accounts for approximately 32.5 percent of all childhood cancers. (For further details, see the section on The Blood in chapter three.)

Are all tumors cancerous?

No. Tumors are either benign or malignant. Benign means favorable, gracious, kindly. Malignant means harmful, hateful, cancerous.

What is the difference between a benign tumor and a malignant tumor?

A benign tumor is an abnormal growth that is almost always enclosed in a fibrous capsule and does not spread to other parts of the body. A malignant tumor – which most people call a cancer – is rarely encapsulated and almost always has the ability to spread.

Although a benign tumor can grow to a very large size – some have been known to weigh as much as ninety pounds – it is rarely fatal. For a benign tumor to kill a person, the tumor must begin in a vital place where there is little room to grow and no chance for the surgeon to operate – for example, in some areas of the brain. The patient then dies from the disabling pressure exerted on the brain by the tumor.

Where does a cancer begin?

In the cells. Every part of the body is composed of cells, which form tissues. Cancer is classified by the type of tissue in which it originates.

ORIGIN	MAJOR CANCER TYPE
1 Connective tissue and muscles: such as bone and cartilage	Sarcoma
2 Lining tissue: such as tissue that makes up the skin or lines the intestine, kidney, mouth, uterus, lung, and other organs	Carcinoma
3 Blood-forming tissue: in the bone marrow and lymph nodes	Leukemia
4 Lymphatic tissue	Lymphoma

The major types of cancer are further divided into sub-types, not included here.

Can more than one cancer begin in the same area at the same time?

Whatever causes one cell to become malignant can cause other cells to become malignant at the same time. Although cancer usually arises from one misguided cell, on rare occasions several cells may become malignant at the same time, causing separate tumors. These tumors are called *multiple primary cancers*. For example: cancer of the colon often occurs as two or more tumors; cancer of the larynx is sometimes accompanied by cancer of the lung; cancer of the skin may develop in several places at once.

What is the "time bomb" effect?

The conversion of a normal cell to a cancerous cell is a slow genetic process that usually takes many years. Cancers that will appear in the year 2000 are being caused *now*. Unlike infectious diseases, cancer does not appear until long after a person has been exposed to the agents that cause it. The radiation a person is exposed to now, for example, may cause cancer in ten to fifty years; or the job a person has at age eighteen may be the cause of a cancer he develops at age sixty-five. This delay between cause and effect is called the "time bomb" effect.

How fast does cancer grow?

Cancer not only *grows* in the original site, but also *spreads* to other sites. Some cancers take twenty or thirty years just to appear. Once they have done so, they grow and spread at different rates. For example, one type of skin cancer – basal cell cancer – grows slowly and rarely spreads; while another type of skin cancer – melanoma – grows quickly and often spreads. Basal cell cancer, in other words, is a low malignancy cancer; and melanoma is a high malignancy cancer. Between these two extremes is a great variety of growth and spread rates.

How does a cancer spread?

Cancer spreads when cells from a cancerous site travel beyond that site. The cells may be spread slowly or quickly by: (i) invading neighboring tissue with amoeba-like movements; (ii) traveling through the lymphatic vessels to the lymph nodes (see note on p. 22); (iii) traveling through the veins to other parts of the body, particularly to the lungs, the bones, and the liver; (iv) invading a body cavity, particularly the abdominal cavity or the chest cavity.

The last three types of spread lead to secondary growths (metastases) in distant parts of the body.

Secondary growths are similar to transplants. Under a microscope, secondary growths may have some of the same fingerprints (structure and secretions) as the primary growth. For this reason, when a secondary growth is discovered before the primary growth, the doctor may be able to tell where the cancer has come from. If, for example, the offspring of a cancerous skin cell (melanoma) has spread to the lungs, the doctor can tell from the presence of skin pigment in the lungs, and from the structure of the cell, that the cancer in the lung is a secondary growth and that the primary growth is a melanoma.

Why doesn't the body's immune system destroy cancerous cells?

To some extent it does, at least in the early stages. But cancerous cells may secrete a substance that eventually blocks the immune system. What this substance is or how it works, scientists have been unable to discover. The substance that allows cancerous cells to disable the immune system is called the "Blocking Factor."

Why are cancerous cells bad cells?

The human body is an enormous factory which, in the course of a day, uses up billions of parts. These parts are called cells. Each cell in the body has a specific function. Some cells carry oxygen, some produce

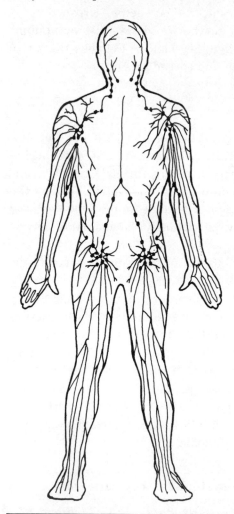

THE LYMPHATIC SYSTEM

Note: The lymphatic system is a drainage system that cleanses the fluid between cells and deposits the wastes from that fluid into the body's blood (circulatory) system. Cancers of the lining tissue (carcinomas) most often spread via the lymphatic system.

blood, some become skin, some build bone, and so on. When cells die, new cells take their place. The body is always manufacturing new cells or parts to replace the old.

But sometimes the manufacturing process goes wrong: one cell becomes defective, or cancerous, and all the descendants of that cell inherit the defect. These cancerous descendants are unable to do the work of healthy cells because cancerous cells are non-functional (un-differentiated); that is, they do not perform the specific function they were meant to perform, like carrying oxygen, or producing blood, or making skin, or building bone. Cancerous cells are faulty parts. They do not work – so the body is denied the working parts that it needs in order to function properly. Imagine a chain minus some links or a gear minus some teeth: cancerous cells are such distortions. And since cancerous cells not only spread, but also reproduce more often and live longer than normal cells, the cancerous cells take over and ruin the body with defective parts.

THE CAUSES OF CANCER

Is cancer a modern disease?

Although often considered a modern disease, cancer is probably as old as the most primitive animals and plants. In any organism composed of numerous cooperating cells, one of those cells may begin to divide wildly at the organism's expense. One of those cells, in other words, may become cancerous. Cancer, then, has very likely occurred in all but the most primitive forms of life. Fossils more than 60 million years old show that cancer afflicted the dinosaurs; and a skeleton from half a million years ago reveals that the Java ape-man suffered cancer of the thighbone. By the time of the early Egyptians, Greeks, and Romans, cancer was known as a common disease that men tried to cure with medication and surgery. Greek doctors, in fact, gave cancer its name: the word "cancer" means sea crab in Greek and was used to describe cancer of the breast, which, in its advanced stages, has the appearance of a central lump with lines (or claws) extending from it. Hence cancer is not peculiar to the twentieth century.

Why is cancer prevalent in the modern world?

Because people have polluted their environment with cancer-causing agents, and because more and more people are living long enough to develop what is primarily a disease of old age.

Can cancer be eradicated from the earth?

Probably not, since no means of prevention can guarantee the good behavior of every dividing cell in the world. Some cells will always become unruly and divide without regard for the organism in which they grow, just as some people will become unlawful and act without regard for the society in which they live.

Nevertheless, people can significantly reduce the rate of cancer by preventing the pollution of earth, air, food, and water.

What are the known causes of cancer?

Radiation, chemicals, viruses, and heredity.

Radiation: How do scientists know that radiation causes cancer?

They know that the cancer rate among people who have been exposed to large doses of radiation rises dramatically. Sailors and farmers, for example, often develop skin cancers on those parts of the body continually exposed to the sun's radiation. The survivors of Hiroshima and Nagasaki, having been exposed to radiation from atom bombs, suffer high rates of leukemia and other cancers. Similarly, people who have been present at test explosions of nuclear devices suffer higher than normal rates of cancer. So, too, do radiologists. In fact, in the early days of X-rays, before the dangers of radiation were sufficiently appreciated, salesmen and technicians developed numerous cancers from demonstrating or using X-ray equipment without adequate protection.

Proof that radiation causes cancer comes from experiments in which X-rays, radioactive substances, and ultraviolet light have been used to induce cancer in test animals.

Radiation: How does radiation cause cancer?

No one knows, just as no one knows exactly how in some cases radiation cures cancer. Doctors know only that radiation – which is nothing more than highly active invisible beams of energy – damages the cells it touches. Presumably, cells exposed to radiation either die or undergo a genetic change. If radiation alters the genes that control reproduction, the cells may become cancerous.

Radiation: What are the common sources of radiation?

Ultraviolet rays from the sun and cosmic rays from outer space are the most common sources of radiation. Another common source is the X-ray machine, used to take routine diagnostic X-rays of the teeth, bones, and body.

Radiation: How can people protect themselves from radiation?

By thoughtfully limiting the amount of sun they take and the number of X-rays they receive.

Sunbathing should be moderated in simple ways. Never sunbathe between 11 A.M. and 1 P.M., when the ultraviolet rays of the sun are strongest; and never sunbathe without first applying a lotion that screens out ultraviolet light. These rules are especially important for fair-skinned people, who lack skin pigment (melanin) to protect them from sunburn.

X-rays should be used only when necessary. Patients should insist that doctors justify the use of X-rays for diagnosis or treatment. Consider: numerous thyroid cancers are now appearing in adults who, as children during the 1920s, 30s, or 40s, had X-ray treatment of the thymus gland. Of course, patients should not refuse X-rays that are strongly recommended. The benefits of X-rays, when they are properly used, far outweigh the risks. To refuse X-rays when they are needed is as foolish as to use them without justification.

Chemicals: How do scientists know that chemicals cause cancer?

From observation and experiment. In 1775, Percival Pott observed that cancer of the scrotum was common in chimney sweeps (small boys who cleaned creosote and ashes out of chimneys while wriggling naked through soot-filled chimney stacks). One hundred years later, Richard von Volkmann observed that cancer of the skin was common on the hands and arms of tar-workers. And in 1895, Ludwig Rehn recognized that cancer of the bladder was common in aniline dye-workers. Although doctors suspected that these cancers were caused by industrial chemicals, their suspicion was not proved until scientists in the twentieth century finally succeeded in using these chemicals to cause cancer in test animals.

Chemicals: How do chemicals cause cancer?

Since most cancer-causing chemicals damage the structure of genes, they probably cause cancer by damaging the genes responsible for cell reproduction. But it may be that a few chemicals alter the function of these genes, without at all changing their structure. Some cancer-causing chemicals appear to be relatively harmless until they are combined with another chemical (a "co-carcinogen"), which may not in itself be cancer-causing, but which somehow induces the first chemical to cause cancer. Only further research will reveal exactly how chemicals make cells cancerous.

Chemicals: How do scientists know which chemicals cause cancer?

A number of industrial chemicals have been identified as cancer-causing because the people who work with them frequently develop a specific type of cancer. For example, people who work with asbestos frequently develop lung cancer; people who work with benzene frequently develop leukemia.

When scientists suspect that a chemical causes cancer, they conduct extensive experiments. Generally, test animals are exposed to large amounts of the chemical under study. If the test animals develop cancer at a higher than normal rate, scientists conclude that the chemical causes cancer.

Chemicals: Aren't experiments with large doses meaningless?

No. Such experiments should not be ridiculed: they do produce meaningful results. When large doses of a chemical cause cancer in test animals, small doses of the same chemical will also cause cancer; but the cancer occurs less often and may develop more slowly when doses are small.

Chemicals: Why do scientists experiment with large doses instead of small doses?

Because it is convenient and economical to do so. When doses are large, the cancer can be induced in a relatively short period of time, and the experiment can be conducted at the lowest cost with the lowest number of test animals. Since the average experiment with large doses takes three years to complete, costs $250,000, and uses hundreds of test animals, scientists can hardly be criticized for economizing.

Chemicals: Is there an inexpensive test to determine if a chemical is cancer-causing?

The Ames test. Developed over a period of ten years by the Berkeley biochemist Bruce Ames, this test identifies chemicals that alter the genetic structure of cells. Ames contends that such chemicals are cancer-causing, and he is probably right. In a trial of its accuracy, the Ames test has identified as cancer-causing 90 percent of all chemicals actually known to cause cancer. Since the Ames test takes only three days to complete and costs only $200, it promises to become a major tool for testing the more than 20,000 new chemicals that are introduced into the environment each year.

Chemicals: What are the common sources of cancer-causing chemicals?

Tobacco smoke contains cancer-causing chemicals. In fact, smoking is the major cause of lung cancer throughout the world. Of all smokers, those who smoke cigarettes run the highest risk of developing lung cancer; and of cigarette smokers, those who smoke more than two packs a day run thirty times the normal risk of dying from the disease. Cigar or pipe smokers are less likely than cigarette smokers to develop lung cancer; but all smokers are equally threatened by cancers of the mouth, throat, and bladder.

Alcohol may also cause cancer. Heavy drinking, for example, is dangerous because it may lead to cancer of the esophagus. But even more dangerous is heavy drinking and heavy smoking – a combination that is frequently associated with cancers of the esophagus, throat, and mouth. In fact, the cancer risk run by heavy drinkers and smokers is greatly reduced when either the drinking or smoking is stopped.

Many industrial chemicals, like asbestos and benzene, are cancer-causing. In addition, certain drugs, insecticides, and food-additives (for example, dyes and nitrite) are known to cause cancer.

Chemicals: Can people get cancer from the air they breathe?

It depends on where they live and work. The greater the pollution, the greater the risk. Most scientists agree that people live in a sea of cancer-causing chemicals, which are found in the air they breathe, the food they eat, the drugs they take, and even the dyes they use to color their hair. The questions is: how much pollution can the body tolerate? Scientists disagree. The point is: whatever degree of pollution people live with, it is usually too great.

Chemicals: How can people protect themselves from cancer-causing chemicals?

1 By not smoking, and by asking that others smoke only in designated smoking areas.
2 By insisting that industry provide workers with adequate filters and safeguards from exposure to cancer-causing chemicals.
3 By urging that the government ban cigarettes, as well as cancer-causing chemicals in clothing, water, food, and air.

Chemicals: Why doesn't the government ban cancer-causing chemicals and cigarettes?

Although some chemicals have been banned, cigarettes and many other cancer-causing agents are tolerated, primarily for economic and political reasons. Several southern states, for example, depend on tobacco for income. In these states, great numbers of people are employed by the tobacco and related industries: from the planters and farm laborers to the advertisers and distributors. Few politicians will recommend that the federal government discontinue subsidies to the tobacco industry when they know how many voters will be put out of work. Until politicians are willing to lose elections and people are willing to give up their jobs in order to prevent cancer, government action will be timid at best and culpable at worst.

Chemicals: Can't "tobacco states" plant other money crops?

Yes. In recent years there has been talk about replacing tobacco crops with peanuts or cotton. Change, however, comes slowly; and to date almost nothing has been accomplished.

Chemicals: Haven't smokers with lung cancer sued the tobacco industry?

Yes, but with no effect. The tobacco companies print warnings that smoking is harmful, but argue that it is impossible to know whether a person has developed cancer from cigarettes or from some other cause. The law courts, unfortunately, have sided with the tobacco companies.

Viruses: How do scientists know that viruses cause cancer?

From animal research scientists know that viruses can cause cancer in chickens, hamsters, and monkeys. They also know that a virus which is cancer-causing (oncogenic) in one type of animal is usually non-cancer-causing (non-oncogenic) in another type of animal. Adenoviruses, for example, often cause cancer when injected into hamsters; yet these same viruses, which are commonly found in the human throat, almost certainly do not cause cancer in human beings.

Viruses: How do scientists know that viruses cause cancer in human beings?

At least one type of cancer – Burkitt's lymphoma, a cancer of the lymph tissue – occasionally attacks two, three, or four people in a small population; but statistics show that this should occur only one time in a million. Such occurrences have led many scientists to think that Burkitt's lymphoma is caused by a virus: the Epstein-Barr virus, which usually causes infectious mononucleosis. It is also suspected that cancer of the cervix may be caused by a virus: the genital herpes virus, which usually causes genital ulcers (genital herpes disease).

Note: Although the Epstein-Barr virus and the genital herpes virus may cause cancer, infectious mononucleosis and the genital herpes disease do *not* lead to cancer.

Some doctors doubt that viruses cause human cancers, arguing that as long as experiments on human beings are forbidden, the viral theory cannot be proved. But in the absence of proof, scientists assert: (i) that viruses have been isolated from cancerous human cells; (ii) that some of these viruses have been used to cause cancer in animals; and (iii) that if viruses cause cancer in animals, it is likely that they can do so in human beings. Man, after all, is only an animal who reasons.

Viruses: How do viruses cause cancer?

In non-cancerous infections, a virus invades a cell and begins reproducing again and again until the cell bursts. The viruses are then set free to invade and kill other cells. This process repeats itself until the viruses are destroyed by the body's immune system, which fights infection.

But if a virus is to cause cancer, it cannot kill the cell it infects. It must somehow unite with the genes in a cell and change their behavior. Some scientists believe that for a virus to cause cancer, the virus-laden cell must be exposed to radiation or chemicals. Only further research will show how viruses cause cancer.

Viruses: Is cancer contagious?

Not in human beings, but definitely in some animals. For example, lymphoma is highly contagious in chickens, and leukemia in cats. But there is no evidence that these cancers – or any other cancers – are contagious in human beings, notwithstanding outbreaks of lymphoma and leukemia in small communities like Rutherford, New Jersey. If cancer were contagious, doctors who treat the disease (oncologists) would have the highest rate of cancer in the world; but they do not. Despite 100 years of research, scientists have never found the least evidence that human cancer is contagious.

Infectious diseases caused by a virus are usually contagious. But cancer – even cancer caused by a virus – is not. Remember: in order to cause cancer, a virus must unite with a cell's genes. In most instances, when such a union takes place, the virus cannot be released from the cell. But even in those few instances when the virus is released, it is released in amounts far too small to infect other people.

Consider the Epstein-Barr virus. It can cause not only infectious mononucleosis, but also cancer (Burkitt's lymphoma). A person with mononucleosis can pass on the virus; a person with Burkitt's lymphoma cannot. Remember: infectious mononucleosis does *not* lead to cancer.

Viruses: Is it safe to come in contact with a person who has cancer?

Definitely yes. Since cancer is not contagious, a cancer patient may engage in all the normal activities of life: work, play, church, friendship, and love.

Viruses: How can people protect themselves from viruses?

Only basic research in cell biology will enable scientists to conquer viruses, either with drugs that can kill them or vaccines that can disable them. At present, drugs are totally ineffective in treating viral infections; and the vaccines that exist prevent only a few of them.

Heredity: How do scientists know that cancer can be inherited?

From experiments with animals they know, for example, that selective breeding can produce cancer of the breast in some strains of mice, cancer of the skin in one type of tropical fish, and cancer of the brain in fruit-flies. These experiments show that certain deficiencies in the genes that control cell reproduction are passed on from one generation to the next.

Heredity: How do scientists know that the tendency to develop cancer can be inherited by human beings?

Heredity in human beings is difficult to study, because mating and environmental factors cannot be controlled. But there is strong evidence that the tendency to develop cancer can sometimes be inherited by human beings. Identical twins, for instance, frequently develop identical cancers within several years of one another. Certain rare cancers of the eye and thyroid recur in families when the odds against recurrence are a million to one. And some families, "cancer families," suffer a much higher rate of cancer than the general population.

Heredity: With which cancers is heredity associated?

Primarily with a rare cancer of the eye (retinoblastoma) and a rare cancer of the thyroid (medullary carcinoma). Because genetic defects give rise to these cancers, the tendency to develop them can be inherited. In fact, the tendency to develop retinoblastoma is passed on to approximately one-half of all children born to a parent who carries the defective gene responsible for the disease.

Some pre-cancerous conditions – for example, polyps in the colon (familial polyposis) and a rare skin disease (xeroderma pigmentosum) – are also passed on within families. Cancer almost always develops in people with familial polyposis. But cancer can be prevented in people with xeroderma pigmentosum because the defective gene responsible for the cancer does not express itself unless the person afflicted with the gene is exposed to strong sunlight. People with pre-cancerous conditions should undergo thorough annual checkups for cancer.

Heredity: Which cancers tend to recur in families?

Cancers of the large intestine, the stomach, the lung, the prostate, the breast, the lining of the uterus (endometrium), and possibly the ovaries tend to recur in families. There is no clear evidence, however, that the tendency to develop these cancers is passed on from parent to child. These cancers may just as easily be caused by diet, occupation, or some other environmental condition that affects many members of a single family.

Heredity: Why must a doctor be told about the cancer history of a patient's family?

Because patients from families with high rates of cancer run a higher than normal risk of developing the disease. Such patients should routinely undergo special cancer checkups. A woman whose mother, sister, and/or maternal aunt has had cancer of the breast, for example, may be advised to have an occasional mammogram (an X-ray examination of the breast). Similarly, a patient whose relatives have had cancer of the colon may be advised to have an occasional proctosigmoidoscopy (examination of the lower intestine through a tubular device that is passed into the colon through the rectum).

In addition, a doctor who knows a family's cancer history may be able to give genetic counseling to prospective parents. Before having children, a couple should know if they are likely to endow those children with a tendency to develop cancer.

Can cancer-causing agents harm babies while they are still in the womb?

Yes. Certain cancers have been linked to drugs and X-rays administered not to the cancer patient, but rather to the patient's mother during pregnancy. A rare form of uterine cancer, for example, occurs at a higher than normal rate in girls and women whose mothers took DES – a drug prescribed during the 1940s, 50s, and 60s to prevent miscarriages in pregnant women.

Note: Children of women who receive pelvic X-rays during the first three months of pregnancy run a higher than normal risk of developing leukemia.

Can the causes of cancer be controlled?

Yes, with the result that the world's cancer rate could be reduced by 75 to 90 percent. But for social and political reasons it is no simple matter to control the behavior of industry or individuals. In fact, people may choose *not* to exert control, if they believe that the benefits of a particular cancer-causing agent will outweigh its risks. But choice must proceed from knowledge, not ignorance: people must understand the causes of cancer before they decide what risks are tolerable and what risks unavoidable. To understand the causes of cancer is to know that, within limits, the disease can be prevented.

Is an ounce of prevention really worth a pound of cure?

Definitely yes! Since it is better to prevent a disease than to undergo the rigors of a cure, people must help themselves by controlling cancer-causing agents. If, for example, all people who smoke cigarettes were to stop, lung cancer would cease to be a major problem; even among those who had smoked for many years, the rate of lung cancer would decrease. And if all the cancer-causing chemicals people breathe in the air and eat in their food were eliminated, the number of people who develop cancer would be drastically reduced. Preventing disease is always preferable to curing it.

THE DETECTION OF CANCER

Can a person have cancer without being aware of it?

Yes. Since a cancer can take years to develop, a person may not be aware of the cancer until it begins to interfere with the normal functions of his body. But even before the appearance of pain, which is a *late* symptom of cancer, there are painless symptoms that may indicate the presence of a cancer in the body.

What are the symptoms or warning signs of cancer?

Change in bowel or bladder habits.
A sore that does not heal.
Unusual bleeding or discharge.
Thickening or lump in the breast or elsewhere.
Indigestion or difficulty in swallowing.
Obvious change in a wart or mole.
Nagging cough or hoarseness.
The American Cancer Society says that if any of these symptoms persists for more than two weeks, a doctor should be consulted immediately.

How important is early detection of cancer?

The old saying that a stitch in time saves nine can be applied to cancer. If the original cancer site is detected early enough, the cancer can be removed or destroyed before it travels to nine other sites, or even more. Very few cancers, however, are detected early enough to be cured.

Is cancer easy to detect?

In the late stages yes, in the early stages no. But since cancer kills when it is far advanced, every doctor hopes to achieve early detection. The difficulty is that there is no simple procedure by which to test for early cancer. A throat culture will reveal a "strep" infection, a blood test syphilis, a chest X-ray tuberculosis. But no simple test exists to discover a cancerous cell. Why? Because, with trillions of cells in the body, it is virtually impossible to locate one that is cancerous. The disease can be detected only after a cancerous cell has taken root and produced billions of cancerous descendants.

How does a doctor detect cancer?

The first step is for the doctor to record and analyze the patient's medical history. Because cancer is so difficult to detect in its early stages, a medical history may provide the doctor with clues that will lead to a tentative diagnosis. Cancer of the stomach, for example, may exhibit early warning signs, such as indigestion, nausea, heartburn, and gas.

The second step is for the doctor to give the patient a thorough physical examination, including a careful inspection of accessible body cavities.

Is there an ideal cancer test?

The ideal test would be one that inexpensively revealed, with little or no discomfort to the patient, whether a cancer was present in the body and where it was located. No such test exists; nor are doctors close to devising one. In the near future, doctors may be able to design a simple urine or skin test that will indicate the presence of a cancer – but not its location. A urine or skin test will thus be imperfect. Imagine the mental distress of a person who discovers he has cancer but does not know where it is.

At present, the closest that doctors have come to an ideal test is a marker blood test for cancer of the placenta. Blood is taken from the vein of a patient; the blood is analyzed for the presence of a particular substance that is identified only with placental cancer; and the substance, if found, is measured to determine the nature and degree of the cancer. But since this test is useful only for cancer of the placenta it can hardly be said to be ideal.

What kinds of cancer tests are there?

Cancer tests are classified according to how they are administered and how effective they are. Tests are administered either externally or internally. The first is called a non-invasive test, the second an invasive test. The first is relatively harmless, the second is often painful and even dangerous. Non-invasive means not to invade; a non-invasive test does not invade the body, as in an ultrasound test, or enters the body only to extract or withdraw a substance, as in a blood test. Invasive means to invade; an invasive test invades the body, as in surgery, or injects a substance into the body, as in a dye test. A non-invasive test can easily be made invasive with the injection of a substance into the body during the test.

The effectiveness of a test depends on how sensitive the test is for a certain disease and how specific it is for a certain disease. If a test is *sensitive* for a certain disease, the test is almost always right when it shows that the disease is *not* present. But the test may be wrong when it shows that the disease *is* present, because the test sometimes reacts to diseases other than the one it is looking for. If a test is *specific* for a certain disease, the test is almost always right when it shows that the disease *is* present. But the test may be wrong when it shows that the disease is *not* present, because the test sometimes fails to react to the disease it is looking for.

Sensitive and specific tests may be thought of as magnets. Let us say, for example, that we are looking for pure iron. An ordinary magnet is a *sensitive* test for pure iron: the magnet is right when it tells us that pure iron is *not* present; but it may be wrong when it tells us that pure iron definitely *is* present, because the magnet will pick up steel (which is partially composed of iron) as often as it picks up pure iron. Let us say further that we design a magnet to detect only pure iron that is at least 1 inch thick. This new magnet is a *specific* test for pure iron: the magnet is right when it tells us that the iron *is* present; but it may be wrong when it tells us that the iron is *not* present, because the magnet will fail to pick up pure iron that is less than 1 inch thick.

Some cancer tests are both sensitive and specific, and some are one or the other. A test that is both sensitive and specific, although more accurate than one that is only sensitive or only specific, is by no means error free. Doctors often find themselves in the difficult position of telling a patient that, according to his tests, he does not have cancer – only to learn later that the cancer must have in fact been present, but hidden, at the time of the tests. Doctors who do not tell their patients that cancer tests are imperfect can expect bitter complaint if it turns out that the patient does have cancer.

The following diagram may help demonstrate how sensitive and specific tests work.

	SENSITIVE TEST	SPECIFIC TEST
THE TEST SAYS NO	A negative reading means: stop looking. There is probably no cancer.	A negative reading means: keep looking. There may or may not be a cancer present.
THE TEST SAYS YES	A positive reading means: keep looking. There may or may not be a cancer present.	A positive reading means: stop looking. There is probably a cancer.

What are the non-invasive tests?

1 DIAGNOSTIC X-RAYS This test involves the use of X-ray pictures to locate cancer. On the pictures, abnormal growths and accumulations of tissue appear darker than normal organs. Sometimes a dye is injected into a patient's blood vessel with a needle in order to sharpen the image on the pictures.

Discomfort: none, unless the test is made invasive by the injection of dye into a blood vessel. (See Radiologic Catheter Invasion, p. 39.)

Risk: exposure to radiation; and if dye is used, allergic reaction, clotting, and stroke.

Reliability: both sensitive and specific for diagnosing cancer of the bone and lung.

2 COMPUTER SCAN This test involves the use of X-rays and a computer. Extensive X-ray pictures are taken of a particular area of the body. By means of a computer, the pictures are analyzed to determine the cellular composition of that area. Sometimes during the course of the test, dye is injected into a patient's blood vessel in order to sharpen the images on the pictures.

Discomfort: none, unless the test is made invasive by the injection of dye into a blood vessel.

Risk: exposure to radiation; and if dye is used, allergic reaction, clotting, and stroke.

Reliability: sensitive and, if dye is used, fairly specific for diagnosing cancer of the brain.

3 ULTRASOUND This test involves the use of a flashlight-type device, which is run over the patient's body in order to sound out the vital

organs. Sound waves issuing from the device are recorded on a screen. In some instances, a Polaroid camera is used to take pictures of the screen so that the doctor will have a record of the test. In a healthy body, the sound waves appear as straight lines and normal arcs. In an unhealthy body, with diseased organs or a tumor in a body cavity, the sound waves show up as irregular lines and distorted arcs.

Discomfort: none.

Risk: none known.

Reliability: sometimes sensitive but never specific. Because this test must be performed skillfully in order to be meaningful, the test is only as sensitive as the doctor and technician performing it. In skilled hands, it is very useful; in unskilled hands, it is not.

4 CHEMICAL TEST This test involves drawing blood from a vessel in order to evaluate the health of certain organs. Particular chemical substances in the blood are analyzed to determine the presence of cancer.

Discomfort: none, except from the needle.

Risk: none.

Reliability: both sensitive and specific for diagnosing cancer of the placenta. Sensitive and moderately specific for diagnosing cancer of the testicle. Moderately sensitive and moderately specific for diagnosing a form of cancer of the bone (multiple myeloma). Sometimes specific for diagnosing cancer of the colon.

5 CYTOLOGY This test involves analysis of cells taken from urine, from sputum, from smears of the nose, mouth, lungs, or cervix, or from washings of the stomach.

Discomfort: none when cells are taken from the urine or sputum; slight when cells are taken from the nose, mouth, or cervix; painful when cells are taken from the stomach or lungs.

Risk: none.

Reliability: both sensitive and specific for diagnosing cancer of the cervix or lung; slightly less so for cancer of the stomach.

6 BONE MARROW TEST This test involves extracting marrow from a bone in order to determine its health.

Discomfort: moderately painful.

Risk: none.

Reliability: both sensitive and specific for diagnosing leukemia. Specific for diagnosing cancers that have spread to the bone.

What are the invasive tests?

1 RADIOLOGIC CATHETER INVASION This test involves the injection of a dye into a catheter – a slim hollow tube that is passed through a blood vessel or a lymph vessel to the site that the doctor wants to examine. The injected site is then X-rayed. The dye – an iodine compound – makes the vessels show up clearly, enabling the doctor to detect those irregularities that occur when tumors push blood and lymph vessels out of place or increase their size.

Discomfort: slight to moderate.

Risk: exposure to radiation, allergic reaction, clotting and stroke.

Reliability: sensitive but not specific. This test is most useful for diagnosing cancers of the kidney, brain, and liver.

2 ISOTOPE SCANNING This test involves the injection of a radioactive substance, by means of a needle, into a blood vessel. The radioactive emissions from the injected area are then measured to see if there are any alterations in the normal function of the organs. The scanning test measures how well a particular organ is functioning.

Discomfort: little, if any.

Risk: exposure to radiation.

Reliability: sensitive but not specific. This test is most useful for diagnosing cancer that has spread to the bone or brain, and slightly less useful for detecting cancer that has spread to the liver.

3 BIOPSY This test involves minor surgery. A local or general anaesthetic is administered to the patient, an incision is made in the area of the suspected cancer, and a section of flesh or tissue is removed from the body. The tissue must be removed from just the right spot and in such a manner as not to spread the cancer to other parts of the body. The tissue is then examined under a microscope. If the tissue must be examined immediately, it will be prepared as a "frozen section"; if a delay of one to three days is possible, the tissue will be prepared in paraffin as a permanent section. The pathologist (the doctor who looks at the tissue under the microscope) is specially trained to determine if the tissue is cancerous.

Discomfort: the degree of discomfort depends on the location and extent of the surgery; but of all the tests, biopsy is probably the most painful.

Risk: as in any operation, the risks include infection and hemorrhage.

Reliability: specific for the particular area of the body that is tested, but useless for all other areas.

Note: Large-scale operations conducted for nonspecific diagnostic purposes (exploratory surgery) are disparagingly called "fishing expeditions." Once common, they are now frowned upon.

Staging operations, which are performed only when a cancer is known to be present, are not to be confused with exploratory surgery. In a staging operation, the surgeon performs a series of biopsies on various organs and lymph nodes to determine how far a cancer has spread.

Is cancer easy to detect under a microscope?

No. The difficulty is that cancerous cells sometimes look like normal cells.

Most people think that normal cells and cancerous cells look very different. And often they do look very different. Normal cells have a regular shape; cancerous cells do not. Normal cells are arranged in an orderly pattern; cancerous cells are not. Normal cells have a well-proportioned nucleus; cancerous cells have an enlarged, distorted nucleus. Normal cells during cell division behave predictably; cancerous cells during cell division behave unpredictably.

But sometimes cancerous cells look so much like normal cells that the pathologist cannot decide whether they are cancerous. For this reason, cytology, biopsy, and bone marrow tests are only as good as the sample of tissue and as the pathologist who looks into the microscope.

To probe or not to probe?

In order to decide how far to probe for cancer, the doctor must determine how much physical injury he is willing to allow and how much discomfort the patient is willing to endure. If a test is worse than the cancer, or if a test is unlikely to yield significant results, the test ought not to be done. When tests are recommended, the patient has every right to ask the doctor to justify them. When test results are negative, the patient should ask the doctor whether further testing is necessary. When tests reveal the presence of another disease, the patient should ask the doctor whether it is best to continue testing for cancer, or to treat the other disease, or both. Remember: the primary function of a cancer test is to determine the location and extent of a possible cancer.

How are tests selected and treatment determined?

The doctor's initial examination of the patient will suggest the use of particular cancer tests. When the tests are complete, the doctor will assess the patient, the test results, the disease, and the resources of the hospital in order to decide upon a particular treatment.

Should the patient seek a second opinion?

Yes, if he wishes to do so. But the doctor has probably already sought the advice of other doctors. In recent years, cancer specialists (oncologists) have tended to favor a team approach to diagnosis and treatment. Most participate in "tumor boards" or consult with other oncologists. Even after treatment has begun, oncologists frequently confer with one another in order to evaluate the success of a particular treatment and its side effects.

If changes in treatment are necessary, the doctor should discuss these changes with his patient.

When will the patient know if his cancer is gone?

This question, perhaps the most important to cancer patients, is the most difficult for doctors to answer. Everyone thinks that after the first few weeks of treatment the doctor will know whether the patient has been cured. But only time will tell. The longer a patient is free from symptoms, the greater the prospect that the cancer is completely gone.

Generally, the doctor can tell in four to six weeks whether a cancer is responding to chemotherapy, and in one to two years whether surgery or radiotherapy has been effective. Although patients may ask the doctor to test again and again in order to prove that the cancer is gone, it is better to wait, since retesting can cause pain and, in rare cases, even death.

What does "cured" mean?

A cancer is considered "cured" if after treatment the patient remains free from symptoms for five years. But just as an infection may appear to be cured only to recur, so too may a cancer appear to be cured only to recur. And just as one infection may be cured only to be followed by a different, unrelated infection, so too may one cancer be cured only to be followed by a different, unrelated cancer. For this reason, doctors talk about "cures" in terms of years: "a five year cure," "a six year cure," "a ten year cure." A person, in short, may be cured for a lifetime or only for an indefinite number of years.

What can the patient do to help himself?

There is very little the patient can do to help himself physically; but he can help himself mentally in the following ways: (i) by participating in group discussions; (ii) by inviting help from the hospital social workers, who are there to assist him; (iii) by seeking moral support from his family; (iv) by affirming life; (v) by returning to work; (vi) by becoming as active as possible in hobbies and sports; (vii) by maintaining normal relationships; (viii) by talking openly about the cancer.

Are there instances when the treatment is worse than the cancer?

Yes. Surgery may alter the body radically; radiotherapy and chemotherapy may sicken the body. Unless survival is an end in itself, a patient may wish to refuse treatment that threatens to destroy the quality of his life. Since one person's happiness may be another's hell, every patient must judge for himself whether treatment is desirable.

THE VITAL STATISTICS OF CANCER

Isn't cancer the number one killer?

No. If we omitted cancers of the lung, breast, and colon-rectum – the three greatest cancer killers – the number of deaths from cancer would be far fewer each year than the number of deaths from stroke. Even when these cancers are included, heart disease kills more people each year than cancer. In the United States, heart disease accounts for approximately 38 percent of all deaths, while cancer accounts for approximately 19 percent.

It may be better at age fifty to have cancer of the vocal cords than to have a serious heart attack. The first is curable, the second is not.

15 leading causes of death: United States, 1975*

Cause of Death	Number of Deaths	% of Total Deaths
1 Diseases of Heart	716,215	37.8
2 Cancer	365,693	19.3
3 Stroke	194,038	10.3
4 Accidents	103,030	5.4
5 Influenza & Pneumonia	55,664	2.9
6 Diabetes Mellitus	35,230	1.9
7 Cirrhosis of Liver	31,623	1.7
8 Arteriosclerosis	28,887	1.5
9 Suicide	27,063	1.4
10 Diseases of Infancy	26,616	1.4
11 Homicide	21,310	1.1
12 Emphysema	18,795	1.0
13 Congenital Anomalies	13,245	0.7
14 Nephritis & Nephrosis (Kidney Disease)	8,072	0.4
15 Ulcers	6,743	0.4
Other & Ill-defined Causes	240,655	12.8

*These are the most recent statistics.

Which type of cancer is the most common?

Of the four major types – carcinomas, sarcomas, leukemias, and lymphomas – carcinomas are the most common.

Which type of cancer is the most difficult to treat?

In general, sarcomas are the most difficult to treat because they begin deep in the tissue. But the effectiveness of any treatment depends less on the type of cancer than on the stage of the cancer at the time it is discovered, its size, its location, and its rate of spread.

Which individual cancers are the most common?

The lung, breast, and colon-rectum account for almost 42 percent of all cancers.

Which individual cancers are the most common in men?

The lung, prostate, and colon-rectum account for approximately 52 percent of all cancers in men.

Which individual cancers are the most common in women?

The breast, colon-rectum, and uterus account for approximately 55 percent of all cancers in women.

Which individual cancers are the most common in children?

Leukemia and cancer of the brain account for 54 percent of all cancers in children.

Which individual cancers are the most curable?

Slightly more than half the patients treated for the following cancers are alive after five years.

Bladder	Lip	Skin (melanoma)
Breast	Lymph nodes	Testes
Cervix	Penis	Thyroid
Eye	Prostate	Uterus
Larynx	Salivary gland	Vulva

Which individual cancers do people most often die from?

Cancer of the lung is the number one killer, followed by cancers of the colon-rectum and breast.

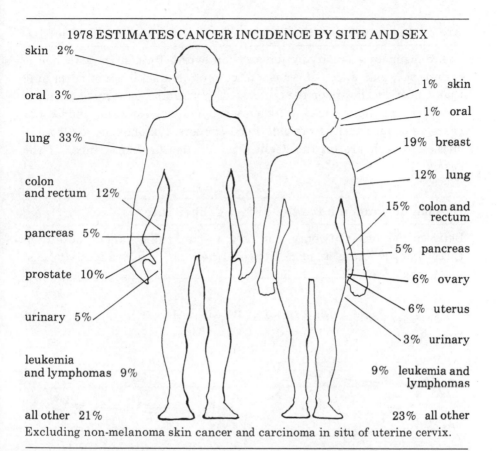

1978 ESTIMATES CANCER INCIDENCE BY SITE AND SEX

skin 2%

oral 3%

lung 33%

colon
and rectum 12%

pancreas 5%

prostate 10%

urinary 5%

leukemia
and lymphomas 9%

all other 21%

1% skin

1% oral

19% breast

12% lung

15% colon and
rectum

5% pancreas

6% ovary

6% uterus

3% urinary

9% leukemia and
lymphomas

23% all other

Excluding non-melanoma skin cancer and carcinoma in situ of uterine cervix.

Which individual cancers do men most often die from?

Cancers of the lung, colon-rectum, and prostate account for approximately 55 percent of all cancer deaths in men.

Which individual cancers do women most often die from?

Cancers of the breast, colon-rectum, and lung account for approximately 46 percent of all cancer deaths in women.

Which individual cancers do children under fifteen most often die from?

Leukemia, the most common form of childhood cancer, accounts for approximately 52 percent of all cancer deaths in children under fifteen.

Are cancer deaths on the increase?

Yes. Since people are living longer than ever before, since pollution is widespread, and since cancer is a disease of old age, it is not surprising that cancer deaths are on the increase. In particular, cancers of the lung, pancreas, and kidney are killing more people today than they did twenty years ago. But deaths from childhood cancers, lymphomas, and cancer of the stomach are on the decline, as are deaths from cancer of the cervix.

Do men or women have the higher cancer rate?

Between the ages of twenty and forty, women suffer cancer more than three times as often as men. Between the ages of fifty and sixty, men

CANCER DEATHS BY SITE AND SEX

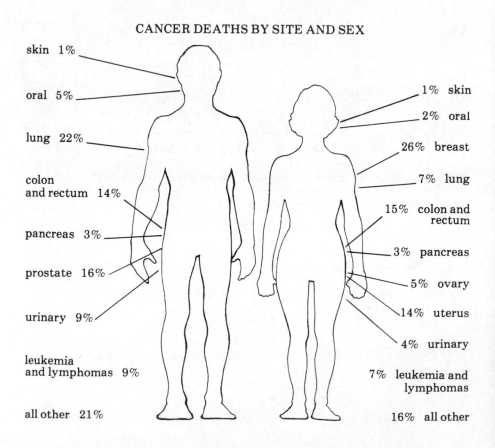

skin 1%

oral 5%

lung 22%

colon and rectum 14%

pancreas 3%

prostate 16%

urinary 9%

leukemia and lymphomas 9%

all other 21%

1% skin

2% oral

26% breast

7% lung

15% colon and rectum

3% pancreas

5% ovary

14% uterus

4% urinary

7% leukemia and lymphomas

16% all other

account for more cancers than women. In total, however, women account for more cancer cases than men.

Do whites or non-whites have the higher cancer rate?

For whites under sixty-five, the cancer rate is slightly higher than for non-whites. For whites over sixty-five, the cancer rate is slightly lower.

What age group does cancer most often strike?

Cancer is generally a disease of old and middle age. Years ago, in fact, cancer occurred far less often than it does today because people died at an early age from accidents, influenza, pneumonia, and other diseases.

The highest cancer rate occurs in the age group sixty-five and older. The second highest rate is in the age group fifty to sixty-five. In children and young adults, cancer is rare. In adults, cancer kills one out of five people; in children, cancer (usually leukemia) kills one out of twenty-eight of all those who die under the age of fifteen.

What does cancer cost in dollars?

When a cancer patient is hospitalized, the average length of his stay in the hospital is sixteen days at a total cost of about $400 a day ($6,400). There are approximately 1.5 million cancer patients hospitalized each year. The cost: $9.6 billion. This figure does not include doctor bills, outpatient treatment, therapy, and time lost from work. The total cost is well over $30 billion.

2 Proven Methods of Treatment

There are three proven methods for treating cancer: surgery, radiotherapy, and chemotherapy. In surgery, the doctor removes cancerous tissue from the body by operating. In radiotherapy, he destroys cancerous cells with X-rays. In chemotherapy, he destroys cancerous cells with drugs.

SURGERY

Surgery is the oldest proven treatment for cancer. For thousands of years, cancerous tumors have been surgically removed from the surface of the body; and as long ago as the first century after Christ, the Roman doctor Celsus treated breast cancer by amputating the breast (mastectomy). But only in this century have surgeons learned to enter the body and cut away cancerous tumors that grow inside. Before the discovery in the mid-nineteenth century of anaesthetics and of antiseptic procedures, surgery caused unbearable pain and exposed patients to serious risk of infection. In the last century, however, surgery has become a relatively safe and painless method for treating numerous diseases – among them cancer.

Many modern surgical procedures for treating cancer have been used for more than twenty-five years, and few are less than five years old. But surgery is constantly improving, as doctors refine not only surgical techniques, but also anaesthetics, blood banking, and antibiotics. Most new surgical treatments for cancer use surgery, radiotherapy, and chemotherapy in unique combinations.

How does surgery work in the treatment of cancer?

A surgeon treats cancer by cutting a cancerous tumor out of the body. The success of an operation depends on the surgeon's ability to remove the entire cancer. The surgeon seeks to cut away as little healthy tissue as possible, but as much tissue as necessary to insure a cure.

Different surgeons will have different opinions about the required extent of surgery and about the patient's physical and emotional ability to tolerate surgery. Unfortunately, there is no perfect opinion: in surgery for cancer, the patient must be either overtreated or undertreated. When he is overtreated, he may suffer complications from the removal of too much healthy tissue. When he is undertreated, he may find that his cancer has not been cured.

When is surgery used?

A surgeon operates when he is reasonably sure that he can remove the cancerous tumor and all surrounding tissue invaded by the cancer. During the operation, the surgeon will perform numerous biopsies in order to learn if the cancer has spread. The surgeon's goal is to remove the entire cancer without severely damaging the quality of the patient's life. But until he operates, the surgeon cannot know for certain whether this goal can be achieved.

Which cancers cannot be treated surgically?

Widespread cancer cannot be removed through surgery. In widespread cancer, the cancerous cells are not confined to the site of the tumor and to the regional lymph nodes, but have traveled to other parts of the body.

Cancers that involve vital parts of the body cannot, in general, be treated surgically, because vital parts cannot be removed. When cancer of the lung occurs close to the heart, for example, surgery may be impossible: if any portion of the heart is removed, the patient may die. Surgery may also be impossible when cancer attacks the major bones in the pelvic area: if the lower half of the body is cut off, the patient will suffer horrible mutilation. To be helpful, surgery must not only preserve life, but also respect the integrity of the human form.

Which cancers respond poorly to surgery?

Rapidly spreading cancers – for example, oat cell cancer of the lung, or cancer of the stomach – respond poorly to surgery. Generally, these cancers have become widespread before they are detected. But even when they are confined to one place in the body, they often grow so quickly that they cannot be entirely removed. Although partial removal of such cancers is sometimes desirable, the surgeon must be careful not to cut through the tumor, since the cancer will rapidly spread if cells from the tumor spill out.

Cancerous tumors that flow like lava, breaking through neighboring organs, do not respond to surgery so well as cancerous tumors that grow like balloons, pushing away neighboring organs. (Cancer that starts in the lower throat spreads like lava; while cancer that starts in the vocal cords, which are only one-half inch away from the lower throat, grows like a balloon.) Lava tumors are difficult to remove because they fragment and invade neighboring tissue early in the disease. Balloon tumors, on the other hand, can be removed completely, because they enlarge in encapsulated form and do not invade neighboring tissue until late in the disease.

Is surgery for cancer an emergency procedure?

No. Surgery can generally cure cancer only before it has spread beyond the site of origin or beyond the regional lymph nodes. Since over one-third of all cancers spread in a slow, predictable manner, a surgeon should not operate until he has tried to determine whether a cancer has become widespread. It is inadvisable for a patient to rush into surgery when a well-planned evaluation might show that an alternative treatment is preferable.

How extensive must surgery be?

The extent of surgery depends primarily on the location and size of the tumor. Inevitably, some types of surgery for cancer permanently alter the body's normal functions. If parts of the mouth or the throat are removed, for example, the surgery must affect swallowing and speaking. If the bladder or the rectum is removed, a new opening for urine (a urostomy) or for feces (a colostomy) must be constructed in the abdominal wall. Surgery, then, may preserve life while altering the quality of life.

Occasionally, in treating a particular cancer, a doctor may be able to choose among several surgical procedures. He may treat cancer of the breast, for example, by performing maximum surgery or by combining limited surgery with radiotherapy and/or chemotherapy. When different procedures are likely to produce a cure, patients generally prefer limited surgery, since the less extensive the surgery, the less the cosmetic disfigurement.

Before an operation, the patient must understand how surgery will change his life. He must also consider how he can accommodate his life to these changes. The patient must not hesitate to insist that his doctor explain the full consequences of his operation.

How is surgery performed?

Before surgery, the patient is often sedated with medication, so that he will be comfortable during his presurgical treatments. The surgery is performed while the patient is anaesthetized.

The area of the body in which the surgeon makes his incision must be shaved and cleansed to reduce the risk of infection. Because the successful removal of a cancer requires that the entire tumor and neighboring normal tissues be exposed, the incision must often be long.

During surgery, which always involves the cutting and tying of blood vessels and the cutting of nerves, the patient is given blood transfusions as needed. Since surgery for cancer often requires the surgeon to cut important blood vessels, the patient may need five or six pints of blood.

It is essential that the patient's heart and lungs function normally while he is anaesthetized – often as long as four to eight hours. By monitoring these organs throughout the surgery and by adjusting medication as required, the anaesthesiologist can prevent breathing and heartbeat from becoming dangerously depressed.

In surgery, exposed organs are always handled gently so that later complications do not occur. Even extensive surgery is now relatively safe, because of modern antibiotics and methods of blood replacement.

What are the drawbacks of surgery?

At worst, surgery can cause death, either from the anaesthetic or the surgical procedure. Cancer patients, however, rarely die from surgery, although they may suffer disfigurement. Surgery of the mouth or throat, for example, may deform the patient's face and make subsequent cosmetic surgery necessary. Surgery for cancer of the cervix may alter the patient's sex life by shortening or removing the vagina. Surgery to remove the stomach or the colon may lead to difficulty in digesting food. When a surgeon must cause physical deformity in order to save the patient's life, he should fully explain the consequences of the surgery, so that the patient can decide whether or not to have the operation.

Is recovery painful?

After surgery, there is normally some pain, which can often be relieved with medication. In addition, some patients feel abnormal stabbing pains at the site of the incision. These pains, which can be controlled, arise from cut nerves.

How long must the patient remain in the hospital?

It all depends on the type and extent of his surgery. The removal of a larynx or uterus may require a stay of no longer than one or two weeks. The removal of a bladder or rectum may require a stay of as long as three to six weeks.

Can the patient return to work after surgery for cancer?

Most patients – even those who have undergone major surgery – can return to work after a period of recovery and rehabilitation. Some employers, however, hesitate to rehire cancer patients. For information about rehabilitation programs and for assistance in educating employers, patients should consult their social service department or the American Cancer Society.

When can the patient be certain that surgery has been successful?

A patient is considered to be cured if five years after surgery he has suffered no recurrence of the cancer. But periodic checkups are essential for all cancer patients throughout their lives, even for those who have been cured. An adequate examination can be performed by any doctor familiar with the patient's cancer history.

RADIOTHERAPY

In radiotherapy the doctor attempts to destroy cancerous cells with highly active, invisible beams of energy called X-rays or gamma rays. X-rays are produced by machines – for example, linear accelerators and betatrons. Gamma rays, which are a type of X-ray, are given off by radioactive substances like cobalt and cesium, iridium and radium. When radioactive substances are used in the treatment of cancer, they may be (i) housed in a machine that delivers their rays; or (ii) placed in a small container that is inserted into a body cavity – for example, the uterine cavity; or (iii) put directly into a tumor, as in the treatment of tongue cancer by needle implants.

Radiotherapy has been used for fewer than seventy-five years. Soon after Wilhelm Roentgen discovered the X-ray in 1895, doctors learned that X-rays could not only cause cancer, but also cure it. By 1900, X-rays were reported to have been used successfully in treating cancers of the face; and within several years, experiments were undertaken to test the effectiveness of X-rays in treating leukemia and other cancers. But several decades passed before doctors learned to use X-rays skillfully – that is, to control dosage in the X-rays they administered, and to predict accurately the effect of particular dosages. Developed largely in Europe, radiotherapy has matured more rapidly abroad than in the United States, where it has only recently come to rank with surgery and chemotherapy as an accepted treatment for cancer.

Doctors speak of X-ray treatments as *radiations*. To *irradiate* means to give X-ray treatment.

How does radiotherapy work in the treatment of cancer?

X-rays, which can be neither seen nor felt, deposit their energy in the cells they touch. Although doctors are uncertain how X-rays alter these cells, they know that the cells die, probably because the X-rays have damaged their genes. Some irradiated cells die instantly; but most die only when they attempt to divide. Because selected cells can be killed by bombardment with X-rays, radiotherapy can cure cancer in two ways:

(i) by destroying the cancerous cells that comprise a tumor; and (ii) by damaging the blood vessels that nourish the tumor.

When is radiotherapy used?

Radiotherapy is best suited for treating cancers that are considerably more sensitive than normal tissue to the destructive effects of X-rays: namely, cancer of the lymph nodes, certain cancers of the testicle, and most childhood cancers. When these cancers are treated with X-rays, the doctor can irradiate large parts of the body without causing excessive damage to normal tissue.

The majority of cancers are only slightly more sensitive than normal tissue. Radiotherapy, then, is generally used only when the area to be treated is small, so that the body can tolerate the destruction of the irradiated normal tissue. When cancer becomes widespread, radiotherapy can seldom produce a cure, although it may be used to alleviate the symptoms associated with the cancer.

Most often, radiotherapy is used to treat cancers that cannot be surgically removed. But it may also be used to treat operable cancers in organs that are best not removed because they are vital to the patient's normal activities: organs such as the cervix, the vocal cords, and the tongue. When several treatments are available for a particular cancer, the doctor must weigh the risks and benefits of each treatment. The "best" treatment produces a cure while causing the least possible damage to the normal functions of the body.

When is radiotherapy used in combination with surgery or chemotherapy?

After surgery, radiotherapy is used when the doctor fears that cancerous cells are alive in tissues just beyond those that have been removed. In addition, some surgeons have recently begun to use radiotherapy as a routine precautionary measure before and after surgery for cancer of the uterus, bladder, and colon.

During chemotherapy, X-rays are sometimes used to improve a tumor's response to cancer drugs.

Which cancers respond best to radiotherapy?

Because a patient's response to radiotherapy is unpredictable, doctors cannot know whether radiations will succeed in curing a particular tumor. In general, though, radiotherapy is highly effective for treating cancer of the lymph nodes, certain cancers of the testicles, and most childhood cancers. It is also useful in treating cancers of the mouth and throat, the cervix and uterus, the bladder, prostate, lung, breast, esophagus, and brain. Cancer of the kidneys, one cancer of the bone (osteosarcoma) and one cancer of the skin (melanoma) do not respond well to radiotherapy.

What conditions limit the effectiveness of radiotherapy?

Since X-rays always destroy some normal cells along with the cancerous cells, the doctor must attempt to destroy the cancer without unduly injuring neighboring normal tissue. The less radiation administered to the tumor, the less the damage done to normal tissue. But small amounts of radiation are effective only when a cancer is considerably more susceptible than normal tissue to the destructive effects of X-rays. Since most cancers are only slightly more susceptible than normal tissue, radiation sessions are usually spaced so that partially injured normal cells have time to heal. Fortunately, spacing does not assist the cancer to heal because cancerous cells, unlike normal cells, cannot easily survive injury from X-rays.

Is radiotherapy an emergency procedure?

Not usually. Most cancers grow for years before they are discovered. Once the diagnosis of cancer has been confirmed, proper treatment is better than hasty treatment. A program of radiotherapy should always be carefully planned.

How extensive must radiotherapy be?

The extent of radiotherapy depends on:

1 The purpose of the treatment. It takes more radiation to produce a cure than to control the symptoms of widespread cancer. For radiotherapy to produce a cure, X-rays are usually administered four or five days a week for six to nine weeks. For radiotherapy to control symptoms such as bone pain, X-rays are administered in a very short program,

lasting perhaps from one day to three weeks.

2 The character of the treatment. When radiotherapy is the patient's sole treatment, more X-rays are needed than when radiotherapy is part of a combined treatment that includes surgery and/or chemotherapy. For example, if the largest portion of a tumor has been or will be surgically removed, as in cancer of the lymph nodes or the breast, the program of radiotherapy may be reduced to five or six weeks.

3 The sensitivity of the tumor to the destructive effects of X-rays. The most sensitive tumors – those of the lymph nodes and testicle, and those arising from childhood cancers – may be cured by as few as four weeks of daily X-ray treatments. Other tumors may require as many as seven to nine weeks of treatments.

4 The size of the tumor. In any given cancer, the larger the tumor, the greater the amount of radiation needed to produce a cure.

Note: The extent of therapy is determined by the amount of radiation administered to the patient. That amount may be administered in a program of any length prescribed by the doctor.

How long must radiotherapy continue?

The length of a program is a matter of professional judgment. The longer the program, the less the damage suffered by normal tissue – and the less the damage suffered by the tumor – at each session. If a patient suffers severe side effects from radiotherapy, his doctor may reduce the amount of radiation he is receiving, or even temporarily cancel his program. An extension or a temporary cancellation does not indicate that the disease has worsened.

How is radiotherapy administered?

Occasionally a doctor administers radiotherapy by placing a small container of radioactive material into one of the body's cavities, or by putting radioactive material directly into a tumor. But more often radiotherapy is administered by a skilled technician operating a highly specialized machine. Following the doctor's instructions, the technician delivers a precise amount of radiation to a particular area of the patient's body. That area is identified by the doctor after he has determined the precise location of the tumor and the preferred path of travel for the X-rays through the body. Since the technician must repeat the doctor's exact prescription at each radiation session, the area to be treated is usually outlined in blue dye.

The patient need not worry if the machine makes noise or emits an odor. The machine is frequently serviced; and during each session the amount of radiation is monitored.

The length of a session may range from forty seconds to ten minutes. At routine intervals during the patient's program of radiotherapy, a technician will take an X-ray picture of the irradiated area so that the doctor can see if the X-rays are reaching the cancerous site.

Is radiotherapy painful?

No. The patient feels nothing, just as he feels nothing when an X-ray picture is taken of his chest or teeth.

For information on painful side effects, see pp. 57–58.

Must the patient be hospitalized during radiotherapy?

Not necessarily. Most radiotherapy is administered to outpatients, who are advised not to treat the irradiated area of their body with heat pads, ice packs, lotions, or other home remedies. Otherwise patients lead relatively normal lives during therapy.

Hospitalization is generally recommended if complications develop or if patients are incapacitated by symptoms of their disease – for example, bone pain, fracture; inability to walk, seizures, or change in personality.

May an outpatient work during radiotherapy?

Yes, so long as he feels well enough to work. Because radiation causes fatigue, most patients need afternoon naps.

What are the early side effects of radiotherapy?

Except for fatigue, the early side effects are usually confined to the irradiated area of the body. When the throat is irradiated, for example, the patient may experience a sore throat and difficulty in swallowing. When the bladder or the rectum is irradiated, he may experience frequent urination, diarrhea, or cramps. When the stomach is irradiated, he may experience nausea. During radiotherapy, the irradiated area of the body often acquires a sunburned appearance.

If the irradiated tissue is diseased or infected, the side effects tend to be worse. If the frequency or intensity of the treatments is increased, the side effects also increase. Most early side effects of radiotherapy can be controlled with medication.

What are the late side effects of radiotherapy?

X-rays leave their mark on all irradiated tissue, especially the small blood vessels. If radiotherapy severely injures normal cells or organs, or if it impairs circulation of the blood by damaging blood vessels, serious late side effects may result. Among the possible side effects are new cancers, caused by the X-rays that cured the first. Late side effects may occur as soon as six months after radiotherapy is discontinued; or they may occur many years later.

Serious late side effects develop in fewer than one out of twenty patients. But every patient should ask his doctor about the possible dangers associated with a program of radiotherapy. If the patient is a child, his parents should ask how the treatment will affect the child's physical development. Every patient must know and evaluate the dangers of his therapy. Although these dangers can be controlled, they cannot be eliminated if the X-rays are to succeed in producing a cure.

Can the patient have alcohol during radiotherapy?

Yes, in moderate amounts. But patients with cancer of the mouth, throat, esophagus, or bladder should consult their doctors about restrictions on drinking.

When will the patient know whether radiotherapy has been successful?

The patient's best guide is the doctor's estimate of the cancer's response to the X-rays. This estimate will be based on the doctor's previous experience in treating similar cancers with radiotherapy.

The success of radiotherapy cannot be judged by the speed with which an irradiated tumor shrinks. Slowly growing tumors – for example, tumors of the prostate gland – shrink slowly when irradiated.

Rapidly growing tumors shrink rapidly when irradiated. But no tumor disappears suddenly, because after cell death the body's "scavengers" (the macrophages) need time to remove the dead cells.

Some tumors disappear during radiotherapy. Others – in particular, large tumors and tumors containing large amounts of scar tissue – remain present to the touch even after radiotherapy is complete. Although these tumors may shrink or disappear as time passes, their failure to shrink need not be a sign that the cancer persists.

CHEMOTHERAPY

At least from the time of the ancient Egyptians, people have attempted to cure cancer with drugs. But effective chemotherapy dates only from World War II, when an American ship loaded with poisonous mustard gas was bombed and sunk off the coast of Italy. The sailors who died in the attack were found to have suffered a radical change in their blood: the mustard gas had destroyed the lymph cells. This discovery led to the development of a drug – a derivative of mustard gas – that is used to treat cancer of the lymph nodes. Subsequently, additional drugs were developed to treat a wide variety of cancers.

Nearly fifty different cancer drugs are now in use. Some have been identified during experiments unrelated to cancer; some have emerged from government-sponsored cancer research. Still others have been created by refinement of already existing drugs. New drugs must be shown to be safe and effective in animals before they can be tested in human beings. On the average, no more than one in every fifteen thousand new drugs is approved for use in the treatment of cancer.

How does chemotherapy work in the treatment of cancer?

Drugs destroy cells by interfering with their life-sustaining functions. One type of drug prevents cells from forming the proteins and enzymes that keep them alive. Another type kills by disrupting a step in the process of cell division. A third type, by upsetting the balance of hormones in a patient's body, creates conditions unsuitable for the survival of some cancers.

All drugs that kill cancerous cells kill normal cells as well. But drugs that are used in the treatment of cancer selectively kill more cancerous cells than normal cells. Drugs that disrupt cell division, for example, are effective because the cells in cancerous tissue divide more often than those in normal tissue.

In chemotherapy, a doctor often prescribes drugs in combination with one another. Each drug is chosen for its ability to attack cells at a unique point in their life cycle. When properly combined, several drugs may be more effective in treating a particular cancer than any single drug.

When is chemotherapy used?

Chemotherapy is used when cancerous cells have spread throughout the body, so that their locations cannot be precisely determined. Neither surgery nor radiotherapy can destroy widespread cancer. But drugs can circulate throughout the entire body and kill the cancerous cells that surgery and radiotherapy miss.

Most cancers, though, cannot be cured by drugs. Typically, a cancer either develops a resistance to drugs or spreads so extensively through the body that an effective dose of drugs would kill the patient. Drugs are generally able to cure only the following cancers: acute leukemia, cancer of the placenta, cancer of the ovary, and cancer of the testicle.

But even when drugs cannot produce a cure, chemotherapy may still be useful, since drugs often extend the lives of patients who respond to them. Drugs may be used during radiotherapy to "radiosensitize" a tumor – that is, to improve the tumor's response to X-rays. They may also be used in adjuvant chemotherapy (see the next question).

What is adjuvant chemotherapy?

Doctors sometimes use chemotherapy as a precautionary measure when they are uncertain if a cancer has spread. This use of drugs is called "adjuvant chemotherapy." The drugs are intended to destroy cancerous cells that may be alive, but undetected, in the body.

Adjuvant chemotherapy is commonly used when cancer has been discovered in several lymph nodes. Once cancerous cells have reached the nodes, it is likely that some of the cells have traveled beyond the nodes to infect other parts of the body.

Although initial expectations have not been realized, adjuvant chemotherapy has had modest success, particularly in cancer of the breast among young women, in cancer of the testicle, and in most childhood cancers. Patients for whom adjuvant chemotherapy is recommended should understand its risks and benefits.

Which cancers respond to chemotherapy?

Specific cancers respond differently to different drugs. A drug that is useful for cancer of the colon may be useless for cancer of the breast. The doctor must choose the proper drug or combination of drugs for the cancer he is treating. Since very few drugs penetrate the brain and central nervous system, chemotherapy is of limited use for cancers that have spread to these areas.

Because cancer drugs destroy cells only when they are dividing, chemotherapy is best suited for small, rapidly growing tumors. Large, well-established tumors have many non-dividing cells that survive the effects of most drugs.

What conditions limit the effectiveness of chemotherapy?

Normal cells, like cancerous cells, are killed during chemotherapy. If a patient suffers severe side effects from the death of normal cells, his program of chemotherapy must be adjusted. Since most cancer drugs disrupt cell division, side effects tend to occur in those parts of the body comprised of frequently dividing cells – the stomach and intestines; the mucous membranes, which lubricate the mouth, throat, and anus; the hair follicles; and the bone marrow.

Is chemotherapy an emergency procedure?

Usually not, although proper timing is important. Since a cancer drug can kill cells at only one point in their life cycle – for example, during cell division – treatments must be spaced so that the drug is administered when the cancerous cells are most susceptible to injury and death. Before doctors learned how to space treatments, drugs were administered in doses far larger than necessary, with generally poor results. Now that drugs are administered according to an exact schedule, results have dramatically improved.

Adjuvant chemotherapy is not an emergency procedure. But when a primary tumor has been destroyed through surgery or radiotherapy, any cancerous cells that remain tend to multiply quickly. Adjuvant chemotherapy, therefore, is usually most effective when drugs are administered within a month after surgery or treatment with X-rays.

How extensive must chemotherapy be?

The extent of chemotherapy depends on:

1 The type of treatment. A drug may be administered in one amount for adjuvant chemotherapy, in another amount for radiosensitizing a tumor, and in still another amount for long-term control of disease.

2 The choice of drugs. Some cancers respond well to one drug, others to a combination of drugs.

3 The sensitivity of the cancer to drugs. Some cancers – for example, cancer of the lymph nodes – respond readily to drugs. Other cancers resist chemotherapy and must be flooded with drugs before they begin to respond.

4 The size of the cancer. Well-established cancers may require a longer course of treatment than cancers that are just beginning to grow.

5 The health of vital organs. Drugs are passed out of the body through specific organs – for example, the kidneys. These organs must function adequately during chemotherapy, or the drugs will poison the patient.

How long must chemotherapy continue?

In therapy to control a growing cancer, drugs are administered as long as they prove effective. If a drug ceases to work or reaches a dangerous level in the blood, it must be replaced by another drug. Therapy ends when the cancer has been cured or when the drugs present a greater danger to life than the cancer itself.

In adjuvant chemotherapy, drugs are administered for at least a year and often longer.

How is chemotherapy administered?

Some drugs must be given by mouth. Others must be injected under the skin or into a muscle, as in an ordinary shot. Still others must be dripped through a needle that is placed in a vein, an artery, or the space surrounding the spinal cord. When a single drug can be administered in several ways, the doctor chooses the way best suited to the particular cancer, to the prescribed dosage, and to the patient's comfort and convenience.

Drugs are administered weekly or monthly, though for short periods of time they may be administered daily.

Is chemotherapy painful?

Only occasionally. When drugs are dripped through the veins, the patient may feel a burning sensation, and a mild discomfort may persist for several days.

For information on painful side effects, see pp. 63–64.

Must the patient be hospitalized during chemotherapy?

Chemotherapy is usually administered to outpatients. But when drugs must be given on schedule or when they must be slowly dripped into the veins over many hours or days, the patient will be hospitalized. A stay in the hospital may also be required if the patient is incapacitated by symptoms of his cancer, or if the side effects of his drug must be carefully watched.

May an outpatient work during chemotherapy?

Yes, so long as he feels well enough to work. For several days after each treatment, many patients are sick with symptoms like those of the flu.

What are the immediate side effects of chemotherapy?

Chemotherapy damages most tissues, but in particular, tissue comprised of frequently dividing cells: the stomach and intestines, the mucous membranes, the hair follicles, and the bone marrow. Nausea, vomiting, and diarrhea result from damage to the stomach and intestines; dryness and soreness of the mouth from damage to the mucous membranes; and partial loss of hair from damage to the hair follicles. When damage to the bone marrow occurs, the marrow ceases to supply the blood with a normal amount of white blood cells, platelets, and red blood cells, so that the body cannot properly control infection, bruising, or fatigue.

Frequent blood counts are needed to warn the doctor of potentially dangerous deficiencies in the blood.

Drugs may cause additional side effects, such as muscular weakness, loss of appetite, rashes, discoloration of the skin, irregular menstrual periods, and sterility in both men and women. Since most of these effects disappear when chemotherapy ends, the doctor can control severe or dangerous side effects by discontinuing or changing a drug. Other means of controlling side effects include: prescribing medication to counteract the toxic effects of the drug; choosing an alternate method of administering the drug; giving blood transfusions to a patient who bruises, bleeds, or tires easily; confining to a germ-free isolation chamber a patient who is unable to fight off infection.

The range and intensity of immediate side effects differ so radically among individual patients that predictions are generally fruitless. But side effects tend to increase when the number of drugs is increased.

What are the late side effects of chemotherapy?

In adults, late side effects can usually be avoided if the doctor is attentive to early warning signs. Rare but possible late effects include permanent discoloration of the skin, suppression of the bone marrow's ability to supply the blood with platelets and with red and white blood cells, kidney disease, lung failure, heart failure, and the development of new cancers.

In children, late side effects include permanent sterility and permanent injury to the heart, lungs, kidneys, and liver. A combined treatment of radiotherapy and chemotherapy may cause children to develop new cancers. Although drugs may retard a child's physical development, surprisingly few children remain abnormally small because of chemotherapy.

Can the patient have alcohol during chemotherapy?

A moderate amount of alcohol is usually permissible, but not encouraged. Patients should consult their doctors about restrictions on drinking.

When will the patient know whether chemotherapy has been successful?

It takes three to six weeks before a doctor can determine whether the patient is responding to chemotherapy. Response is measured by chemical tests and by physical or X-ray examinations to see if the tumor has decreased in size.

Since chemotherapy is improving all the time, every patient should request current information about the usefulness of particular drugs in treating his cancer.

3 Individual Cancers

This chapter describes the twenty-one most common individual cancers. The cancers are arranged alphabetically by the name of the organ in which they originate. Cancer of the lung, for example, is described in the section on The Lung; Hodgkin's lymphoma, in the section on The Lymph Nodes; and leukemia, in the section on The Blood. The only major organ that is not discussed is the liver, because cancer that originates in the liver is rare.

Most readers will use this chapter primarily for reference. Thus each section has been divided into clearly defined units: (i) description of the organ, (ii) function of the organ, (iii) description of the disease, (iv) symptoms, (v) diagnosis, (vi) treatment, (vii) possible side effects of treatment, (viii) prognosis, (ix) geographic pattern, (x) ethnic pattern, (xi) occupational pattern, (xii) age pattern, and (xiii) specific causes. All information is easily accessible.

Readers who doubt that cancer is many different diseases may wish to read at one sitting all the units entitled Description of the Disease, or all those entitled Treatment or Prognosis. They will find that cancer of the colon, for example, begins in the lining of the organ, while cancer of the testicle begins in the interior; that cancer of the prostate spreads slowly, while cancer of the lung spreads quickly; that cancer of the ovary responds to all proven treatments, while cancer of the stomach responds only to surgery; that cancer of the vocal cords (see the section on The Throat) is almost always curable, while cancer of the pancreas is not. Even an individual section – like that on The Bladder, or The Skin, or The Thyroid – can show that cancer is a varied disease: in the bladder, a cancerous polyp is nothing like a cancerous tumor that invades the muscle wall; in the skin, a basal cell cancer is nothing like a melanoma; and in the thyroid, a well-differentiated tumor is nothing like an undifferentiated one.

Although this chapter may appear to be independent, it is best understood in relation to the first two chapters, which give general information on the disease and on the ways it is diagnosed and treated. In addition, the reader should see the material on widespread cancer (chapter four), so that he may understand why the rate of cure for cancer is often remarkably low, even when patients have received appropriate treatment from excellent doctors. Until widespread cancer can be controlled, most of the various cancers will be alike in at least one regard: that is, in their ability to defy all present means to cure them.

THE BLADDER

DESCRIPTION OF THE ORGAN Located directly behind the pubic bones, the bladder is a muscular sack that serves as a reservoir for urine. When empty, it is small and limp. When full, it expands into the lower abdomen and assumes a spherical shape.

FUNCTION OF THE ORGAN Urine flows down from the kidneys to the bladder through two long (10 to 12 inch) muscular tubes. These tubes, the ureters, contract one to five times a minute in order to assist the urine's passage to the bladder. Urine collects until specialized nerves cause a muscular action that forces the urine out of the bladder, down through another tube (the urethra), and out of the body. Although primarily a reflex action, urination can be controlled: voluntary contraction of the sphincter muscle at the top of the urethra can prevent urination. In men, the urethra is a fairly long tube, traveling from the bladder, through the prostate gland, to the end of the penis. In women, the urethra is much shorter, running from the bladder to an opening next to the vagina.

DESCRIPTION OF THE DISEASE Generally arising in the lining of the organ, cancer of the bladder takes one of two forms. It may grow like a balloon, remaining entirely within the bladder and connected to the bladder wall by a thin stalk. Or it may spread like lava, often breaking through the muscles of the bladder wall early in the course of the disease. Balloon tumors are often called polyps.

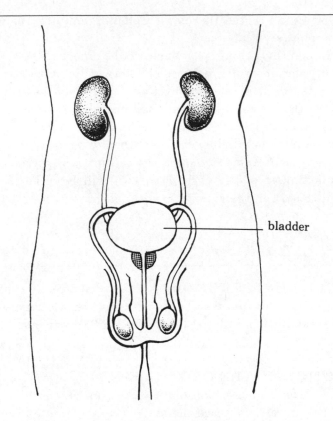

bladder

SYMPTOMS The usual symptom is blood in the urine. When bleeding is heavy, the urine will be deep red in color; when light, it will be rusty. The character of the bleeding – heavy or light, frequent or infrequent – reveals nothing about the size or stage of the cancer. In fact, the bleeding may disappear for days, weeks, or even months while the cancer continues to grow. For this reason, blood in the urine should be reported to a doctor even if the symptom goes away.

In addition to bleeding, some patients experience the need to urinate more often than usual. Others suffer discomfort during urination because of muscle spasms in the bladder.

DIAGNOSIS The doctor reaches a preliminary diagnosis by taking X-ray pictures of the patient's kidneys in order to learn if they are the source of his bleeding, and by analyzing the patient's urine (urinalysis). If the kidneys are not diseased, the doctor will proceed by examining the bladder through a cystoscope – a narrow tube that is passed into the bladder through the urethra. The cystoscope, which resembles a pencil flashlight with a slot for a knife at its end, allows the doctor not only to see inside the bladder, but also to remove or take biopsies of any tumors he may find there. When a cystoscope is used only to examine the bladder, no anaesthetic is needed; when it is used to perform a biopsy, a general anaesthetic must be given to the patient.

TREATMENT Surgery is used to treat both balloon tumors and lava tumors that grow in the bladder. Balloon tumors (polyps) are easy to remove: because they grow into the bladder cavity without invading the muscles of the bladder wall, they can be scooped out with a knife inserted into the end of a cystoscope, a process called a transurethral resection. Lava tumors require more extensive surgery: because they destroy the bladder wall, they cannot be surgically removed unless the entire bladder is removed with them.

Whether radiotherapy is useful in combination with surgery for treating cancer of the bladder is a question now being studied. Occasionally, radiotherapy is used as the sole treatment for lava tumors; but X-rays are generally able to cure only those lava tumors that have not invaded the bladder wall extensively.

Chemotherapy is seldom effective for treating cancer of the bladder.

POSSIBLE SIDE EFFECTS OF TREATMENT When balloon tumors (polyps) have been removed from the bladder, the patient may need to urinate frequently.

When the bladder has been removed, the patient must learn to live with an artificial bladder made from a portion of small intestine (an ileal bladder). An ileal bladder empties through a hole (stoma) constructed in the wall of the abdomen. Because patients with ileal bladders cannot control urination, they must wear a plastic bag to collect the urine that constantly drips from the stoma. When properly maintained, the bag emits no odor and causes no telltale bulge on the patient's body. Patients with ileal bladders may thus engage in nearly all the normal activities of life. But they are unusually susceptible to urinary infection, chemical imbalance in the blood, and kidney damage. And they must expect to suffer impotence or sexual dysfunction: when the bladder is removed, so too are the nerves responsible in men for erections of the penis and in women for sexual pleasure during intercourse. Although removal of the bladder causes impotence in men, it does not disable women from bearing healthy children.

For the usual side effects of radiotherapy, see pp. 57–58. Additional side effects may include frequent need to urinate, burning pain during urination, blood in the urine, diarrhea, and sometimes an impairment of the intestine that may eventually require surgical correction.

PROGNOSIS The prognosis for patients with cancer of the bladder ranges from very poor to very good. Patients whose cancers have spread to the lymph nodes are rarely curable; but all others have fair hope of survival. Among patients with lava tumors that have penetrated or broken through the wall of the bladder, 20 percent are alive five years after treatment. Among those with polyps that are confined to the lining of the bladder or only superficially embedded in the muscle wall, 60 percent are alive five years after treatment. Patients with low malignancy polyps survive in nine cases out of ten; although most are cured by transurethral resection, some must undergo removal of the bladder to prevent the cancer from recurring.

GEOGRAPHIC PATTERN Egypt shows the highest rate for cancer of the bladder; Europe and the United States, the next highest; Japan, Sweden, and New Zealand, the lowest.

ETHNIC PATTERN None known. But four out of every five cancers of the bladder occur in men.

OCCUPATIONAL PATTERN Cancer of the bladder occurs most often in dye workers, tobacco smokers, and employees in some chemical industries.

AGE PATTERN Cancer of the bladder occurs most often in people between the ages of fifty-five and sixty-nine.

SPECIFIC CAUSES The chemical compound betanaphthylamine, an aromatic amine used in the manufacture of aniline dyes, can cause cancer of the bladder. So, too, can the other aromatic amines.

In Egypt, cancer of the bladder has been associated with the parasitic fluke *Schistosoma haematobium* – a Nile-bred worm that enters the body through the foot, buries itself in the wall of the bladder, and causes changes that can lead to cancer.

THE BLOOD

DESCRIPTION OF THE ORGAN The blood is a liquid tissue that circulates to the skin, the bones, and all the internal organs – that is, circulates throughout the entire body. Traveling through an elaborate system of blood vessels that penetrate deeply into every tissue, the blood bears nutrients to the cells of the body and takes away their waste products. Nutrients are gathered by the blood as it circulates through the lungs, where it absorbs oxygen, and through the small intestine, where it absorbs the products of digestion. Wastes are removed from the blood as it circulates through the spleen, liver, lungs, and kidneys.

The liquid portion of the blood consists of plasma, which contains water, proteins, sugars, and assorted chemicals to nourish the body. The solid portion consists of three types of cells: red blood cells, which are produced in the bone marrow; platelets, also produced in the marrow; and white blood cells, which are produced in both the marrow and the lymph nodes. The red blood cells gather oxygen from the lungs. The platelets help the blood to clot when the body has been injured. And the white blood cells, of which there are several different kinds, help the body to fight infection.

blood cells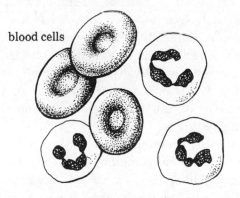

FUNCTION OF THE ORGAN The blood nourishes the tissues of the body by supplying them with oxygen and the products of digestion. It bears away from these tissues waste products that are discharged from the kidneys as urine, from the sweat glands as perspiration, and from the lungs as carbon dioxide. It protects the body from foreign substances by delivering white blood cells to the sites of infection or injury. It helps to maintain the proper temperature in the body. And it regulates the amount of fluid that resides in and between the body's cells.

DESCRIPTION OF THE DISEASE Leukemia is a cancer of the
bone marrow or the lymph nodes; but it expresses itself as a disease of
the blood. The cancer affects the white-blood-cell-forming tissues of the
marrow and the nodes, causing them to produce immature white blood
cells in endless numbers. These immature, or leukemic, cells replace
normal white blood cells, so that the body may become subject to infectious disease. In addition, the leukemic cells glut the blood, crowding
out platelets and red blood cells so that the body bleeds easily and
receives insufficient supplies of oxygen. For this reason, patients with
leukemia usually die from secondary causes such as rampant infection
or massive internal bleeding.

There are four different types of leukemia:

1 Acute lymphocytic leukemia – also called acute lymphoblastic
leukemia. This cancer generally occurs in children. Leukemic white
blood cells rapidly glut the bone marrow, pour over into the bloodstream, and invade the lymph nodes, the spleen, and such vital organs
of the body as the liver, brain, and kidneys. In addition, the cells may
spill into the stomach and the testicles or ovaries. As the leukemic
cells spread, internal bleeding (hemorrhaging) may occur.

2 Acute myelocytic leukemia – also called granulocytic leukemia or
myelogenous leukemia. Generally occurring in adults, this cancer affects
the granulocytes, which are one of several different kinds of white blood
cells produced in the bone marrow. The leukemic granulocytes prolifer-
ate rapidly, invading the lymph nodes, the spleen, and eventually the
vital organs of the body. As the leukemic cells spread, internal bleeding
(hemorrhaging) may occur.

3 Chronic myelocytic leukemia – also called chronic granulocytic
leukemia, chronic myeloid leukemia, or chronic myelogenous leukemia.
Like acute myelocytic leukemia (see 2 above), this cancer occurs mainly
in adults and causes uncontrolled proliferation of the granulocytes in
the bone marrow. At first, the cancer progresses slowly, sometimes re-
gressing on one or more occasions. But in its later stages (that is, about
three years after diagnosis), chronic myelocytic leukemia behaves very
much like the acute leukemias described above.

4 Chronic lymphocytic leukemia. In this cancer, which occurs in
adults, the leukemic cells accumulate slowly and when examined under
a microscope look very much like normal cells. Proliferating in the

lymph nodes, the leukemic white blood cells collect in the bone marrow and the blood vessels, eventually lodging in the lymph nodes, liver, and spleen.

Note: In some discussions of leukemia, the disease is divided into only two categories: acute leukemia and chronic leukemia.

SYMPTOMS All leukemias produce very much the same symptoms: weakness, fatigue, loss of appetite and weight, bruising, bleeding, susceptibility to infection, low-grade fever, and swelling of the lymph nodes, liver, and spleen. In addition, patients with acute leukemia may experience bone pain; and patients with chronic leukemia may experience fatigue and excessive sweating.

The symptoms of acute leukemias appear suddenly. Those of chronic myelocytic leukemia appear gradually. But chronic lymphocytic leukemia may be silent for many years, often producing no symptoms for as long as a decade.

DIAGNOSIS The doctor examines samples of blood and bone marrow under a microscope to determine if a patient has leukemia. The blood is withdrawn through a needle inserted into a blood vessel, and the marrow through a needle inserted into a bone, while the patient is awake. In chronic leukemias, the white blood cells in the blood and in the marrow are far more numerous than they should be; in acute leukemias, the white blood cells are not only more numerous, but also entirely abnormal in appearance.

TREATMENT Acute lymphocytic leukemia in children is treated – and sometimes cured – with chemotherapy. Combinations of drugs are administered to leukemic children in large doses over long periods of time. In addition, antibiotics are prescribed to control infection; and blood transfusions – or platelet transfusions – are given to control hemorrhaging. If the doctor suspects that leukemic cells have spread to the brain, where drugs are unable to reach them, he may irradiate the brain as adjuvant treatment. An additional treatment for acute lymphocytic leukemia is bone marrow transplantation – a procedure in which the patient's diseased marrow is removed and replaced with healthy tissue. As in all transplant procedures, the donor of the tissue must be carefully chosen, so that the patient's immune system does not cause death by attacking the new marrow as a foreign substance.

Acute myelocytic leukemia in adults is treated in much the same way as acute lymphocytic leukemia in children. Although chemotherapy in adults is much more rigorous than in children, it produces no cures in the disease and shorter periods of remission.

Chronic myelocytic leukemia and chronic lymphocytic leukemia can, to various degrees, be controlled – but never cured – with chemotherapy. In adults with these leukemias, drugs are administered in modest doses for as long as they are effective. Although some doctors apply X-rays to the entire body instead of using chemotherapy as the sole treatment for patients with chronic leukemias, radiotherapy is generally used only to shrink organs enlarged by accumulations of leukemic white blood cells.

POSSIBLE SIDE EFFECTS OF TREATMENT For the usual side effects of chemotherapy, see pp. 63–64. During the course of treatment, drugs – like leukemia itself – make the body susceptible to infection and hemorrhaging. In addition, chemotherapy may weaken the bones, damage the liver, and scar the lungs. Children treated with chemotherapy may remain abnormally small; they may also become infertile.

For the usual side effects of radiotherapy, see pp. 57–58. When radiotherapy is used in adults, the doses of X-rays are generally modest and the side effects minimal. In children, radiotherapy, when it is administered with the drug methotrexate, may damage the brain.

Bone marrow transplantation is a hazardous procedure, and the side effects may be numerous. Patients undergoing transplants should discuss these effects with their doctors.

PROGNOSIS Among children who receive a full schedule of treatment for acute lymphocytic leukemia, 90 to 95 percent experience a remission of the disease; and approximately 50 percent survive for five years. Some of these children are undoubtedly cured. But cures are least likely in children with a low number of red blood cells and platelets, a high number of circulating leukemic white blood cells, enlarged organs, and the presence of leukemic cells in the spinal fluid.

Adults with acute myelocytic leukemia survive only a few months without treatment. But among some patients, chemotherapy may extend their lives for as long as several years.

Among adults who are treated for chronic myelocytic leukemia, 50 percent survive for three years; 10 percent survive for five years.

Among adults who are treated for chronic lymphocytic leukemia, 90 percent experience a temporary remission of the disease; 40 to 50 percent survive for five years; 30 percent survive for ten years. Although there is little evidence that treatment significantly extends the lives of patients with chronic lymphocytic leukemia, which progresses very slowly, chemotherapy and radiotherapy administered at appropriate intervals can greatly improve their quality of life.

GEOGRAPHIC PATTERN None known, although chronic leukemias are almost nonexistent in Japan.

ETHNIC PATTERN Acute leukemia is more common among whites than among blacks; but the rate of cure is higher among whites. Chronic leukemia occurs more often in men than in women.

OCCUPATIONAL PATTERN Benzene workers suffer a higher than normal rate of acute leukemia.

AGE PATTERN Acute lymphocytic leukemia occurs most often in children between the ages of three and ten. All other leukemias occur most often in adults over the age of thirty-five.

SPECIFIC CAUSES Exposure to radiation can cause acute leukemia, as it did among children who survived the atom bomb explosions at Hiroshima and Nagasaki. Among children who have been treated with therapeutic – not diagnostic – doses of radiation, the disease occurs at a slightly higher than normal rate. Among cancer patients who have received radiotherapy for cancers other than leukemia, the rate of leukemia is not much higher than it is in the general population. But among patients who have received a combined treatment of radiotherapy and chemotherapy for Hodgkin's lymphoma (see the section on The Lymph Nodes), the rate of leukemia is somewhat higher than normal.

Benzene has been identified as the cause of some leukemias. In addition, doctors are investigating a possible relationship between leukemia and viruses.

High-risk children include those with genetic abnormalities. In particular, children with Down's syndrome (mongolism) are susceptible to acute myelocytic leukemia.

THE BONE

DESCRIPTION OF THE ORGAN The skeleton of the body contains over 200 bones joined together by cartilage and connective tissue (ligaments). Individual bones may be long, short, flat, or irregular in shape; but all of them are made of the same elements – water, protein, and mineral salts (calcium and phosphorus). The protein and salts form a framework to house living bone cells (osteocytes). The mineral salts, which are hardened or calcified, give the bone its usual hardness and rigidity.

A typical bone contains three structural parts: (i) at each end, a knobby protrusion composed of smooth lubricated cartilage that makes up one-half of a joint; (ii) a long rigid shaft composed of bony tissue that forms canals to house nutrients for the bone-making cells; and (iii) within the shaft, a cavity for bone marrow (blood-forming tissue). Long bones, like the thigh or the forearm, function as struts. Flat bones, like the pelvis or ribs, are a major source of bone marrow. The jaw and the

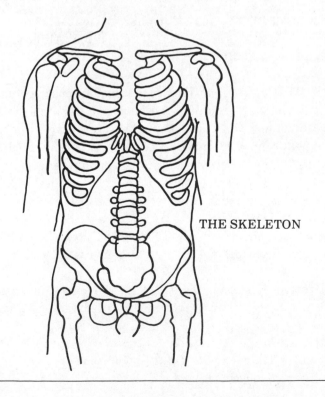

THE SKELETON

skull, at least in an adult, contain very little marrow and serve mainly a protective function. Individual bones, then, differ somewhat in shape and character, depending on their position and function within the body.

FUNCTION OF THE ORGAN The bones provide the body with support. They work as levers for the muscles that are attached to them. They protect the body's organs from injury: the skull, for example, protects the brain; and the ribcage protects the heart and the lungs. They store minerals – in particular, calcium and phosphorus – for use by the body. And they house, in their numerous cavities for marrow, the cells that form the blood.

DESCRIPTION OF THE DISEASE Usually occurring in the leg, arm, rib, or pelvis, cancer of the bone may arise from any living cell in the bone or in the marrow. But cancers that originate within these cells (primary cancers of the bone) are relatively rare, except among teen-agers and young adults. Most cancers in the bone are secondary tumors that have spread (metastasized) from distant parts of the body – usually from the breast, kidney, thyroid, or prostate.

The most common primary cancer of the bone is osteosarcoma – a cancer that arises from a bone-forming cell. Usually beginning near the knee, an osteosarcoma makes the bone soft and mushy, so that the grain that streaks the bone looks like a highway that ends abruptly in a swamp. As the cancer grows, it breaks through the bone and flows into surrounding muscles and tendons.

Other primary cancers of the bone include chondrosarcoma, which arises from a cell in the cartilage; lymphomas of the bone, which arise from blood-forming cells in the marrow; and Ewing's sarcoma, which appears to arise from primitive cells in the bone.

SYMPTOMS Symptoms do not occur until the disease is well advanced. Then the patient may experience pain and swelling in the area of the cancer, and occasionally fever. Even these symptoms, however, are difficult to recognize as signs of cancer. They are often mistaken for signs of muscle strain, bursitis, arthritis, or sprain.

DIAGNOSIS As a preliminary step, the doctor takes X-ray pictures of the bone and examines the chemistry of the patient's blood. If a cancer is suspected, a biopsy must be performed by means of surgery, while the patient is under a general anaesthetic.

TREATMENT Surgery is the usual treatment for osteosarcoma and chondrosarcoma. Since these cancers tend to spread into the marrow and into the muscle attached to the bone, the diseased limb is usually amputated at a joint above the tumor. But recently, in order to preserve the limbs of children, particularly their arms and hands, pediatricians have begun experimenting with a surgical procedure less radical than amputation. In this procedure, only the cancerous section of bone is removed. Set in its place is a substitute, which is sometimes a new piece of bone taken from a deceased person. Because the procedure is quite new, doctors do not yet know whether it produces a cure and whether the rebuilt bone is strong enough to last for many years.

Radiotherapy is the usual treatment for Ewing's sarcoma and for lymphomas of the bone.

Chemotherapy has proved useful as adjuvant treatment (see pp. 60–61) for both osteosarcoma and Ewing's sarcoma. In some patients, a new way of administering chemotherapy is being investigated: powerful, and hence possibly lethal, doses of a cancer drug are dripped directly into the patient's blood vessel; then, several hours later, the patient receives multiple doses of an antidote that prevents the cancer drug from causing death.

When an arrested primary cancer of the bone has spread to the lungs, but to no other part of the body, surgery to remove a secondary tumor in the lungs can sometimes cure the patient.

POSSIBLE SIDE EFFECTS OF TREATMENT Amputation of a leg or an arm must be followed by a period of rehabilitation, during which the patient may learn to use an artificial limb. Such a limb is usually quite functional when the leg has been amputated at a point just above the knee. But when the leg has been amputated at the hip or pelvis, an artificial limb may have only a cosmetic purpose, and many patients find it easier to walk with crutches. When the hand has been removed, an artificial hand can be constructed; but patients who prefer function to appearance generally choose to wear a hook.

For the usual side effects of radiotherapy, see pp. 57–58. Additional side effects may include a gradual withering of the limb over a period of months or years; a devitalization of bone tissue, so that the bone is easily fractured; and a swelling or accumulation of fluid in the irradiated limb. When radiotherapy is used as adjuvant treatment after amputation, these side effects can cause an artificial limb to fit poorly.

For the usual side effects of chemotherapy, see pp. 63–64. Additional side effects may include hemorrhaging of the bladder and damage to the vital organs – namely, the heart, kidneys, and liver.

PROGNOSIS Among patients who undergo amputation for osteosarcoma, 15 to 20 percent are alive five years after treatment. When the surgery is followed by adjuvant chemotherapy, the drugs retard the development of secondary tumors (metastases) in distant parts of the body; but doctors do not yet know whether adjuvant chemotherapy improves the five-year rate of cure among these patients.

Among patients with chondrosarcomas, 50 percent are alive five years after surgery.

Among patients with Ewing's sarcoma, 15 percent survive for five years. The rate of cure is lower for patients who have experienced late symptoms like fever and loss of weight; but new types of adjuvant treatment are improving these patients' chances for survival.

Among patients with lymphomas that are confined to the bone, 50 percent are alive five years after radiotherapy.

GEOGRAPHIC PATTERN None known.

ETHNIC PATTERN None known.

OCCUPATIONAL PATTERN Cancer of the bone occurred frequently among workers who painted radium dials on the faces of clocks and watches. Most susceptible were those workers who ingested radium while shaping the tips of their brushes against their tongues.

AGE PATTERN Osteosarcoma occurs most often in people between the ages of fifteen and thirty; chondrosarcoma, in people between the ages of thirty and fifty; lymphomas of the bone, in people between the ages of twenty and thirty; Ewing's sarcoma, in people between the ages of fifteen and twenty-five.

SPECIFIC CAUSES Cancer of the bone is associated with radiation; hence it occurs frequently among people who have been exposed to nuclear fallout from atom bomb explosions and among people who have been treated with intense doses of low voltage (orthovoltage) X-rays. The disease occurs most often among those who have ingested radio-active compounds – for example, radium dial workers.

THE BRAIN

DESCRIPTION OF THE ORGAN The brain is located in the upper portion of the head within a cavity protected by the rigid bones of the skull. Gelatin-like in texture, the brain is encased in three membranes. Between two of these membranes flows a thin layer of spinal fluid, which delivers and bears away chemicals and cushions the brain from shock. The three major parts of the brain are: the cerebrum, which fills most of the skull; the cerebellum, which occupies the lower back of the head; and the brainstem, which forms the base of the brain and leads into the spinal cord.

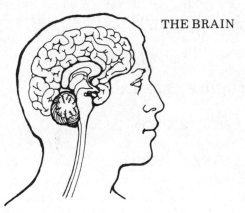

THE BRAIN

FUNCTION OF THE ORGAN Each part of the brain has a unique structure and function. The cerebrum governs thought, emotion, move-ment, speech, sight, smell, touch, taste, and hearing. The cerebellum governs balance and coordination. The brainstem governs heartbeat and breathing, swallowing, salivation, and sleep.

DESCRIPTION OF THE DISEASE In adults, brain cancers usually arise deep within the cerebrum; the tumors spread like lava, causing the brain to become soupy. In children, brain cancers usually arise in the cerebellum or brainstem; the tumors grow like balloons, obstructing the circulation of spinal fluid or pressing on nerves that serve the eyes and the face.

SYMPTOMS Symptoms depend on the area of the brain affected by the cancer. Adults may suffer headaches, seizures, a general decline in awareness, impairment of speech, difficulty in moving arms and legs, loss of memory generally involving recent events, and decreased ability to conduct such mental processes as addition and subtraction. Children may experience nausea and vomiting; they may suffer eye disorders, including double vision, crossed eyes, and occasionally blindness; and they may appear to walk drunkenly, taking frequent falls.

DIAGNOSIS As a first step, the doctor generally performs a computer scan or an isotope scan of the brain. During a computer scan, he may use dye, which will show whether a tumor has eroded any blood vessels. When a scan reveals a tumor in an accessible region of the brain, a surgeon will perform a biopsy in order to learn if the tumor is cancerous.

TREATMENT In adults, brain cancers are usually treated by surgery in combination with radiotherapy and chemotherapy. A surgeon removes as much as he can of the soupy tumor that has formed in the cerebrum. X-rays and drugs are then used to destroy the remaining cancerous cells. Throughout treatment, cortisone is prescribed to control swelling of the brain – a condition that causes death if the brain presses too tightly against the skull.

In children, tumors of the cerebellum – for example, cerebellar astrocytomas – can be completely removed through surgery. But tumors of the brainstem – for example, brainstem gliomas – cannot be treated surgically, because the brainstem controls heartbeat, swallowing, and breathing. Thus for tumors of the brainstem, radiotherapy is the only possible treatment. For a medulloblastoma – the tumor that most often in children obstructs the pathway of the spinal fluid around the brain – surgery is combined with radiotherapy. When a medulloblastoma is irradiated, treatment may take as long as twelve weeks, since X-rays are applied not only to the brain, but also to the entire length of the spinal cord. Chemotherapy has not proved effective for prolonging life in children with brain cancer.

POSSIBLE SIDE EFFECTS OF TREATMENT In both children and adults, brain surgery involves a high risk of death. When the patient survives an operation, his original symptoms may persist as permanent side effects of the surgery.

For the usual side effects of radiotherapy, see pp. 57–58. Additional late side effects include permanent baldness in adults, and slowness in learning and retarded growth in children.

For the usual side effects of chemotherapy, see pp. 63–64.

PROGNOSIS In adults, brain cancer is usually incurable, because the cerebrum can rarely tolerate the doses of X-rays and drugs necessary to destroy cancerous brain tissue. Most adults who undergo conventional treatment die within two years. Those who refuse treatment die sooner. In either case, the quality of the life remaining to the patient depends primarily on the area of the brain affected by the cancer.

In children, brain tumors that can be completely removed through surgery (for example, cerebellar astrocytomas) are often curable. Medulloblastomas are curable in a third to a half of all patients. But brainstem gliomas can rarely be cured. Although treatment can both lengthen the patient's life and improve the quality of his life, most children with brainstem gliomas die in two to five years.

GEOGRAPHIC PATTERN None known.

ETHNIC PATTERN None known.

OCCUPATIONAL PATTERN None known.

AGE PATTERN Brain cancers occur most frequently in adults between the ages of forty and sixty-five, and in children between the ages of five and fifteen.

SPECIFIC CAUSES None known.

THE BREAST

DESCRIPTION OF THE ORGAN Originating beneath the skin of the chest wall and lying against the muscles of the chest, the firm round breast of the adult female contains a network of glands, but is primarily composed of supporting connective tissue and soft yellow fat. During the menstrual cycle, the breast undergoes small changes in size and shape; during pregnancy and nursing, it enlarges considerably.

THE BREAST

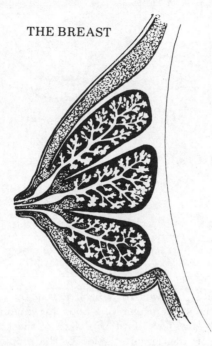

FUNCTION OF THE ORGAN The breast contains specialized glands designed to produce milk for the newborn infant. These glands, which are connected to the nipple through a system of pathways called ducts, begin to function during pregnancy and cease when the infant has been weaned.

DESCRIPTION OF THE DISEASE Cancers of the breast usually begin as gristly, grayish tumors that form within a duct and spread into the fatty part of the breast.

SYMPTOMS The usual symptom is a lump within the breast, sometimes accompanied by pain. Occasionally, areas of the breast may turn red; or the skin of the breast may dimple or ulcerate; or the nipple may release a discharge or retract.

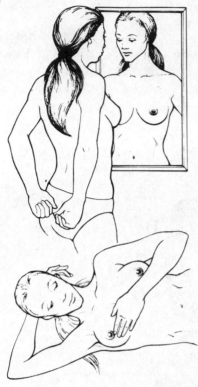

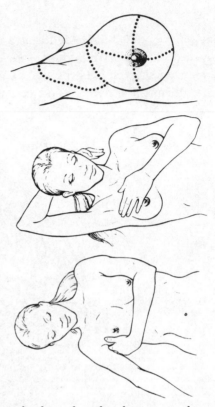

During self-examination, a woman looks for changes in the shape of her breasts. In addition, she feels for lumps in the breast or the armpit. Women who regularly examine their breasts soon learn the character of each breast, so that they can distinguish between normal and abnormal tissue. Every woman should examine her breasts at the end of each menstrual cycle or, if menopause has occurred, at monthly intervals.

INSTRUCTIONS

Unclothed before a mirror, stand straight with arms at the sides; lean forward slightly, with hands behind the back at the level of the buttocks; stand straight, place hands on hips, and tighten the muscles of the chest and arms; stand straight, place hands behind the neck and draw the elbows back so that the chest protrudes.

Look for dimpling or puckering in the skin of the breasts, or for retraction of the nipples. Also squeeze the nipples to see if blood, or any other discharge, is released.

Feel for lumps while lying with a pillow or a folded towel beneath the shoulders.

To examine the right breast, place the right hand behind the neck. Then, use the fingers of the left hand to examine the breast part by part, starting at the top of the breast, proceeding to the sides and the underside of the breast, and ending at the nipple. Then, feel for lumps in the armpit.

To examine the left breast, reverse the position of the arms and repeat the procedure.

DIAGNOSIS Most lumps are detected during self-examination of the breast – a simple, painless procedure that every woman should perform at the end of each menstrual cycle or, if menopause has occurred, at monthly intervals. (For instructions on examining the breast, see opposite.)

X-ray examination of the breast (mammography) can be used to detect lumps while they are still too small to be felt during physical examination. (Xerography, which is similar to mammography, involves more radiation and produces clearer pictures.) Some doctors think that mammography is unsafe, because the mammograph may, by exposing the breast to radiation, cause the cancer it was meant to detect. Even though modern machines expose the breast to very small – and hence relatively safe – amounts of radiation, mammography is still recommended only for high-risk patients over the age of thirty-five. The interval between mammographs should be at least one year.

A new diagnostic procedure currently under study is thermography, which measures heat patterns in the breast. Because the temperature of the skin sometimes rises in those parts of the breast that harbor a cancer, thermography may one day provide a safe means for detecting a tumor early in the disease. At present, however, thermography is useful only when combined with mammography.

A lump, of course, need not mean cancer. In fact, 80 percent of all breast tumors are not cancerous. *But any lump or change in the breast should be brought to a doctor's attention immediately.* If the doctor is not sure that the disorder is benign, he will perform a biopsy in order to reach a diagnosis. The biopsy can be performed while the patient is under a local anaesthetic, by means of a needle that withdraws tissue from the breast; or while the patient is under a general anaesthetic, by means of surgery. If the biopsy reveals a cancer, the doctor may perform additional biopsies in order to learn if the cancer has spread to the lymph nodes in the armpit.

TREATMENT In Europe and Canada, radiotherapy is frequently used as the sole treatment for cancer of the breast, particularly when the disease is discovered early. In some patients, radiotherapy can cure the cancer without altering the appearance of the breast. In other patients, radiotherapy may cause the breast to change in size and shape.

In the United States, surgery is generally the primary treatment for cancer of the breast. The surgeon may perform (i) a lumpectomy –

removal of the cancerous tumor; or (ii) a mastectomy – removal of the breast; or (iii) a modified radical mastectomy – removal of the breast and the lymph nodes in the armpit; or (iv) a radical mastectomy – removal of the breast, the lymph nodes in the armpit, and the muscles that lie beneath the breast. The surgeon's choice will depend on his evaluation of the cancer: its size, its spread, and its likelihood of recurring if maximum surgery is not performed. After surgery, radiotherapy may be administered either as a routine precautionary measure or as a means of treating cancerous cells that are thought to remain in neighboring tissue.

When cancer of the breast has spread throughout the body, treatments that may be used to supplement surgery and/or radiotherapy include: (i) chemotherapy; (ii) removal of the ovary, the adrenal gland, and/or the pituitary gland – organs that produce hormones favorable to the growth of cancerous breast tissue; (iii) therapy with hormones, which may be given by pill or by injection.

Although drugs and hormones can sometimes produce a temporary remission of the disease, at present no drug can cure cancer of the breast once it has spread to other parts of the body.

POSSIBLE SIDE EFFECTS OF TREATMENT Surgery may cause a feeling of tightness in the chest and arm, as well as numbness and discomfort in the area where the surgery was performed. Swelling of the arm may result from accumulation of fluid in the tissue. Although many women fear that a mastectomy is horribly disfiguring, it leaves only a thin scar that runs from the midpoint of the torso to the armpit, so that the woman's chest looks rather like that of a young boy. After the surgical incision has healed, a woman may wear a prosthetic device that cannot be distinguished beneath her clothing from a normal breast. About a year after surgery for a mastectomy, she may undergo cosmetic surgery to have her breast rebuilt. But women who choose cosmetic surgery must understand that a rebuilt breast never entirely resembles the one that has been removed.

For the usual side effects of radiotherapy, see pp. 57–58. Additional side effects include a tightening and thickening of the skin in the breast – a condition that can last for months and sometimes even years. Although in some women radiotherapy preserves the original appearance of the breast, in others it causes the breast to change radically in size and shape.

For the usual side effects of chemotherapy, see pp. 63–64. Additional side effects include fatigue, bladder irritation, and severe cold sores in the mouth. When female hormones are administered, the patient may experience vaginal bleeding. When male hormones are administered, the patient may notice increased sexual desire and she may become virilized – that is, she may develop acne, a beard, and other body hair; her clitoris may become enlarged; and her voice may deepen.

PROGNOSIS When cancer of the breast is discovered before it has spread to the lymph nodes, the patient can often be cured. Of these patients, 70 percent are alive ten years after treatment.

But when cancer of the breast has spread to the lymph nodes, the patient is less often cured. In general, only 30 percent of these patients are alive ten years after treatment. The survival rate, however, depends on the extent of the spread. Among patients with extensive spread to the lymph nodes, the cure rate is somewhat lower than 30 percent; among patients with minimal spread, the cure rate is somewhat higher.

The larger a malignant breast tumor, the greater the chance that the cancer has spread to the lymph nodes. In tumors larger than $2\frac{1}{2}$ inches, 75 percent will have spread to the nodes. In tumors less than $2\frac{1}{2}$ inches, 50 percent will have spread to the nodes. In tumors detectable only by means of mammography – those less than $\frac{1}{4}$ inch in size – no more than 10 percent will have spread to the nodes.

GEOGRAPHIC PATTERN None known, although it has been observed that cancer of the breast occurs far less often in Japanese women than in American and European women. If cultural differences account for this disparity, as many researchers believe, cancer of the breast may increase in Japan as the country becomes more westernized.

ETHNIC PATTERN Ethnic patterns reveal little about a woman's risk of developing cancer of the breast. More significant are a woman's economic status, marital status, and family history. Cancer of the breast tends to strike women who have rich diets and who are relatively wealthy, unmarried, and childless. High-risk women are those whose mothers, aunts, and/or sisters have suffered cancer of the breast. Every woman from a family in which cancer of the breast is common should advise her doctor of her family's cancer history.

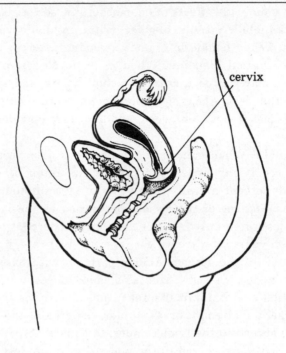

cervix

OCCUPATIONAL PATTERN None known.

AGE PATTERN Cancer of the breast occurs most often in women between the ages of forty and sixty-five.

SPECIFIC CAUSES None known. Despite folk belief, cancer of the breast has never been shown to arise from an injury to the breast.

THE CERVIX

DESCRIPTION OF THE ORGAN The cervix is the neck of the uterus. For a description of that organ and its function, see the section on The Uterus.

FUNCTION OF THE ORGAN The cervix functions as the passageway, or canal, that connects the uterus to the vagina. The menstrual tissues use this canal when they flow from the uterus into the vagina and out of the body. Sperm also use the canal to pass from the vagina into the uterus as they travel toward the unfertilized egg during conception.

DESCRIPTION OF THE DISEASE Cancer of the cervix arises in the lining at the lip of the cervix. The cancer, which resembles a tiny cauliflower, remains confined to the cervix for most of its course. But if it invades and destroys the muscle wall, cancer of the cervix can spread to the lymph nodes and to the rectum or the bladder. Eventually the cancer obstructs the ureters – the tubes through which urine flows to the bladder from the kidneys.

SYMPTOMS The usual symptom is vaginal bleeding after intercourse. Additional symptoms include pain during intercourse, unusual vaginal discharge, abnormal menstrual flow, and spotting between periods.

DIAGNOSIS The Pap test, sometimes called the Pap smear, can detect cancer of the cervix while it is 100 percent curable – that is, before a tumor can be seen or felt. Developed in the 1920s by Dr. George N. Papanicolaou, the test is painless and simple: cells are scraped from the vagina and cervix; they are smeared onto a glass plate and then examined under a microscope. If the test shows no abnormality, the patient is free of infection and cancer; *but as a precaution, she should repeat the test in a year*. If the test is classified as atypical, the patient may have an infection; after suitable treatment, she should be tested again. If the test is classified as suspicious or positive, the patient has either cancer of the cervix or dysplasia (an abnormal disposition of cells that may develop into cancer); a biopsy must be performed.

When a tumor is visible in the cervix, the doctor can perform a simple biopsy in his office by removing from the tumor some tissue to be examined under a microscope. If no tumor is visible, the doctor may perform a biopsy with the aid of a colposcope, a microscope for viewing living tissue at the top of the vagina. Or he may remove from the cervix a cone-shaped piece of tissue (conization) – a procedure performed in the hospital while the patient is under a general anaesthetic.

TREATMENT When detected early, cancer of the cervix can be treated with either surgery or radiotherapy. If surgery is used, the surgeon removes the uterus, Fallopian tubes, and lymph nodes. Although the ovaries may sometimes be removed as well, they are often allowed to remain, so that the patient can continue to produce normal amounts of estrogen. If radiotherapy is used, the doctor may administer radiation by machine or by inserting a radioactive material into the uterine cavity. Small cancers of the cervix respond equally well to surgery and radiotherapy. But X-rays have one great advantage: they can destroy cancerous cells that may have spread beyond the cervix to the lymph nodes and to other tissue. Since cancers of the cervix tend to spread, radiotherapy is generally the preferred method of treatment.

When cancer of the cervix is detected late, and when radiotherapy fails to produce a cure, extensive surgery may be performed as a last resort. In some patients with advanced cancers, it is sufficient for the surgeon to remove only the uterus, Fallopian tubes, and ovaries, along with the surrounding tissue and lymph nodes. But more often, the bladder and rectum must also be removed.

Chemotherapy is not generally effective for treating cancer of the cervix, although doctors have recently found some combinations of drugs that may prove useful.

POSSIBLE SIDE EFFECTS OF TREATMENT Surgery causes loss of fertility in premenopausal women and shortening of the vagina in all patients. It may also cause the patient to lose control of urination or to experience swelling in the arms and legs. Removal of the bladder requires the construction of an ileal bladder for the elimination of urine (see the section on The Bladder). Removal of the rectum requires construction of a colostomy for the elimination of feces (see the section on The Colon-Rectum).

For the usual side effects of radiotherapy, see pp. 57–58. Additional side effects include narrowing of the vagina and loss of fertility. (Patients who continue to have intercourse during radiotherapy are less inclined to experience narrowing of the vagina than those who practice abstinence.) Patients may also suffer impairments of the small intestine, the large intestine, and the bladder – conditions that may eventually require surgical correction.

PROGNOSIS The rate of cure for patients with cancer of the cervix ranges from excellent to poor. Among patients whose tumors are not visible, nearly 100 percent can be cured. Among those whose tumors are confined to the cervix, 70 to 90 percent are alive five years after treatment. The smaller the tumor, the better the rate of cure. When the cancer has invaded the tissues neighboring the cervix, 40 to 60 percent of the patients survive the disease; when it has eroded the bladder or rectum, only 20 percent survive. For patients whose cancers have spread to the lymph nodes, each of the above percentages must be reduced by half.

GEOGRAPHIC PATTERN Cancer of the cervix tends to occur in areas of low socio-economic status.

ETHNIC PATTERN Black women suffer cancer of the cervix twice as often as white women, perhaps for social and economic reasons. In addition, women whose sexual partners have not been circumcised suffer a higher rate of the disease than women whose sexual partners have been circumcised. The disease also tends to strike women who begin sexual intercourse early in life and who have many pregnancies or many sexual partners. Cancer of the cervix, however, is *not* prima facie evidence of promiscuity.

As a precaution, all sexually active women over the age of eighteen should have a Pap test once a year, every year of their lives. No woman need die from cancer of the cervix; when discovered early, the disease is curable.

OCCUPATIONAL PATTERN None known.

AGE PATTERN Cancer of the cervix occurs most often in women between the ages of forty and fifty-five.

SPECIFIC CAUSES None known.* But doctors are investigating the possibility that cancer of the cervix is associated with the genital herpes virus (see p. 29).

---

*DES – a drug prescribed during the 1940s, 50s, and 60s to prevent miscarriages in pregnant women – has been associated with a rare form of cancer sometimes found in the daughters of women who took the drug. When discovered early, this cancer, which occurs in the vagina *near*, but not in, the cervix, is curable by surgery or radiotherapy. DES, incidentally, has never been proven effective in preventing miscarriages.

THE COLON-RECTUM

DESCRIPTION OF THE ORGAN A muscular tube about $5\frac{1}{2}$ feet long, the colon-rectum (large intestine) forms the last part of the body's digestive tract, which consists of the mouth, throat, esophagus, stomach, small intestine, and large intestine. Beginning in the lower right side of the abdomen, the colon ascends to a point just above the waist, crosses to the left side of the body, and descends into the pelvic cavity. There it loops back into an S-shaped curve and becomes the rectum, which is merely a continuation of the colon. Descending toward the back of the body, the rectum narrows into the anal canal, which opens from the body at the anus.

FUNCTION OF THE ORGAN The colon and rectum receive the

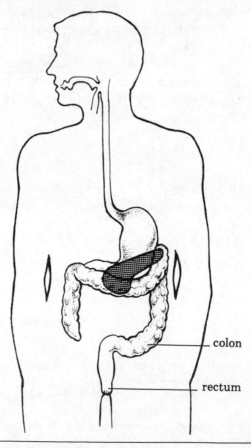

colon

rectum

waste products that remain from food digested in the small intestine. Sugars, fats, proteins, and vitamins are absorbed into the bloodstream as they travel through more than 30 feet of small intestine coiled in the abdominal cavity. Feces, composed of solid residue and excess water, pass into the colon and the rectum.

Within the colon, water is absorbed from the feces so that they become pasty. Muscular contractions force the feces into the rectum and then, by a reflex action, out of the body. Although defecation is largely governed by involuntary muscles, the process can be controlled: voluntary contraction of the anal sphincter muscle can prevent defecation, while voluntary contraction of certain abdominal muscles may initiate it.

DESCRIPTION OF THE DISEASE Cancer begins in the lining of the colon. As it enlarges, the cancer protrudes into the cavity through which the feces pass, eventually causing an obstruction.

SYMPTOMS Rectal bleeding, abdominal cramps, and persistent constipation or diarrhea are all symptoms of cancer in the colon. If bleeding is heavy, the patient may suffer from general weakness caused by loss of blood.

DIAGNOSIS Even before the symptoms of cancer occur, tumors near the anus may be discovered by digital (finger) examination of the rectum – a procedure that should be part of every patient's annual checkup after the age of forty. Other tumors may be found during examination with a proctosigmoidoscope – an inflexible lighted tube that reaches into the colon, enabling the doctor to see about 12 inches of the organ's interior. Since cancer of the colon is usually curable if it is discovered early, some doctors think that a "procto," which causes only mild discomfort, should be performed every three to five years in all adults over the age of forty-five. Other doctors think that a "procto" is necessary only when a prior test – a hemoccult – reveals the presence of occult, or hidden, blood in a smear of the patient's feces. Although a hemoccult cannot reveal the presence of a cancer, it can alert the doctor to the existence of a lesion that should be promptly diagnosed in case it is malignant.

When cancer of the colon or the rectum is suspected, the doctor may look for a tumor through a proctosigmoidoscope or through a flexible tube – a fiberoptic colonoscope – that can be threaded through the entire length of the colon. But more often he takes X-ray pictures of the colon and the rectum after the patient has been given an enema containing a mixture of dyes (a barium enema). If a tumor is discovered, a biopsy is necessary. Often the biopsy can be performed through a proctosigmoidoscope or a fiberoptic colonoscope – a procedure for which the patient requires only a mild sedative. But occasionally, the doctor must perform a biopsy by making an incision in the abdominal wall (laparotomy), while the patient is under a general anaesthetic.

TREATMENT Surgery is the primary treatment for cancer of the colon or the rectum. The surgeon removes not only the portion of intestine that contains the cancer, but also any lymph nodes to which the cancer may have spread. When a tumor occurs within 4 inches of the anus, the entire rectum must be removed, and a new opening for feces (a colostomy) constructed in the abdominal wall. But with most other tumors, the rectum can be preserved; by sewing together the severed ends of the colon, the surgeon enables the feces to pass through the colon to the rectum and out of the body.

Radiotherapy produces very few cures in patients with cancer of the colon or the rectum. Since recurrence happens frequently in cancers that have broken through the wall of the intestine, some doctors use radiotherapy as a precautionary measure after surgery; but the value of such adjuvant treatment has not yet been proved.

Chemotherapy cannot cure cancer of the colon or the rectum. But it may improve the patient's condition when the cancer has spread to distant parts of the body.

POSSIBLE SIDE EFFECTS OF TREATMENT When the rectum is removed, patients must learn to live with a colostomy – a new opening for feces constructed in the abdominal wall. By avoiding foods that disagree with them and by "irrigating" the colostomy with enemas every day or so, these patients (colostomates) can learn to regulate their bowel movements so that they need not wear a bag over the colostomy nor worry about embarrassing accidents. Once colostomates have made the necessary physical and psychological adjustments, they can participate in all the normal activities of life.

For the usual side effects of radiotherapy, see pp. 57–58.

For the usual side effects of chemotherapy, see pp. 63–64.

PROGNOSIS Half of all patients with cancer of the colon or the rectum are alive five years after treatment. Among patients whose cancers have not spread to the lymph nodes, 70 percent survive the disease.

GEOGRAPHIC PATTERN Europe and the United States show the highest rates for cancer of the colon and the rectum; Africa and Chile, the lowest. The disease rarely occurs in areas where cancer of the stomach is common.

ETHNIC PATTERN None known.

OCCUPATIONAL PATTERN None known. But scientists are investigating the possibility that asbestos workers suffer a higher than normal rate of the disease.

AGE PATTERN Cancer of the colon and the rectum occurs most often in adults between the ages of forty and seventy-nine.

SPECIFIC CAUSES None known. But diet has been suggested as a possible cause, since cancer of the colon and the rectum is common among people who eat low-fiber diets containing large quantities of beef, carbohydrates, fats, and refined foods. Currently, scientists are attempting to identify in the feces chemicals that may initiate the growth of a cancer.

High-risk adults include those with chronic ulcerative colitis, multiple polyps of the colon, or a strong family history of polyps or cancer of the colon and rectum.

THE ESOPHAGUS

DESCRIPTION OF THE ORGAN Beginning just above and behind the Adam's apple, the esophagus is a 10 inch tube that connects the throat to the stomach. Lined with mucous tissue that keeps it moist, the esophagus is composed of two very thin layers of muscle.

FUNCTION OF THE ORGAN When food, liquid, or saliva enters the esophagus from the throat, the esophageal muscles contract, in a con-

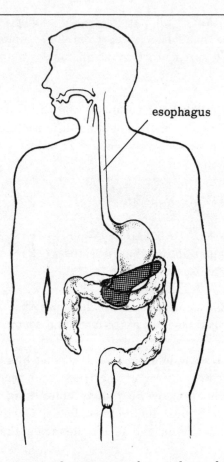

esophagus

tinuous wave from top to bottom, to force the substance into the stomach.

SYMPTOMS Cancer of the esophagus produces no reliable early warning symptoms. Late in the disease, the patient may experience pain or difficulty in swallowing, choking sensations during attempts to drink liquids, and gradual but extreme loss of weight.

DIAGNOSIS When the doctor suspects the presence of cancer, he performs a fluoroscopy – that is, he takes X-ray pictures of the esophagus while the patient swallows a mixture of dyes (barium). Although on X-ray pictures a cancerous tumor of the esophagus is often easy to distinguish from a benign tumor, the diagnosis of cancer must be confirmed by a biopsy. While the patient is under a general anaesthetic, the doctor performs the biopsy with an esophagoscope – a long tube that is passed down the mouth and throat into the esophagus, where tissue is removed from the tumor to be examined under a microscope.

TREATMENT If cancer of the esophagus is discovered early while it is confined to the lining of the organ, radical surgery is generally performed. A large portion of the esophagus is removed and, in some patients, replaced with a piece of intestine. But more often the stomach is tilted up from the abdomen into the chest and connected to the remaining piece of esophagus. Although the surgery is intended to alleviate the patient's difficulties in swallowing, it does not always do so. In a few patients, radiotherapy may be used after surgery as adjuvant treatment.

When an early cancer is discovered high in the esophagus, radical radiotherapy is generally used. During six to eight weeks of treatment, X-rays are applied to a large portion of the organ.

Unfortunately, cancer of the esophagus is usually discovered only when it is far advanced and cannot be cured. Radiotherapy may then be used to relieve distressing symptoms of the disease. In addition, surgery may be used to place in the esophagus a permanent tube that restores the patient's ability to swallow normally.

Chemotherapy has not proved effective in treating cancer of the esophagus.

POSSIBLE SIDE EFFECTS OF TREATMENT After surgery, because the wall of the esophagus is very thin, tears may occur in the surgical seam that joins the original part of the organ to the artificially constructed part. Leaks that arise in these tears may lead to infection and possibly even death.

For the usual side effects of radiotherapy, see pp. 57–58. Additional side effects include further loss of weight, further difficulty in swallowing, shortness of breath, hoarseness, and injury to neighboring portions of the lung or spinal cord.

PROGNOSIS Despite all treatment, cancer of the esophagus tends to progress relentlessly. Fewer than 10 percent of all patients are alive five years after treatment. On the average, patients live only nine months after their symptoms first appear.

GEOGRAPHIC PATTERN Cancer of the esophagus occurs frequently among men in Puerto Rico, Bantus in South Africa, and blacks in eastern South Carolina. Japan, France, Finland, Southern Russia, and the Honan province in China also show high rates of the disease.

ETHNIC PATTERN None known.

OCCUPATIONAL PATTERN None known.

AGE PATTERN Cancer of the esophagus occurs most often among adults between the ages of sixty and seventy.

SPECIFIC CAUSES Heavy smoking and heavy consumption of alcohol can cause cancer of the esophagus. Recent studies suggest that those who both smoke heavily and drink heavily are far more likely to develop cancer of the esophagus than are those who only smoke or only drink.

High-risk adults include those who have been afflicted with cancer of the throat and those who have suffered inflammation and scarring of the esophagus as a consequence of having swallowed lye.

THE KIDNEY

DESCRIPTION OF THE ORGAN Located at the back of the body just above the waist are two kidneys. Each kidney is bean-shaped and relatively small, weighing only a third of a pound in the average adult and measuring about 5 inches long, 3 inches wide, and 1 inch thick. Blood flows into each kidney through a large artery (a renal artery) and passes out through a large vein (the renal vein). Urine also passes out of each kidney, flowing through a muscular tube (a ureter) that leads into the bladder. Each kidney is covered by a thin, white membrane and supported on a bed of fatty tissue.

FUNCTION OF THE ORGAN The kidneys form urine by removing from the blood substances that the body cannot use. Some of these substances are potentially poisonous chemicals derived from digested food and drugs; if these chemicals are not excreted, the body will die. Other substances gained from digestion – for example, salt, sugar, amino acids, and water – are necessary to the body, but only in appropriate amounts; if excess amounts of these substances are not excreted, the body will sicken. By continuously filtering the blood, the kidneys preserve the proper balance of chemicals in the body and regulate the amount of fluid that the body retains.

Among the hardest working of all organs, the kidneys filter the entire volume of blood in the body every four to five minutes and produce about two quarts of urine a day. The exact amount and chemical composition of the urine varies with changes in food, fluid, and exercise. For example, when fluids are ingested in large amounts, the urine is clear and plentiful; when they are ingested in small amounts, the urine is dark yellow and scant. Highly efficient, the kidneys can function adequately even when disease has destroyed 80 percent of their capacity to work. Sometimes they can support life in the body even after their capacity has been reduced by as much as 90 to 95 percent.

DESCRIPTION OF THE DISEASE Because the kidneys can with-

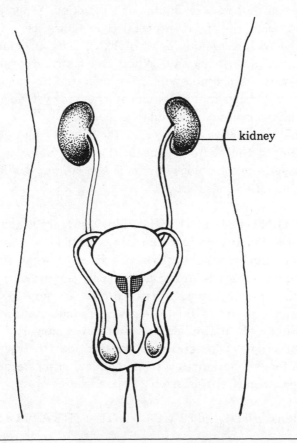

kidney

stand extensive injury, cancer of the kidney is often silent: that is, it may destroy a large part of the organ before it is detected. Forming a soft and bloody tumor as it grows, the cancer generally spreads to the renal vein and breaks through the membrane that covers the kidney.

SYMPTOMS Cancer of the kidney is the great imitator. By causing pain and fever, it may imitate infection; by causing loss of blood, it may imitate anemia; by causing changes in the body's hormones, it may imitate polycythemia (a disease in which the blood becomes sludgy from a surplus of red blood cells). Even blood in the urine – the most common and reliable symptom – may be associated with diseases other than cancer. In patients whose cancers are well advanced, pain may occur in the back or side; and a lump in the side may be present to the touch.

DIAGNOSIS When a doctor suspects that the kidneys are cancerous, he reaches a preliminary diagnosis by taking X-ray pictures of the kidneys. During the X-ray procedure, dye may be injected into the patient's vein (intravenous pylography) or into a blood vessel of the kidney (renal arteriography). When the X-rays reveal a tumor, the doctor must perform a biopsy in order to learn if the tumor is cancerous. If the doctor suspects that the tumor is a benign cyst, he may perform the biopsy while the patient is under a local anaesthetic, by means of a needle that withdraws tissue from the kidney (percutaneous needle biopsy). But if the doctor suspects that the tumor is cancerous, he generally performs the biopsy by means of surgery while the patient is under a general anaesthetic.

TREATMENT For cancer of the kidney, surgery is at present the only proven cure. Since a patient can live a normal life with one healthy kidney, the surgeon removes the entire diseased organ and all surrounding tissue, including the ureter and a large portion of the renal vein.

Radiotherapy may be administered after surgery to destroy any remaining cancerous cells. But recent studies indicate that X-rays may be more useful for shrinking large tumors before surgery is performed.

Chemotherapy is generally ineffective for treating cancer of the kidney, although hormones – in particular, progesterone – may occasionally cause partial remission of the disease.

POSSIBLE SIDE EFFECTS OF TREATMENT Permanent

damage from surgery is rare.

For the usual side effects of radiotherapy, see pp. 57–58. Additional side effects may include stomach ulcers and impairment of the small intestine – conditions that may eventually require surgical correction. These additional side effects occur most often when X-rays are administered after surgery.

When hormones are used to treat cancer of the kidney, no serious side effects occur.

PROGNOSIS In patients whose tumors are discovered before they have spread beyond the kidney, 50 percent are alive ten years after treatment. The rate of cure is lower for patients whose tumors have spread to the renal vein, invaded the lymph nodes, or broken through the membrane that covers the kidney.

GEOGRAPHIC PATTERN Denmark shows the highest rate for cancer of the kidney; Japan, the lowest.

ETHNIC PATTERN None known. But men suffer cancer of the kidney more often than women; and the rate of the disease in men is rising.

OCCUPATIONAL PATTERN None known.

AGE PATTERN Cancer of the kidney occurs most often in adults between the ages of fifty and eighty.

SPECIFIC CAUSES Kidney stones and phenacetin, a drug used to control pain, are associated with cancer of the kidney.

Wilms's tumor, a cancer of the kidney that occurs among children, may sometimes be hereditary.

THE LUNG

DESCRIPTION OF THE ORGAN The body's two lungs fill most of the chest cavity, which is formed by the breastbone and bones of the ribcage. The left lung is somewhat smaller than the right, because the heart occupies space on the left side of the chest.

The lungs are each divided into lobes: the left lung into two lobes; the right lung into three. Branching into each of these lobes is the windpipe (trachea), which subdivides within each lobe into thousands of tiny air tubes (bronchial tubes). Along with accompanying blood vessels and arteries, the bronchial tubes extend deep into the lung, eventually terminating in the air sacs that are evenly distributed throughout the organ.

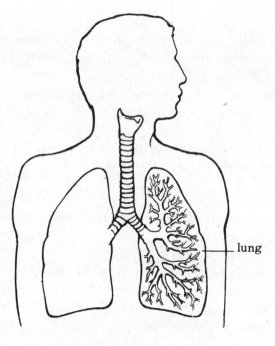

lung

FUNCTION OF THE ORGAN The lungs make use of oxygen that is inhaled in the process of breathing. Whenever a breath is drawn, oxygen-rich air passes through the mouth, throat, and trachea, down into the lungs. There the air travels through a vast network of bronchial tubes into innumerable tiny air sacs. Within these sacs, oxygen from the air is absorbed into the blood, and carbon dioxide from the blood is released into the air. Imbued with carbon dioxide, the air is then exhaled, traveling out of the body by retracing its course through the lungs, throat, and mouth.

Since obstructions in the throat or lungs may prevent air from reaching the air sacs, the body has developed a highly sensitive coughing reflex. When the throat, trachea, or any of a lung's larger bronchial

tubes is obstructed by a foreign body or a tumor, the obstruction provokes coughing to open the clogged passageway. A chronic cough
should thus never be ignored: it may be a sign of serious lung disease.

DESCRIPTION OF THE DISEASE Usually arising in the lining
of a bronchial tube, a cancerous tumor of the lung forms a fibrous lump
amid the air sacs. As it grows, the cancer breaks through the sacs and
spreads to other bronchial tubes, so that the lung's supply of air is
gradually reduced. Eventually, the cancer may invade the heart or extend to the edges of the lung – as far away as 5 or 6 inches from the
original site of the tumor. Cancer of the lung often spreads to distant
parts of the body through the numerous blood and lymphatic vessels
in the lung.

Note: Most cancers arise from a single cancerous cell; but cancer of
the lung may be different. Although doctors cannot yet be sure, they
believe that some cancers of the lung arise at different locations in the
bronchial tubes from cells that have become cancerous at more or less
the same time.

SYMPTOMS In its early stages, cancer of the lung causes a chronic
cough. When the cancer is moderately well advanced, symptoms may
include pneumonia, shortness of breath, and bloody sputum. Late in the
disease, the patient may experience chest pains, loss of weight, extreme
shortness of breath, hoarseness, difficulty in swallowing, and accumulation of fluid (pleural fluid) in the chest cavity.

DIAGNOSIS The doctor makes a preliminary diagnosis by taking
X-ray pictures of the chest and by examining the sputum under a
microscope for the presence of cancerous cells. Often this diagnosis is
definitive. But if the doctor is uncertain whether a tumor is cancerous,
he may perform a biopsy in one of three ways: (i) by administering a
local anaesthetic and withdrawing tissue from the lung through a
needle inserted into the wall of the chest (percutaneous needle biopsy);
(ii) by administering a local anaesthetic and removing tissue from the
lung through a bronchoscope – a tube that is passed through the mouth
and throat into the lung; or (iii) by administering a general anaesthetic
and removing tissue from the lymph nodes of the chest through a medi-
astinoscope – a tube that is inserted into the chest above the breastbone.
If none of these methods is feasible, a biopsy may be performed through

an incision in the wall of the chest (thoracotomy).

Although biannual X-rays of the lungs are sometimes used to achieve early detection of cancer among high-risk patients (that is, among heavy smokers), frequent examinations have not improved these patients' rate of cure.

TREATMENT Cancer of the lung can be cured only by means of surgery. But in 75 percent of all patients, the cancer is discovered too late for surgery to be of use: in 50 out of every 100 patients, surgery is not even attempted because the cancer has invaded distant parts of the body (metastasized); while in another 25 out of every 100 patients, surgery is attempted but fails, because the cancer is more extensive than the surgeon had thought. A surgical cure is possible only for those patients whose cancer is small enough to be entirely removed.

When cancer of the lung is incurable, radiotherapy may be used to relieve painful symptoms of the disease, including cough, shortness of breath and bloody sputum. If fluid accumulates around the lung, the patient is given a local anaesthetic and the fluid is withdrawn through a needle inserted into the chest.

Chemotherapy is effective for prolonging life only in patients with oat cell cancer of the lung – a particularly vicious cancer that rarely benefits from surgery. Occurring in about 20 percent of all patients, oat cell cancer differs from other cancers of the lung in that it spreads more rapidly to distant parts of the body and may produce a variety of hormones. When drugs are first administered, the cancer regresses quickly; but within a year or two, oat cell cancer of the lung almost always recurs and kills the patient.

POSSIBLE SIDE EFFECTS OF TREATMENT Surgery to remove a lung or part of a lung may cause shortness of breath during exercise, and pain at the site of the incision.

For the usual side effects of radiotherapy, see pp. 57–58. Additional side effects may include pneumonia or difficulty in swallowing.

For the usual side effects of chemotherapy, see pp. 63–64. Additional side effects may include constipation, numbness and tingling in the fingers, and possibly failure of the heart.

PROGNOSIS In 25 out of every 100 patients, small cancers of the lung may be entirely removed by surgery before they have spread to the lymph nodes. Of these patients, half – or 13 out of every 100 – are alive five years after treatment.

Patients with oat cell cancer of the lung rarely survive for five years. But radiotherapy and chemotherapy can extend the lives of these patients from three months to one year.

GEOGRAPHIC PATTERN Great Britain and Finland show the highest rates for cancer of the lung; Japan, Norway, and Sweden, the lowest. In the United States, the rate is about half that in Great Britain and Finland.

ETHNIC PATTERN None known. But cancer of the lung occurs more often among residents of urban areas than among residents of rural areas, and more often among men than among women. Cancer of the lung in women was once uncommon; but as smoking among women has increased, so too has the rate of the disease.

OCCUPATIONAL PATTERN Cancer of the lung tends to occur among people who work with chemicals: for example, asbestos workers, textile workers, arsenic smelter workers, manufacturers of insecticides containing arsenic, taxidermists, sheep dip workers, copper smelter workers, chrome workers, nickel refinery workers, iron ore miners and foundry workers, miners of radioactive ores, manufacturers of isopropyl alcohol, coke oven operators, paraffin pressers, mule spinners, and petroleum workers. If these workers smoke, they greatly increase their risk of developing the disease.

AGE PATTERN Cancer of the lung occurs most often in adults between the ages of forty and seventy.

SPECIFIC CAUSES Known causes of lung cancer include asbestos, arsenic, chromium, nickel, iron, isopropyl oil, coal tar fumes, petroleum oil mists, radioactive substances, and even air pollution. *But smoking is the major cause of lung cancer throughout the world.* Of all smokers, those who smoke cigarettes run the highest risk of developing lung cancer; and of cigarette-smokers, those who smoke more than two packs a day run thirty times the normal risk of dying from the disease.

THE LYMPH NODES

DESCRIPTION OF THE ORGAN Ranging from the size of a pin-head to the size of a bean, and tending to cluster in small groups, the lymph nodes are tiny glands distributed throughout the body. The major nodes are located in the neck, armpits, chest, abdomen, pelvis, and groin. Lymph tissue – which, unlike a node, does not form a separate, well-defined body – can also be found in the lining of many organs, especially the stomach, small intestine, and bone.

The lymph nodes act as way stations in the body's lymphatic system – a vast network of vessels that branch, like the blood vessels, deeply into every tissue. The lymphatic vessels both drain the fluid that accumulates within and between the body's cells and carry the fluid along a circuitous route back into the blood from which it came. On its way through the vessels, the fluid must pass through the lymph nodes to be cleansed of impurities.

FUNCTION OF THE ORGAN The lymph nodes produce lymphocytes – one of several different kinds of white blood cells that comprise the body's immune system. (For further information about white blood cells, see the section on The Blood.) When viruses, bacteria, or any other foreign materials are trapped in a node on their way through the lymphatic system, the lymphocytes help to destroy these materials before they can disable the body. Swollen lymph nodes are thus usually a sign that the body's immune system is attacking an intruder. The lymph nodes in the neck, for example, may swell when a virus has invaded the respiratory system; and the lymph nodes in the armpit may swell when a wound in the hand or the arm has become infected.

As most cancer patients know, the lymph nodes are often important in the diagnosis of cancer. Since the nodes are able to trap cancerous cells that have traveled away from the site of a primary tumor, they may succeed in containing a cancer that is only just beginning to spread or they may indicate that the cancer has invaded distant tissue (metastasized).

DESCRIPTION OF THE DISEASE Lymphoma is a cancer that originates in lymph tissue, usually within a lymph node. In most patients, cancer in a lymph node is a secondary tumor that has migrated to the node from another part of the body. But in patients with lym-

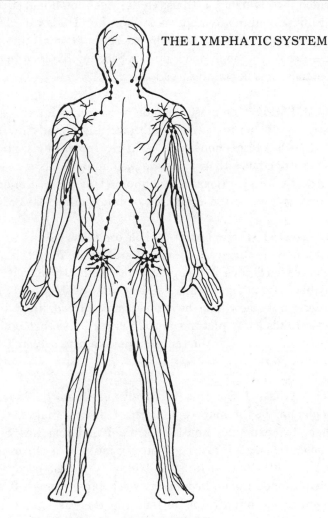

THE LYMPHATIC SYSTEM

phoma, the cancer arises in the lymph node itself.

When a node is diseased with lymphoma, it enlarges with cancerous lymph cells. Sometimes an enlarged node may cause distress by pressing against a neighboring organ – for example, a nerve or a vein, a lung or a part of the stomach. But more often, the cancer is painless. It generally forms a balloon-shaped tumor in the node and eventually spreads to the spleen, liver, and bone.

There are many different kinds of lymphomas. Doctors can identify an individual patient's lymphoma only by studying a sample of cancerous lymph cells under a microscope. In general, lymphomas are divided into two major types: Hodgkin's lymphoma (Hodgkin's disease) and non-Hodgkin's lymphoma. When non-Hodgkin's lymphoma begins in the lymph tissue of the stomach, bone, or small intestine, as it sometimes does, the lymph nodes do not become involved in the disease until the cancer has begun to spread.

SYMPTOMS The most common symptom is a painless swelling in an easily felt lymph node. Although swelling usually indicates that white blood cells in the nodes are fighting infection, a node that remains enlarged for more than three weeks should be examined by a doctor.

Additional symptoms of lymphoma include prolonged fatigue, daily recurring fever, intense itching, or unexplained loss of weight.

DIAGNOSIS Lymphoma can be diagnosed only when a suspicious lymph node is surgically removed and tissue from the node is examined under a microscope. When lymphoma is known to be present, the doctor may use a lymphogram and various tests of the blood and bone marrow to determine how far the cancer has spread. In a lymphogram, the doctor takes X-ray pictures of the lymph nodes throughout the abdomen and pelvis after injecting an opaque dye into a lymphatic vessel in the patient's foot.

TREATMENT Surgery is rarely used as the sole treatment for lymphoma, but it may be important during diagnosis and treatment. When, for example, non-Hodgkin's lymphoma has originated in the stomach or small intestine, a biopsy must be performed either through a tube that is passed into the stomach (a gastroscope) or through an incision made in the abdominal wall (laparotomy). If a non-Hodgkin's lymphoma is found to be obstructing the passage of food through the digestive tract, a part of the stomach or small intestine may, at the time of the biopsy, have to be surgically removed. In Hodgkin's lymphoma, which is best treated when the extent of the disease is fully known, exploratory surgery of the abdomen may be used to reveal whether the cancer has spread to the liver, spleen, or abdominal lymph nodes.

Whenever lymphoma is confined to small areas of the body – for example, to a few lymph nodes or to the stomach – radiotherapy is the most effective treatment. Sometimes, as a precautionary measure, X-rays are applied to a large part of the torso, whether or not the cancer is known to have spread.

Chemotherapy is an effective treatment for lymphomas that have become widespread – that is, for lymphomas that have established tumors both above and below the waistline. Drugs are especially useful for patients with advanced symptoms, like fever and loss of weight. In general, non-Hodgkin's lymphoma tends to become widespread more often than Hodgkin's lymphoma.

POSSIBLE SIDE EFFECTS OF TREATMENT When surgery is used only to perform biopsies on easily accessible lymph nodes, there are no serious side effects. But surgery to remove part of the stomach or small intestine may cause difficulties in the digestion of food. (For further detail, see the section on The Stomach.) Exploratory surgery and removal of the spleen may incline the patient to infection and may increase the side effects caused by subsequent radiotherapy.

For the usual side effects of radiotherapy, see pp. 57–58. Additional side effects include inflammation of the lining of the heart, when X-rays are applied to the chest; and pneumonia, when X-rays are combined with chemotherapy.

For the usual side effects of chemotherapy, see pp. 63–64. Side effects and long-term complications increase when chemotherapy is combined with radiotherapy.

PROGNOSIS The rate of cure varies greatly with the many different kinds of lymphomas that occur in each of the two major categories. When Hodgkin's lymphomas are confined to the lymph nodes, 50 to 90 percent of the patients are alive five years after treatment. When non-Hodgkin's lymphomas are confined to the lymph nodes, 20 to 70 percent of the patients are alive five years after treatment. But if lymphoma spreads beyond the nodes, the rate of cure drops: among patients with widespread Hodgkin's lymphomas, 25 to 35 percent survive for five years; among patients with widespread non-Hodgkin's lymphomas, 0 to 20 percent survive for five years.

Among patients with non-Hodgkin's lymphomas that have arisen outside the lymph nodes in the lymph tissue of the stomach, bone, or small intestine, 40 to 50 percent survive for five years if the cancer is discovered before it has spread to the nodes.

GEOGRAPHIC PATTERN Cali, Colombia, Denmark, and the Netherlands show the highest rates for lymphoma; Japan, the lowest.

ETHNIC PATTERN None known. But men suffer lymphoma more often than women.

OCCUPATIONAL PATTERN None known.

AGE PATTERN Hodgkin's lymphoma occurs most often in adults between the ages of eighteen and thirty-eight. Non-Hodgkin's lymphoma occurs in people of all ages.

SPECIFIC CAUSES Burkitt's lymphoma – a type of non-Hodgkin's lymphoma common among children in Africa – is known to be associated with the Epstein-Barr virus (see p. 29). Scientists are investigating the possibility that other lymphomas are associated with viruses.

High-risk patients include those who have had organ transplants and those who have had long-term treatment with drugs that suppress the body's immune system.

THE MOUTH

DESCRIPTION OF THE ORGAN The mouth, or oral cavity, includes the entire area behind the lips and in front of the tonsils. The upper and lower portions of the mouth are shaped by the jawbones, which hold the teeth; the sides of the mouth are formed by the cheeks. Rooted in the throat at the base of the mouth is the tongue; and forming a roof to separate the mouth from the nasal cavity is the palate. Toward the front of the mouth, the palate is hard and bony; toward the back, it is soft and muscular. Emptying into the mouth are ducts from three pairs of salivary glands located (i) under the jaw, (ii) beneath the tongue at the floor of the mouth, and (iii) at the sides of the face in front of the ears.

FUNCTION OF THE ORGAN The teeth, tongue, and lips form words in the production of speech. They also assist in the process of chewing, tasting, and swallowing food.

When food enters the mouth, it is moistened and softened by the saliva produced in the salivary glands. In this way saliva helps the teeth to chew the food, and the tongue to taste it. As juices from the food pass over the tongue, the taste buds identify flavor: saltiness is identified by

THE MOUTH

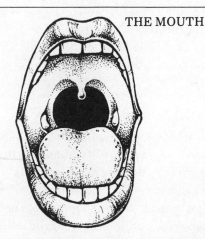

the buds at the front of the tongue; sweetness and sourness, by those in the middle; bitterness, by those at the back. Once the food has been chewed into a mass easy to swallow, the tongue forces the mass to the back of the mouth where a muscular reflex action carries it down through the throat and esophagus into the stomach.

When the mouth is not engaged in chewing and swallowing, saliva keeps it moist and relatively free from foreign matter.

DESCRIPTION OF THE DISEASE Cancer may occur in any part of the mouth. Usually it arises in the lip, the tongue, or the soft tissue under the tongue. Less often it arises in the gums, the palate, the lining of the cheek, or the salivary glands. But wherever the cancer begins, the tissues to which it first spreads are the lymph nodes in the neck.

SYMPTOMS Cancer begins in the mouth as a hard, fibrous sore, which may be either red or white. Sometimes the sore is accompanied by pain. Invariably it fails to heal.

Additional symptoms include pain in chewing, difficulty in speaking or swallowing, toothache, discomfort in wearing dentures, and occasionally unexplained earaches.

Because sores in the mouth occur frequently, many people overlook the first signs of oral cancer. But two precautions can assure that the cancer is discovered early, while it still can be cured: (i) any sore in the mouth that fails to heal within three weeks should be brought to a doctor's attention immediately; (ii) examination for cancerous lesions should be made part of every regular dental checkup.

DIAGNOSIS If a lump or a sore in the mouth appears to be cancerous, a biopsy must be performed. If a tumor can be felt near a salivary gland, X-ray pictures may reveal its location; but an accurate diagnosis cannot be made until the tumor has been surgically removed and examined under a microscope.

TREATMENT Surgery and radiotherapy may be used separately or in combination to treat cancer of the mouth. Small tumors that can be completely removed are generally treated with surgery. Tumors of moderate size are best treated with radiotherapy. Large tumors require a combination of surgery and radiotherapy if they are to be cured. When radiotherapy is used to treat cancer of the mouth, the X-rays are administered by machine and by means of radioactive needles implanted in the tongue, cheek, lip, or floor of the mouth.

Chemotherapy has not proved effective for treating most oral cancers.

POSSIBLE SIDE EFFECTS OF TREATMENT The consequences of surgery depend on the amount of tissue that must be removed. Surgery to remove more than half the tongue may cause serious difficulties in speaking and swallowing. Surgery to remove the lymph nodes in the neck may cause stiffness and pain in the shoulder by severing a nerve in the neck. Surgery to remove parts of the jaw or the cheek may cause difficulties in swallowing and chewing, as well as facial disfigurement. When surgery is disfiguring, prosthetic devices or cosmetic surgery may be used to improve the patient's appearance.

For the usual side effects of radiotherapy, see pp. 57–58. Additional side effects include dryness in the mouth or thickening of the saliva, cavities in the teeth, and weakening of the jawbone, as well as inflammation and scarring of the hinge that works the lower jaw, so that the mouth no longer opens fully.

PROGNOSIS Among patients whose tumors are small, 60 to 75 per cent are alive five years after treatment. Among those whose tumors are of moderate size, 45 to 55 percent are alive 5 years after treatment. Among patients whose cancers are advanced, only 20 percent survive for five years. But in every case, if the cancer has spread to the lymph nodes, the rate of cure decreases.

GEOGRAPHIC PATTERN Cancer of the mouth occurs most often in southern India, Ceylon, Thailand, the Philippines, Indochina, and Sweden.

ETHNIC PATTERN None known.

OCCUPATIONAL PATTERN None known.

AGE PATTERN Cancer of the mouth occurs most often in adults between the ages of fifty-five and seventy-five.

SPECIFIC CAUSES Smoking or chewing tobacco may cause cancer of the mouth; and so, too, may heavy consumption of alcohol. Recent studies suggest that those who both smoke heavily and drink heavily are far more likely to develop cancer of the mouth than are those who only smoke or only drink.

Cancer of the mouth is also associated with frequent chewing of betel nuts and with chronic oral injuries caused by poorly fitting dentures and by jagged teeth or fillings. In addition, cancer may develop from a benign condition in which white patches (leukoplakia) appear on the lips, on the tongue, or in the lining of the mouth.

THE OVARY

DESCRIPTION OF THE ORGAN The female body contains two ovaries, situated on either side of the uterus in the pelvic cavity. Each ovary lies near one of the two Fallopian tubes, which originate at the top of the uterus and terminate near the ovary in numerous finger-like projections.

FUNCTION OF THE ORGAN The ovaries of the adult female produce sex hormones: estrogen, progesterone, and small amounts of androgen. They also produce, from structures called follicles, the eggs (ova) that are fertilized during conception.

The more than 400,000 eggs in the ovaries are all capable of growing to maturity. But on the average, only about 400 of these eggs mature during a woman's reproductive lifetime: approximately one a month for the thirty years or so from puberty to menopause. When a mature egg is produced – usually about the fourteenth day of each menstrual cycle – it is released from the ovary and propelled down a Fallopian tube to the uterus. If the egg is fertilized on its way down the tube, it implants itself in the lining of the uterus (the endometrium) and begins to form a fetus. If the egg is not fertilized, it dies and is shed from the body.

DESCRIPTION OF THE DISEASE Cancers that arise inside the ovary are rare and will not be discussed. The most common cancer of the ovary arises on the organ's surface and forms an encapsulated tumor that is often honeycombed with holes containing fluid. As the cancer grows, it breaks out of its capsule and invades not only the interior of the ovary, but also the neighboring tissues. Because the cancerous cells can float freely from the ovaries throughout the abdominal cavity, the cancer frequently spreads to the surface of one or more abdominal organs: namely, the stomach, intestines, liver, pancreas, spleen, kidneys, and ureters.

SYMPTOMS Although twisting of the tumor sometimes causes pain early in the disease, cancer of the ovary is generally silent until it is far advanced. In its late stages, it gives off fluids that accumulate in the abdominal cavity, causing the belly to swell in a pseudo-pregnancy called ascites.

DIAGNOSIS By digital (finger) examination through the rectum and

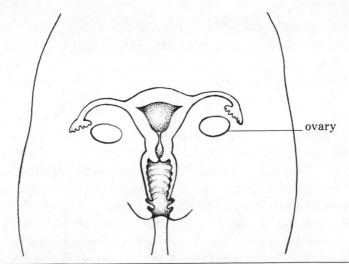

vagina, the doctor can feel the patient's ovaries. If they are enlarged or misshapen, the doctor may examine the abdominal cavity with a peritoneoscope – a lighted scope passed into the abdomen through a small incision near the navel. But if the patient's symptoms clearly indicate the presence of a cancer, a surgeon will make an incision in the abdomen (laparotomy) and remove both ovaries, the uterus, and the Fallopian tubes while the patient is under a general anaesthetic. Tissue from these organs will then be examined under a microscope.

TREATMENT When surgery is used to treat cancer of the ovary, the surgeon removes both ovaries, the uterus, and the Fallopian tubes, as well as the protective blanket of the intestine (the omentum). Since most ovarian tumors cannot be entirely removed, radiotherapy (or adjuvant chemotherapy) is generally used after an operation to destroy cancerous cells that remain in the body. Although most doctors irradiate only the pelvic bed of the ovary, some irradiate the entire abdomen.

If cancer of the ovary is far advanced, as it is in the majority of cases, chemotherapy is used as adjuvant treatment. After drugs have been administered for a year, the doctor may perform exploratory surgery. If no tumor is found, the therapy may be stopped.

POSSIBLE SIDE EFFECTS OF TREATMENT In premenopausal women, surgery causes loss of fertility.

For the usual side effects of radiotherapy, see pp. 57–58. Radiotherapy, when it is confined to the pelvis, is generally well tolerated. When the abdomen is irradiated, the patient may experience severe diarrhea or feel sick as with a case of the flu. She may also suffer serious damage to the kidney, liver, or intestine.

For the usual side effects of chemotherapy, see pp. 63–64. Chemotherapy for cancer of the ovary is generally well tolerated. But if the therapy continues for many years, the patient may develop acute leukemia.

PROGNOSIS When a surgeon completely removes a tumor that is confined to the ovary, 70 percent of the patients are alive five years after treatment. When the cancer has spread beyond the ovary but not beyond the pelvic area, 20 to 50 percent of the patients are alive five years after treatment. The greater the spread, the lower the rate of cure. When the cancer has spread into the upper abdomen, only 10 percent of the patients survive the disease. In these patients, chemotherapy may help to produce a cure; but it usually serves only to ease the distress caused by loss of weight and by the accumulation of fluid in the abdomen.

GEOGRAPHIC PATTERN Scandinavia shows the highest rate for cancer of the ovary; Chile and Japan, the lowest. North America is in between.

ETHNIC PATTERN None known.

OCCUPATIONAL PATTERN None known.

AGE PATTERN Cancer of the ovary occurs most often in women between the ages of forty and sixty.

SPECIFIC CAUSES None known.

THE PANCREAS

DESCRIPTION OF THE ORGAN The pancreas is located at the back of the abdominal cavity, behind and beneath the stomach. The "head" of the organ is attached to the duodenum – the first portion of the small intestine. The "body" and "tail" of the organ extend to the left along the lower curve of the stomach. Lying very close to the pancreas are the major nerves and blood vessels that serve all the organs within the abdominal cavity.

FUNCTION OF THE ORGAN The pancreas produces both hormones and digestive juices. The hormones – insulin and glucagon, which control the body's use of sugar (glucose) – are secreted from small groups of specialized cells called the islets of Langerhans. The digestive juices, which are used in the duodenum, are also produced by specialized cells. Juices (secretions) from these cells travel through an intricate system of tiny ducts into the principal pancreatic duct, which traverses the entire length of the pancreas and enters the duodenum after joining with the common bile duct. Whenever food from the stomach is released into the duodenum, digestive juices from the pancreas and bile from the gall bladder flow into the duodenum to promote the process of digestion.

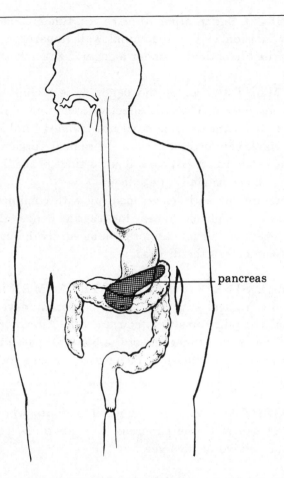

pancreas

DESCRIPTION OF THE DISEASE Cancer begins in the lining of a pancreatic duct and spreads into the tissue of the organ. Eventually it burrows into the blood vessels and nerves surrounding the pancreas, obstructs the passage of bile through the common bile duct, and spreads to all the vital organs in the abdomen.

SYMPTOMS The most common symptoms are persistent abdominal pain, loss of weight, and yellow jaundice caused by the body's absorption of bile that can no longer reach the duodenum.

DIAGNOSIS The doctor may discover a tumor by taking X-ray pictures of the pancreas after injecting an opaque dye into the organ, or by performing an ultrasound test or a computer scan of the pancreas (see pp. 31–32). But in order to learn if a tumor is cancerous, he must make an incision in the abdominal wall (laparotomy) and perform a biopsy while the patient is under a general anaesthetic.

TREATMENT Cancer of the pancreas is usually incurable by the time it is discovered. The only effective treatment is radical surgery for those very few cancers that have not invaded vital blood vessels and organs, which cannot be removed. In radical surgery, the surgeon removes the entire pancreas, as well as portions of the intestine, bile duct, stomach, and occasionally the spleen.

Doctors are currently experimenting with combinations of surgery, radiotherapy, and chemotherapy for treating cancer of the pancreas. At present, X-rays and drugs cannot prolong survival; but they may control painful symptoms of the disease.

POSSIBLE SIDE EFFECTS OF TREATMENT Among patients who survive radical surgery, 15 to 30 percent develop infections or abdominal complications that cause death. After surgery, in order to maintain the normal functions of the body, all patients must take insulin by injection and digestive enzymes by mouth for the rest of their lives.

PROGNOSIS Out of every hundred patients who undergo radical surgery for cancer of the pancreas, thirty-two die from the operation. Only eight survive for five years.

GEOGRAPHIC PATTERN None known.

ETHNIC PATTERN None known. But cancer of the pancreas occurs more often in men than in women.

OCCUPATIONAL PATTERN None known.

AGE PATTERN Cancer of the pancreas occurs most often in adults between the ages of thirty-five and seventy.

SPECIFIC CAUSES None known; but tobacco and alcohol are being investigated as possible causes.

THE PROSTATE

DESCRIPTION OF THE ORGAN A gland found only in men, the prostate is located just below the bladder in the pelvis. About the size of a walnut, the prostate encircles the top of the urethra – the tube through which urine and semen flow out of the body. (For further detail, see the sections on The Bladder and The Testicle.)

FUNCTION OF THE ORGAN The full importance of the prostate is not yet known. But the gland's major function is to produce a milky-white fluid that forms semen by mixing with sperm just prior to ejaculation.

DESCRIPTION OF THE DISEASE Cancer usually arises at the back of the prostate, spreading through the gland like lava and hardening as it enlarges. Because the prostate encircles the urethra, the cancer

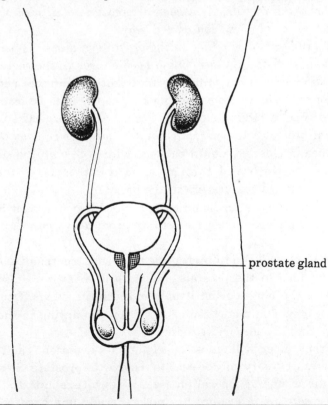

prostate gland

eventually obstructs the flow of urine from the bladder as the tumor grows toward the front of the gland. Late in the disease, the cancer may break out of the prostate and spread to other parts of the body, most often the bones.

SYMPTOMS Cancer of the prostate is usually silent. But when the disease is locally advanced, the patient may experience pain or difficulty in starting to urinate, frequent need to urinate, or blood in the urine. In addition, the flow of urine may be weak, interrupted, or difficult to stop. Very late in the disease, the patient may suffer pain in the pelvic area. Though all these symptoms occur in non-cancerous conditions of the prostate, which are far more common than cancer, they should be brought to a doctor's attention immediately.

DIAGNOSIS Because cancer of the prostate tends to arise at the back of the organ, tumors are often discovered during digital (finger) examination of the rectum. *As a general precaution, all men over fifty should have a rectal examination once a year.*

If a tumor is discovered in the prostate, a biopsy is performed with a local anaesthetic. By inserting a needle through the rectum, or through the skin between the anus and the scrotum (perineal needle biopsy), a doctor can remove from the tumor some tissue to be examined under a microscope. A biopsy is also performed when surgery is used to correct benign prostatic hypertrophy (BPH) – an enlargement of the prostate common in elderly men. In patients with BPH, both the surgery and the biopsy are performed through a narrow tube (a cystoscope) that is passed through the urethra to the prostate.

Under study is an immunologic blood test designed to reveal prostatic acid phosphatase – a substance produced by cancer of the prostate.

TREATMENT Radiotherapy is the usual treatment for cancers that are confined to the prostate and its bed. X-rays are also effective for treating the neighboring lymph nodes in the pelvis. Occasionally, the doctor may administer radiotherapy by implanting in the tumor radioactive gold or radioactive iodine seeds.

If the cancer is diagnosed early and if the patient can tolerate a long operation, surgery may be used to remove the prostate. Some doctors also perform a staging operation (see p. 40) to examine the pelvic lymph nodes; but this procedure has not generally improved the rate of cure for the disease.

Since cancer of the prostate generally occurs in elderly men, many patients are unable to withstand exhausting treatment. Fortunately, cure is less important in most patients than control of symptoms, because the cancer grows very slowly and can often be contained by hormone therapy for the duration of a patient's natural life. The female hormone estrogen, for example, can control the cancer even when it has spread to distant parts of the body. In addition, surgery to remove the testicles is often beneficial, since the testicles produce male hormones favorable to the cancer's growth.

POSSIBLE SIDE EFFECTS OF TREATMENT For the usual side effects of radiotherapy, see pp. 57–58. Additional side effects include damage to the intestines – a serious complication in fewer than 5 percent of all patients – or a narrowing of the urethra that may cause urinary difficulties.

Surgery to remove the prostate causes impotence. It may also cause the patient to lose control of urination. (For the consequences of surgery to remove the testicles, see the section on The Testicle.) When the lymph nodes are removed in a staging operation, sacs of lymph fluid may collect where the nodes used to be; and intestinal difficulties caused by radiotherapy may be aggravated.

Female hormones produce impotence, swelling of the breasts, fluid retention, and progressive hardening of the arteries.

PROGNOSIS Surgery can cure very small cancers that are confined to the prostate. Radiotherapy can cure cancers that have invaded neighboring tissues. But cancer of the prostate can only be controlled – never cured – once it has spread (metastasized) to distant parts of the body.

Among patients over the age of sixty, 50 percent outlive cancer of the prostate to die from such causes as heart attack, stroke, or hardening of the arteries. Among patients who are younger than sixty, cancer of the prostate is often the cause of death, although in most patients the disease can be controlled with hormones for long periods of time.

GEOGRAPHIC PATTERN The Union of South Africa shows the highest rate for cancer of the prostate; Israel, China, and Italy, the lowest.

ETHNIC PATTERN None known.

OCCUPATIONAL PATTERN None known.

AGE PATTERN Cancer of the prostate rarely afflicts young or middle-aged men. But the disease occurs relatively often in men over the age of sixty.

SPECIFIC CAUSES None known, although some doctors think that a hormone imbalance may cause the disease. Doctors are also investigating the possibility that sexual behavior may be associated with cancer of the prostate, as it is with cancer of the cervix; but at present, the information is inconclusive. Unfortunately, cancer of the prostate is difficult to study because it occurs primarily in human beings and cannot be induced in test animals.

THE SKIN

DESCRIPTION OF THE ORGAN A vast organ that covers the entire body, the skin is composed of two layers: an inner layer called the dermis, and an outer layer called the epidermis.

THE SKIN

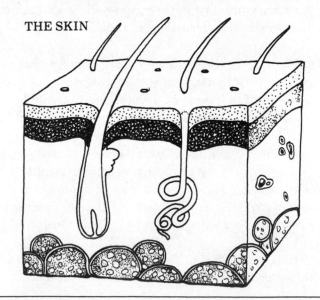

The dermis, which is relatively thick over most of the body, is tough and elastic in quality. Conforming to the shape of the muscles and bones that lie beneath it, the dermis contains the roots of the hair, the glands that produce sweat and oil, fat cells that cushion the skin, blood vessels, lymphatic vessels, and nerves.

The epidermis, which is about a millimeter thick, is composed primarily of dead cells containing large amounts of keratin — a protein that resists heat, cold, and the corrosive effects of most chemicals. Because the dead cells of the epidermis easily flake away, they must constantly be replaced. Near the bottom of the epidermis are two different kinds of living cells: cube-shaped basal cells, and oval-shaped squamous cells. As they divide, the basal and squamous cells push older, dying cells up toward the surface of the skin to replace those that have been lost. The epidermis contains few nerves and no blood vessels; but in its deepest level, it contains the pigment cells (melanocytes) that produce melanin — the substance that gives the skin its color and protects it from ultraviolet light by causing the skin to tan.

FUNCTION OF THE ORGAN The skin protects the body from injury. It wards off bacteria, which can easily enter the body through even the smallest wound. It releases excess water and regulates body temperature by means of sweating — either invisible (insensible) sweating, which occurs continuously, or profuse sweating, which occurs when the body is exposed to heat or exercise. Finally, through the sense of touch, it enables the body to feel temperature, pressure, and pain.

DESCRIPTION OF THE DISEASE Cancer of the skin can be divided into two types: (i) basal and squamous cell cancers, which arise from the epidermal cells that name them; and (ii) melanomas, which arise from the pigment cells (melanocytes) that are scattered in the deepest level of the epidermis.

Basal and squamous cell cancers tend to occur on parts of the body exposed to the sun, especially the hands, face, and ears. Forming pearly nodules or red patches on the surface of the skin, these cancers grow either outward or inward, eventually developing into lumps that may be smooth, knobby, or concave. Although squamous cell cancers grow more quickly and spread more often than basal cell cancers, both grow slowly and tend to remain confined to the site of the original tumor.

Melanomas form dark black moles that spread over the surface of the skin or grow downward into the dermis. More than half of all melanomas arise from pre-existing moles on the patient's body. Often a fast-growing cancer, melanoma may quickly spread to distant parts of the body, including internal organs like the lung.

SYMPTOMS Cancers of the skin usually present no early symptoms beyond the appearance of a lump or a mole that is painless and steadily enlarges. But ulceration, bleeding, or rapid changes in the character of a mole may indicate the presence of a melanoma.

DIAGNOSIS Cancers of the skin are easily diagnosed. The doctor removes either the entire tumor or a portion of tissue from the tumor and examines it under a microscope.

TREATMENT Surgery is the usual treatment for all cancers of the skin. For basal and squamous cell cancers, the surgeon removes the tumor and a relatively small area of healthy neighboring skin. For melanomas, the surgeon removes the tumor and a very wide area of healthy neighboring skin both around and below the tumor; he may also remove the lymph nodes near the cancer, if the melanoma has burrowed deeply into the dermis.

Radiotherapy – because it produces better cosmetic results than surgery – is often used to treat basal and squamous cell cancers that occur on the lip, nose, eyelids, or ears. Chemical lotions (chemotherapy) are generally reserved for basal and squamous cell cancers that have formed tumors on different parts of the patient's skin. Since multiple surgical wounds may be disfiguring, and since radiotherapy is unsuited for treating numerous sites on the body, lotions may produce the most effective cure in these patients. On rare occasions, radiotherapy or chemotherapy may be used to treat internal organs that have been invaded by a melanoma.

Alternative treatments for cancers of the skin include the destruction of cancerous cells with liquid nitrogen (cryosurgery), with heat (electro-cautery), or with cauterizing pastes.

POSSIBLE SIDE EFFECTS OF TREATMENT Surgery may cause disfigurement, especially when moderately advanced tumors are removed from the nose, ears, lips, or the skin around the eyes. Surgery for a melanoma usually leaves a large crater that must eventually be covered with a graft of skin taken from another part of the body. When lymph nodes are removed in surgery for a melanoma, fluids may later accumulate in the areas of the body formerly drained by the nodes.

Radiotherapy generally preserves the skin's normal appearance. But in some patients, the skin may become thin; small blood vessels may become visible in the area that has been irradiated; and a small depression, or crater, may develop in the skin.

Chemical lotions generally cause the skin to turn intensely red and to peel away in layers.

PROGNOSIS When less than 1 inch in size, basal and squamous cell cancers can be cured in nearly 100 percent of all patients.

Very early melanomas can be cured in 80 percent of all patients. But among patients with melanomas that have spread to the lymph nodes, only 20 percent are alive five years after treatment, and 12 percent are alive ten years after treatment. Although removal of the lymph nodes during surgery may reveal how far a melanoma has spread, this surgical procedure has not generally improved the rate of cure for the disease. In a *very small* minority of patients, melanomas have been observed to regress and disappear without treatment.

GEOGRAPHIC PATTERN Basal and squamous cell cancers occur most often in the southern half of the United States. Melanomas occur most often in Australia and India.

ETHNIC PATTERN Cancers of the skin occur most often in fair-skinned people.

OCCUPATIONAL PATTERN Cancers of the skin occur frequently among people who work out-of-doors: for example, sailors, farmers, and construction workers. They also strike workers in various chemical industries: in particular, workers who handle distillation and fractionation products of coal, oil shale, lignite, and petroleum.

AGE PATTERN Basal and squamous cell cancers occur most often in adults over the age of fifty; melanomas, in adults between the ages of fifty and sixty.

SPECIFIC CAUSES Basal and squamous cell cancers are caused by various oils, coal tars, pitch, creosote, nitrate, arsenic, beryllium, nickel, and over 500 chemical compounds. They are also caused by excessive exposure to sunlight and radiation. In addition, these cancers frequently develop in people who are afflicted with a rare skin disease called xeroderma pigmentosum and in people who have developed keratosis (a scaly thickening in small areas of skin).

Melanomas may be caused by excessive exposure to sunlight.

THE STOMACH

DESCRIPTION OF THE ORGAN Located in the upper left-hand portion of the abdominal cavity, the stomach is a hollow organ, shaped somewhat like a J. Mucous tissue containing several different kinds of

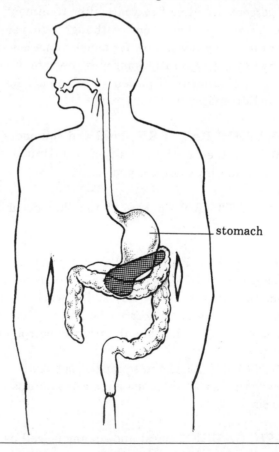

stomach

glands lines the inside of the stomach. Layers of strong muscle compose its outer wall. At the top of the stomach is the esophagus – a muscular 10-inch tube that bears food to the stomach from the throat. At the bottom of the stomach is the duodenum – the start of the body's small intestine, which receives food that the stomach has digested.

FUNCTION OF THE ORGAN By converting solid food into a thick soupy mixture called chyme, the stomach assists in the process of digestion. When food enters the stomach from the esophagus, the glands of the stomach secrete gastric juices that help break down large mole-cules, like the proteins contained in meat. So corrosive are these juices that a special mucous coating is needed to prevent them from eating away the lining of the stomach.

While food remains in the stomach, it is vigorously churned by con-tractions of the stomach's muscle wall. These same contractions move the food toward the duodenum, into which the food passes once it has been converted into chyme. Generally, carbohydrates (for example, potatoes) remain in the stomach only a few hours; proteins (for example, meat) remain longer; while fats (for example, butter) remain longest of all. On the average, food passes out of the stomach into the duodenum within two to six hours after a meal. But emotional tension may slow down digestion, causing food to remain in the stomach twenty-four hours or more.

DESCRIPTION OF THE DISEASE Cancer usually begins in the lining of the stomach as a thick hard ulcer that spreads through the muscle wall. Once it has broken through the wall of the stomach, the cancer quickly spreads to the lymph nodes and the liver.

SYMPTOMS Cancer of the stomach is usually silent until it has grown large enough to spread outside the organ. When the cancer is well advanced, it may cause pain, persistent indigestion, and reduced appetite. Late in the disease, symptoms may include bloody feces, vomiting, and rapid loss of weight.

Because stomach ulcers produce virtually the same symptoms as cancer, one disease may easily be mistaken for the other. If conven-tional treatment for stomach ulcers fails to relieve a patient's symp-toms, the doctor should explore the possibility that the "ulcer" is in fact cancer. Similarly, if a patient with an "ulcer" has achlorhydria (a lack of hydrochloric acid in the gastric juices), the doctor should check his diagnosis, since this condition is common in cancer of the stomach.

DIAGNOSIS As a first step, the doctor performs a fluoroscopy or upper G.I. series – that is, he takes numerous X-ray pictures of the stomach and duodenum after the patient has swallowed a mixture of dyes (barium). If the X-rays reveal an ulcer in the duodenum, the doctor may decide to proceed no further, since these ulcers are usually benign. But if the X-rays reveal a suspicious ulcer in the stomach, the doctor will perform a biopsy with a gastroscope – a flexible tube that is passed through the nose into the stomach, where tissue is removed to be examined under a microscope.

TREATMENT Surgery is the only effective treatment for cancer of the stomach. If the cancer is very large, the entire stomach and neighboring organs – for instance, the spleen and a portion of the intestine – may be removed. For smaller cancers, partial removal of the stomach may be sufficient to produce a cure.

Radiotherapy is ineffective for treating all cancers of the stomach except lymphosarcoma – a cancer of the lymph tissue in the stomach wall. This cancer responds well to a combined treatment of surgery and radiotherapy. (For further detail, see the section on The Lymph Nodes.)

At present, chemotherapy, like radiotherapy, is ineffective for treating all cancers of the stomach, except lymphosarcoma.

POSSIBLE SIDE EFFECTS OF TREATMENT When the entire stomach has been removed, the patient can no longer store large meals in his body; he must therefore learn to eat sparingly but frequently. In addition, he may find carbohydrates difficult to digest; and he may be troubled by vitamin deficiencies – in particular, a vitamin B-12 deficiency that causes fatigue and tingling in the feet and legs (pernicious anemia). When only part of the stomach has been removed, these side effects are less severe. Surgery to remove the spleen generally causes no adverse consequences in adults.

For the usual side effects of radiotherapy, see pp. 57–58.

PROGNOSIS When cancerous tumors of the stomach can be entirely removed, 40 percent of the patients are alive five years after treatment. When lymphosarcoma of the stomach is treated before it has spread beyond the stomach and neighboring lymph nodes, 50 percent of the patients survive for five years. But unfortunately, four out of every five cancers of the stomach are incurable by the time they are discovered.

GEOGRAPHIC PATTERN Japan, Finland, Chile, Austria, Iceland, and eastern Europe show high rates for cancer of the stomach. The United States, Australia, and Canada show low rates. In fact, for reasons that are not understood, the rate of the disease in the United States is rapidly declining.

ETHNIC PATTERN None known. But throughout the world, cancer of the stomach strikes men more often than women and tends to occur in low socio-economic areas. In the United States, it strikes immigrants and their children (especially Japanese immigrants) more often than natives, and blacks more often than whites.

OCCUPATIONAL PATTERN None known.

AGE PATTERN Cancer of the stomach occurs most often in adults between the ages of fifty and sixty.

SPECIFIC CAUSES None known. But diet has been suggested as a possible cause, since the cancer is common among people who eat large quantities of smoked foods.

High-risk adults include those with a history of pernicious anemia and with a strong family history of cancer of the stomach. Some studies have also shown a higher than normal risk for adults with blood type A.

THE TESTICLE

DESCRIPTION OF THE ORGAN The male body has two testicles contained within a sac behind the penis (the scrotum). Each testicle is attached to a duct that passes through the prostate and opens into the urethra – the tube that travels from the bladder to the end of the penis. In men, the urethra serves as the passageway through which both urine and semen flow out of the body. (For further detail, see the sections on The Bladder and The Prostate.)

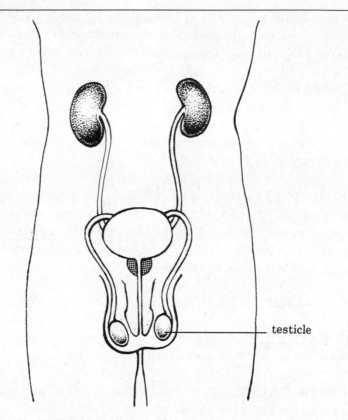

testicle

FUNCTION OF THE ORGAN After puberty, the testicles secrete the sex hormone testosterone. They also make sperm – the germ cells that fertilize the human egg during conception. Produced in the interior of each testicle, the mature sperm are stored until the body is ready to release them. The sperm then travel through ducts to the prostate, mix with the juices of the prostate and the seminal vesicles to form semen, and erupt from the penis in a reflex action called ejaculation.

DESCRIPTION OF THE DISEASE Arising from the cells that make sperm, cancer of the testicle grows like a balloon, only rarely breaking through the organ's covering. The cancer spreads by traveling through the lymphatic vessels to the lymph nodes of the abdomen, chest, and neck, and sometimes to the lungs.

SYMPTOMS The usual symptom is a lump in the testicle, sometimes accompanied by pain.

DIAGNOSIS Painless lumps in the testicle – or painful ones that cannot be cured with antibiotics – are tumors that necessitate removal of the organ. Tissue from the tumor is usually examined under a microscope after the testicle has been removed through an incision made just above the groin (orchiectomy). But on rare occasions, when the doctor is uncertain of his diagnosis, he may leave the testicle in place and perform a biopsy by cutting out a small piece of tissue through an incision in the scrotum.

When a tumor of the testicle is revealed to be cancerous, the doctor may perform a lymphogram to determine if the cancer has spread to the lymph nodes. In lymphography, the doctor takes X-ray pictures of the lymph nodes throughout the body after injecting an opaque dye into a lymphatic vessel. (For a description of the lymphatic system, see the section on The Lymph Nodes.)

After a patient has been treated for cancer of the testicle, the doctor may detect the continued presence of the disease, or a recurrence, by examining the blood for alphafetoprotein and chorionic gonadotropin – substances produced by the cancer.

TREATMENT Surgery is the primary treatment for tumors of the testicle, whether malignant or benign. Through an incision made just above the groin – never through the scrotum, as might be expected – a doctor removes the testicle and all adjoining tubes (orchiectomy). If the tumor proves to be cancerous, the doctor may, in a later operation, remove the lymph nodes in the abdomen (lymphadenectomy); or he may treat the nodes either with X-rays or with a combination of X-rays and surgery.

If radiotherapy is used to treat lymph nodes invaded by cancer of the testicle, X-rays are applied to the nodes in the abdomen, and sometimes to those in the chest and neck as well. Since X-rays are particularly effective for treating lymph nodes invaded by seminoma, one form of cancer of the testicle, patients with seminoma rarely undergo lymphadenectomy.

When distant tissues have been invaded by cancer of the testicle, drugs, and occasionally X-rays, may produce a cure. Since some cancers of the testicle – namely, embryonal carcinoma and teratocarcinoma – tend to become widespread if they reach the lymph nodes, adjuvant chemotherapy is often administered to patients with these cancers, once the testicle has been removed.

POSSIBLE SIDE EFFECTS OF TREATMENT Surgery to re-move a testicle causes no serious side effects; but surgery to remove the lymph nodes may cause infection, hemorrhage, or damage to the kidneys and ureters. When the lymph nodes in the abdomen are removed, the surgeon must cut nerves important to ejaculation, so that the sperm produced in the remaining testicle no longer emerge from the penis, but are absorbed in the body. Surgery may thus cause infertility, *but not impotence.* Even when both testicles have been removed, the patient can experience erection of the penis as long as he receives doses of testo-sterone. For cosmetic purposes, some patients have a surgeon place in the scrotum a prosthetic device resembling a testicle.

For the usual side effects of radiotherapy, see pp. 57–58. Additional side effects include ulcerations of the stomach and the small intestine.

For the usual side effects of chemotherapy, see pp. 63–64. Additional side effects include damage to the kidneys, shortness of breath, sores in the mouth, and numbness or tingling in the limbs, as well as irritation of the skin of the fingers, hands, and elbows.

PROGNOSIS Among patients with seminoma, 85 percent are alive five years after treatment.

Among patients with other cancers of the testicle, 40 to 70 percent are alive five years after treatment. The smaller the spread, the better the rate of cure. If the cancer is treated before it has spread to the lymph nodes, the rate of cure is higher than 70 percent.

The lowest rate of cure occurs for those patients whose cancers have spread to the lung. Although it is too early to be certain, extensive surgery and chemotherapy may cure some of these patients.

GEOGRAPHIC PATTERN None known.

ETHNIC PATTERN Cancer of the testicle is rare in North American blacks and in African Bantus.

OCCUPATIONAL PATTERN None known.

AGE PATTERN Cancer of the testicle occurs most often in men between the ages of twenty and fifty.

SPECIFIC CAUSES None known. But in children, cancer of the testicle often occurs when the organ has failed to descend from the abdomen – the place where the testicles form during development of the fetus – into the scrotum.

THE THROAT

DESCRIPTION OF THE ORGAN A muscular passageway for air and food, the throat starts at the tonsils and ends below the Adam's apple, where the windpipe (trachea) begins. Air passes down the throat into the trachea; but food is diverted into the esophagus – a 10-inch tube that branches off from the throat just above the Adam's apple and descends behind the trachea into the stomach. The tongue is rooted in the throat at the back of the mouth; and the voicebox (larynx) is situated in the throat immediately above the trachea. Stretched across the larynx are muscular membranes called vocal cords, which vibrate to create the voice.

FUNCTION OF THE ORGAN By means of various muscular actions, the throat assists in breathing, swallowing, and speaking. Breathing takes place when air is forced through the throat and the trachea on its

THE THROAT

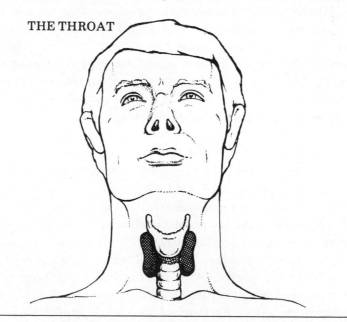

way in and out of the lungs. Swallowing takes place when food, liquid, or saliva is forced down through the throat and esophagus on its way to the stomach. Speaking takes place when air is forced out of the lungs and up through the larynx, causing the vocal cords to vibrate.

The tonsils are small pieces of lymph tissue (see the section on The Lymph Nodes). They have no muscular function.

DESCRIPTION OF THE DISEASE When cancer arises in the tonsil, the root of the tongue, or the lining of the throat, it forms a thick fibrous tumor that spreads like lava. When cancer arises in the vocal cords, it forms a tumor that grows like a balloon.

SYMPTOMS Most cancers of the throat are silent until the tumor has grown quite large. When the disease is advanced, symptoms often include soreness or a lump in the throat, difficulty in swallowing or breathing, and occasionally unexplained earaches. As a rule, cancer of the vocal cords is detected earlier than other cancers of the throat, since it causes persistent hoarseness or changes in the voice early in the disease. If hoarseness lasts for more than three weeks, it should be brought to the attention of a doctor.

DIAGNOSIS With a mirror that is placed in the mouth, the doctor can see any tumors that require biopsy. If the tumor is easy to reach, he may perform a biopsy while the patient is sedated with a local anaesthetic. Otherwise, he will administer a general anaesthetic and perform the biopsy with a laryngoscope – a narrow tube that is passed through the mouth into the throat, where tissue is removed from the tumor to be examined under a microscope.

TREATMENT Cancer in the lining of the throat is usually treated with radiotherapy. Cancer of the tonsil, especially when it has invaded the root of the tongue, is treated with radiotherapy, or with a combination of radiotherapy and surgery. But cancer that originates in the root of the tongue responds poorly to all treatments.

Cancer of the vocal cords is treated in various ways, depending on how far the cancer has spread. For small tumors that are confined to the cords, radiotherapy is used as the sole treatment. For large tumors that impair movement of the cords, surgery is generally used to remove the larynx (laryngectomy). For tumors that have spread throughout the lower throat, surgery to remove the larynx is usually followed by radiotherapy to destroy any cancerous cells that remain after the operation.

Chemotherapy cannot cure cancer of the throat. But it may be used for temporary relief of symptoms when the cancer is incurable.

POSSIBLE SIDE EFFECTS OF TREATMENT The consequences of surgery depend on the type and amount of tissue that must be removed. If the jaw and lining of the throat are removed, the patient suffers facial disfigurement, which may be corrected with cosmetic surgery. If large parts of the tongue are removed, serious difficulties in speaking and swallowing occur. If a single vocal cord is removed, hoarseness is the only result; but if the entire larynx is removed (laryngectomy), the surgeon must create near the bottom of the neck an opening into the trachea, through which the patient breathes. Patients with a laryngectomy may learn to speak by drawing air into the esophagus and expelling it forcefully (esophageal speech); but those who cannot learn esophageal speech may hold against the throat a mechanical or electrical device to simulate a voice. Although patients with a laryngectomy must not swim, since water can flood the lungs through the opening in the trachea, they can participate in most other normal activities of life.

For the usual side effects of radiotherapy, see pp. 57–58. Additional side effects include thickening of the saliva, loss of taste, hoarseness, and cavities in the teeth, as well as inflammation and scarring of the hinge that works the lower jaw, so that the mouth no longer opens fully.

PROGNOSIS Cancer of the root of the tongue is difficult to cure. So, too, is cancer of the lining of the throat.

When cancer of the tonsil is diagnosed early, 70 percent of the patients are alive five years after treatment. When the cancer has spread to the lymph nodes, 40 percent survive for five years; but if the lymph nodes are large and stiff, the rate of cure drops to 17 percent. On the average, 45 percent of all patients with cancer of the tonsil survive the disease.

Cancer of the vocal cords is usually curable. For patients whose tumors are small, 85 to 90 percent are alive five years after treatment. For patients whose tumors have spread to the lymph nodes, 33 percent are alive after five years.

GEOGRAPHIC PATTERN Cancers of the throat occur frequently in Puerto Rico, India, and Sweden. France shows the highest rate for cancer of the vocal cords; Norway, the lowest.

ETHNIC PATTERN None known. But cancer of the vocal cords occurs seven times more often in men than in women.

OCCUPATIONAL PATTERN None known.

AGE PATTERN Cancers of the throat occur most often in adults between the ages of sixty-five and seventy-five.

SPECIFIC CAUSES Smoking or chewing tobacco can cause cancer of the throat. So, too, can heavy consumption of alcohol. Recent studies suggest that those who both smoke heavily and drink heavily are far more likely to develop cancer of the throat than are those who only smoke or only drink.

THE THYROID

DESCRIPTION OF THE ORGAN A gland located in the lower front of the neck beneath the Adam's apple, the thyroid straddles the windpipe (the trachea) with two pecan-shaped lobes. These lobes are connected to one another by a narrow strip of tissue that runs across the front of the windpipe.

FUNCTION OF THE ORGAN The thyroid produces hormones that control the body's rate of metabolism – the rate at which cells make use of the chemicals that keep them alive. Removal of the entire thyroid causes death because the body's metabolism falls too low. In children, abnormalities of the thyroid may cause mental retardation or stunted growth.

DESCRIPTION OF THE DISEASE Cancers of the thyroid generally form slow-growing tumors that cause the gland to enlarge. The tumor may be composed of cells that are completely unlike normal thyroid cells (undifferentiated); or it may be composed of cells that are very much like normal thyroid cells (well-differentiated). Undifferen-

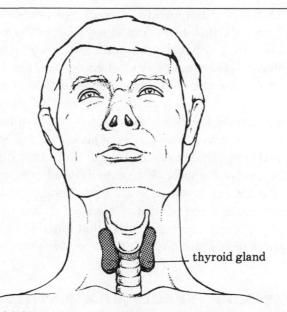

thyroid gland

tiated tumors, which are rare, usually spread to the tissues of the neck: the esophagus, windpipe, and nerves of the vocal cords. Well-differentiated tumors, by contrast, almost always remain confined to the thyroid and to the lymph nodes of the neck, although a few may behave like undifferentiated tumors.

SYMPTOMS The earliest symptom is enlargement of the thyroid – a condition often caused by lack of iodine in the diet (goiter). Late symptoms include choking, hoarseness, difficulty in swallowing or breathing, and the appearance of lumps (swollen lymph nodes) in the neck.

DIAGNOSIS A single hard lump in the thyroid suggests the presence of a cancerous tumor; numerous soft lumps suggest goiter. When the doctor suspects that a lump is cancerous, he performs a scan of the thyroid while the patient swallows a radioactive substance. If the scan is inconclusive, the doctor may treat the lump with oral medication. But if medication does not reduce the size of the lump, or if the scan reveals the presence of a definite tumor, a biopsy must be performed. Since a reliable diagnosis can be made only when a large portion of the thyroid is examined under a microscope, most of the gland is removed during biopsy.

TREATMENT Undifferentiated tumors respond poorly to all treatments. In fact, once they have spread beyond the thyroid, these tumors can rarely be cured, although symptoms may be relieved by X-rays.

Well-differentiated tumors can often be treated by surgery. The surgeon removes most of the thyroid and all swollen lymph nodes in the neck, leaving only a small portion of thyroid to maintain the body's metabolism. Thyroid hormones are then used to control the growth of cancerous cells that may remain. By suppressing the body's production of thyroid-stimulating hormones, hormone therapy can succeed in keeping the cancer dormant. For well-differentiated tumors that have spread to the tissues of the throat, radiotherapy is used as adjuvant treatment. Generally, the outside of the neck is irradiated by machine; the inside, by a "radioactive cocktail" that must be swallowed.

Chemotherapy has not proved effective for treating cancer of the thyroid.

POSSIBLE SIDE EFFECTS OF TREATMENT Surgery may cause permanent hoarseness by damaging the nerves of the vocal cords. It may also cause a calcium deficiency that can be corrected with tablets of calcium and vitamin D.

For the usual side effects of radiotherapy, see pp. 57–58. On rare occasions, radioactive cocktails may cause fatal pneumonia.

Hormone therapy, when properly administered, causes no side effects.

PROGNOSIS Among patients whose tumors are well differentiated and confined to the thyroid and lymph nodes, 80 percent are alive fifteen years after treatment.

When a tumor of the thyroid is undifferentiated, or when it has spread to the tissues of the neck, only one out of six patients survives for fifteen years.

Note: Spread to the lymph nodes is *not* a bad sign in cancer of the thyroid, as it is in almost all other cancers.

GEOGRAPHIC PATTERN Hawaii shows a high rate of cancer of the thyroid.

ETHNIC PATTERN None known.

OCCUPATIONAL PATTERN None known.

AGE PATTERN Cancer of the thyroid occurs most often in adults between the ages of forty and fifty.

SPECIFIC CAUSES In rare instances, cancer of the thyroid may develop from goiter, a condition caused by lack of iodine in the diet. The cancer is also caused by radiation; hence it occurs at higher than normal rates in Japanese who have survived the atom bombs at Hiroshima or Nagasaki, and in adults who have undergone X-ray treatment for enlargement of the thymus or for infections of the ears and tonsils during childhood.

THE UTERUS

DESCRIPTION OF THE ORGAN Part of the female reproductive system, the uterus is a pear-shaped organ situated in the pelvic cavity. It lies behind the bladder and in front of the rectum, immediately above

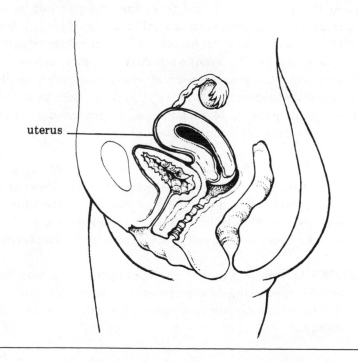

uterus

the vagina – a 4- to 6-inch muscular passageway slanting upward toward the back of the body from an opening between the woman's legs. The short neck of the pear-like uterus (the cervix) points downward and obtrudes into the vagina. The rest of the organ (the fundus) tilts away from the vagina and points upward toward the front of the woman's body. At the top of the uterus are two tubes (the Fallopian tubes), which extend to the ovaries lying on either side of the uterus. (For further detail, see the sections on The Cervix and The Ovary.)

Primarily composed of muscle, the uterus has a hollow center, or cavity, lined with a thick layer of mucous tissue (the endometrium). This cavity is connected to the vagina by a small canal in the cervix.

FUNCTION OF THE ORGAN The uterus is the womb – the home of the unborn child during pregnancy. Soon after fertilization, a fertilized egg embeds itself in the lining of the uterus (the endometrium). As the egg begins to develop into a fetus, the endometrium helps form the placenta, which nourishes the fetus until birth.

In women of child-bearing age, the endometrium continually prepares for pregnancy. During the approximately twenty days of the menstrual cycle when there is no menstrual flow, the endometrium grows and thickens in order to accommodate a fertilized egg. If fertilization does not take place, the uterus sloughs off the endometrium as part of the menstrual tissue during the woman's period. But even before the menstrual flow is over, the endometrium starts to regenerate so that the menstrual cycle can repeat itself. This cycle, which continues for about thirty years from puberty to menopause, is governed by hormones produced in the ovaries and the pituitary gland.

DESCRIPTION OF THE DISEASE Cancer of the uterus generally occurs in the lining of the uterus (the endometrium). Growing until it fills the uterine cavity and spreading downward into the lining of the cervix, the cancer eventually invades the organ's muscle wall. Late in the disease, the cancer may spread into the bladder or the rectum.

SYMPTOMS In women who are past menopause, the most frequent symptom is vaginal bleeding. In menstruating women, symptoms include abnormal menstrual flow, spotting between periods, or vaginal bleeding after intercourse.

DIAGNOSIS The Pap test, which is used to detect cancer of the cervix (see the section on The Cervix), does not reach into the cavity of the uterus and so is usually unable to detect uterine cancer. Diagnosis must be made by D&C (dilatation and curettage) – a procedure in which the doctor scrapes, from the lining of the patient's uterus, tissue to be examined under a microscope. Although the patient is usually hospitalized and given a general anaesthetic during the D&C, a modified D&C (an endobiopsy) may be performed with a local anaesthetic in the doctor's office.

TREATMENT The most effective treatment is surgery to remove the uterus, the Fallopian tubes, and the ovaries. In patients whose cancers are advanced, radiotherapy may be used to supplement surgery either before or after the operation.

When patients cannot withstand surgery, radiotherapy is used as the sole treatment. The doctor may administer X-rays by machine or by inserting into the uterine cavity a small container of radioactive material.

Chemotherapy has not proved effective in treating cancer of the uterus. But when the cancer has spread to other parts of the body, hormones – in particular, progesterone – may cause the cancer to regress.

POSSIBLE SIDE EFFECTS OF TREATMENT Surgery causes loss of fertility in premenopausal women.

For the usual side effects of radiotherapy, see pp. 57–58. When radiotherapy is used in combination with surgery, the doses of X-rays are modest and the side effects minimal. When radiotherapy is used as the sole treatment, the side effects always include loss of fertility and some times narrowing of the vagina. (Patients who continue to have intercourse during radiotherapy are less inclined to experienced narrowing of the vagina than those who practice abstinence.) Patients may also suffer impairments of the small intestine, the large intestine, and the bladder – conditions that may eventually require surgical correction.

Hormones, when they cause the body to retain fluid, produce bloating in the region of the stomach.

PROGNOSIS Among patients whose cancers are confined to the lining of the uterus (the endometrium), 85 percent are alive after five years. Among those whose cancers have spread into the deep muscle layers of the uterus, 60 to 70 percent are alive after five years. But once the cancer has spread to a great many lymph nodes, cure is rare.

GEOGRAPHIC PATTERN None known.

ETHNIC PATTERN Cancer of the uterus occurs more often in white women than in black, perhaps for social and economic reasons. The disease tends to strike women who are hypertensive, obese, relatively wealthy, and childless. Diabetic women also suffer a higher than normal rate of uterine cancer.

OCCUPATIONAL PATTERN None known.

AGE PATTERN Cancer of the uterus occurs most often in women between the ages of forty and seventy.

SPECIFIC CAUSES None known. But it has been suggested that estrogen may cause or stimulate cancer of the uterus, particularly when the hormone is administered without interruption for many years.

4 Widespread Cancer and Terminal Care

Widespread cancer is usually incurable, unless the patient experiences a spontaneous remission, which is the subject matter of miracles and not of medicine. The most a patient with incurable cancer can expect is that radiotherapy or chemotherapy will be able to slow the advance of the disease and briefly prolong the patient's life.

Although it is sad to contemplate that people who have widespread cancer are living under a sentence of death, it is also sad to think that the moment a person is born, his body begins to grow toward death. Life is like a terminal illness. People die from it. When and how they will die are, of course, questions that no thinking person can escape. Presumably, most people want to live long lives and die painlessly in their sleep. Anything less – an early death, for example, or a painful death – is mournfully to be regretted. But as the medieval play makes clear, death, early or late, will come for Everyman.

Rarely a happy subject, death touches the living as well as the dying. In earlier ages, when death was a common street scene, people prepared for death by surrounding themselves with reminders of mortality (memento mori): images of skulls, skeletons, graves, and the like; quotations from the Bible, proverbs, philosophical sayings; and personifications of death in plays and poems. In the present century, because material affluence has removed death from the streets and enabled people to live lives relatively free from plagues and poorhouses, they have put death out of memory. But the old saying "out of sight, out of mind" does not mean out of existence.

It is therefore appropriate that a chapter on widespread cancer should treat both metastasis and terminal care – that is, the care of the dying. Terminal care occupies most of the chapter not only because death is inevitable, but also because the dying should be treated in such a way that they live until they die.

What is widespread cancer?

When cancerous cells travel beyond the original tumor and lodge in other parts of the body, the cancer has become widespread. The word doctors use to describe this spread is *metastasis*, from the Greek term meaning "beyond stability." The original tumor is called the primary tumor and distant tumors are called secondary tumors or metastases.

Some cancers spread quickly, some slowly; some spread is fatal, some not. Cancer that spreads from the pancreas, for example, is fast moving and fatal; cancer that spreads from the prostate is, in an elderly man, slow moving and unlikely to kill the patient. Most rates of spread lie somewhere in between these two extremes.

What percentage of cancer patients have widespread cancer?

Two-thirds of all cancer patients develop widespread cancer. Half of these patients have widespread cancer at the time of diagnosis. The other half are treated for cancer, but the disease nonetheless spreads. Example:

99 people have cancer
66 (of the 99) develop widespread cancer
33 (of the 66) have widespread cancer at first diagnosis
33 (of the 66) are treated for cancer, but the disease nonetheless spreads.

In short, only one-third of all cancer patients are curable. The other two-thirds will die from the disease.

How does cancer become widespread?

Because cancerous cells can become unglued from the primary tumor, they may invade a body cavity, particularly the stomach or the chest, or they may pass into the lymphatic system and the bloodstream, where they are swept along to distant parts of the body. Although thousands of cancerous cells are killed daily by the body's defenses and by the velocity of the bloodstream, some survive. Remember: it takes only one tiny clump of cancerous cells to spread the disease. If a new tumor (a secondary tumor) arises, it usually resembles in character the primary tumor. The cells of a secondary tumor may also invade and metastasize, causing further spread of the disease.

When does cancer spread?

Cancer usually develops over a period of years – for example, an average of eight years for cancer of the breast. If the cancer becomes widespread, the spread will probably occur before the primary tumor is discovered and treated. Only rarely does cancer spread because the primary tumor recurs after treatment. In the majority of cases, spread predates the initial detection of the disease.

Are most metastases multiple or single?

Multiple. Rarely does cancer spread to one site only. Reason: once cancerous cells have entered the lymphatic system and the bloodstream, they can be carried to virtually every part of the body. When a single metastasis does occur, it is usually to be found in the lungs, or the lymph nodes, or the brain.

A single metastasis may be treated with surgery or radiotherapy. Multiple metastases are usually treated with chemotherapy, except in England, where chemotherapy is used far less often than it is in the United States.

Does metastatic spread tend to follow a pattern?

Yes. Cancer tends to spread, with exceptions, from the primary tumor to a specific organ or organs. This pattern can be explained by the pathways that cancerous cells follow once they have left the primary tumor and entered the bloodstream or the lymphatic system. The road from Chicago to Denver, for example, passes through Omaha; so it should come as no surprise that travelers between these cities often spend a night in Omaha. Since all the blood in the body eventually travels through the lungs, most metastases affect the lungs.

In general metastatic spread conforms to the following pattern.

INDIVIDUAL CANCERS	AVENUE(S) OF SPREAD	DESTINATION(S) OF SPREAD
Bladder (cancerous tumors, not polyps)	Veins and lymph nodes	Liver, bones, and lung
Blood	Veins	Bone marrow
Bone	Veins	Lungs
Brain	Spinal fluid	Spinal cord
Breast	Primarily lymph nodes, but also the veins	Bone, lung, and liver
Cervix	Primarily lymph nodes, but also the veins	Lung
Colon-rectum	Primarily lymph nodes, but also the veins	Liver and lung
Esophagus	Lymph nodes	Lung and liver
Kidney	Veins and lymph nodes	Lung and bone
Lung	Primarily veins, but also the lymph nodes	Bone, liver, adrenal glands, and brain
Lymph Nodes	Primarily lymph nodes, but also the veins	Liver, bone, marrow, and spleen
Mouth	Primarily lymph nodes, but also the veins	Lung
Ovary	Lining of the abdominal cavity	Entire abdomen
Pancreas	Veins and lymph nodes	Liver and lung

Prostate	Veins and lymph nodes	Bone
Skin	Lymph nodes	Lymph nodes
Stomach	Veins and lymph nodes	Liver and lung
Testicle	Primarily lymph nodes, but also the veins	Lung
Throat	Primarily lymph nodes	Lung
Thyroid	Veins	Lung and bone
Uterus	Primarily lymph nodes, but also the veins	Lung

How do doctors test for metastatic spread?

Most cancerous cells (but not all) spread to what is called the Big Three – the lungs, liver, and bones – and then to what is called the Little Four – the brain. Hence these sites are usually examined first. To determine the extent of spread, doctors normally use the following tests.

AREA OF SPREAD	TEST
Bone	Radioisotope scan and X-rays
Brain	Radioisotope scan and computer scan with dye injection
Liver	Blood tests and radioisotope scan
Lung	X-rays
Lymph Nodes	Biopsy and, occasionally, lymphogram

Do doctors always test for metastatic spread?

No, but they should. Before the doctor begins treating a primary tumor, he should order tests based on the routes that cancerous cells generally follow (metastatic pathways) to determine whether the cancer has spread.

After the doctor treats a primary tumor, he may, at any time from six months to five years later, order tests to see whether the cancer has been completely eradicated. But tests are not always necessary. By judging the size and location of the cancer, the degree of spread to the lymph nodes and veins, and the appearance of the tumor under a microscope, the doctor can often predict rather accurately, without ordering further tests, if the patient has been cured.

Is pain in other parts of the body a sign of metastasis?

No. Fear often leads a patient to believe that pain is a sign of metastasis. But in a cancer patient, as in any other person, pain may be caused by stress or by benign diseases, such as ulcers or infection.

Why may a patient who suspects that his cancer has spread delay seeing his doctor?

For the same reasons that a person who first suspects that he has cancer delays seeing his doctor. He is afraid to have his worst fears confirmed. So he ignores or evades what he cannot face. Evasion makes it possible for a person to maintain his fantasies and persuade himself that his symptoms are the result of an innocent disorder or innocuous inflammation.

Some patients blame the doctor for the recurrence of the disease. They reason that if the doctor failed to cure them the first time, then it is a waste of time and money to see him a second time. Other patients may have initially disbelieved in conventional treatment and subsequently argue that the recurrence of the disease means that it is time to try unproven treatments.

Still other patients blame themselves if their cancers recur or spread. They feel they are being punished for some misdeed, like adultery or child-beating or desertion. They regard themselves as unworthy and therefore deserving of cancer.

Needless to say, it is important for the doctor to understand why some patients delay seeking treatment – and to alleviate their fears.

Why is metastasis considered a major turning point in the progress of cancer?

Before metastasis there is one tumor, after metastasis there are many. The one is curable, the many are usually not. If a tumor is discovered early enough – that is, before the cancerous cells take root somewhere else – the tumor can be destroyed and the cancer completely eradicated. But once the cancerous cells have metastasized – to the liver or lung or bone, for example – treatment can seldom produce a cure. Even massive doses of radiotherapy and chemotherapy may not be enough to kill the millions of cancerous cells circulating throughout the body.

How do doctors treat widespread cancer?

With chemotherapy. The specific drugs the doctor uses depend on the character of the primary tumor. When, for example, a tumor of the breast becomes widespread, the doctor treats the spread with drugs specifically suited for cancer of the breast.

What is meant by "the unknown primary"?

In rare instances, the doctor may be unable to find the site of the primary tumor, although he knows the sites of the secondary tumors. In other words, the primary tumor is unknown. An unknown primary tumor is a problem because the doctor cannot adequately treat secondary tumors until he knows the source of the disease.

Why do some patients refuse treatment for the recurrence of cancer?

Usually because they feel that the treatment is worse than the disease. Surgery scars the body, radiotherapy burns the body, chemotherapy poisons the body. Some patients, having already suffered scarring, burning, and poisoning, choose to let the disease run its course rather than seek further treatment. Such patients, however, are in a minority. When the choice is between life and looks, most patients are willing to endure scars, changes in skin color, and toxic side effects for an extension of life.

Some patients refuse treatment because they regard their disease as punishment for their previous behavior; or because they feel that to receive treatment is foolishly to resist the inevitable; or because they wish to pursue a course of unproven treatments.

Whatever reasons a patient gives, the doctor should make every effort to tell him what alternatives and choices are available.

When is curative treatment appropriate and when is it not?

Curative treatment is appropriate when the patient continues to improve and inappropriate when the patient continues to decline. The difficulty is that no clear line divides improvement from decline. For the doctor to be certain that the patient is no longer curable, he may have to subject the patient to considerable pain and expense. The doctor's dilemma may be stated in this way: he must, by means of imperfect tests, determine when the patient has crossed the line from curable to incurable. A perfect test, by showing the extent of the cancer, would, of course, save discomfort, time, and money; but in the absence of such a test the doctor must often rely on inconclusive data, the judgment of other doctors, and his own experience. The patient, needless to say, wants the doctor to persist in trying to find a cure. The doctor, in turn, may feel that if he stops trying, he is sentencing the patient to death.

So long as there is hope of recovery, the doctor is justified in ruthlessly pursuing a cure. Someone once observed that in order to eradicate cancer the doctor must have a killer instinct – even if that instinct results in discomfort to the patient. Better to be in pain now and live later than to suffer the spread of cancer because of the doctor's initial timidity.

But once the line has been crossed and the patient cannot be cured, the doctor must shift from active treatment to symptomatic treatment (see the next question). In those cases where the patient has been receiving antibiotics, intravenous feedings, dialysis, blood transfusions, and the like, the doctor and the patient must decide whether such aids – normally used in curative treatment – ought to be continued. The decision is not an easy one. If the patient can, by means of drugs and mechanical aids, still enjoy a period of his life, then it would seem unfair to deny him such assistance. But if mechanical aids are used to keep alive a patient who is unconscious or close to death, it would seem cruel to force him to live. Most dying patients prefer to die with dignity, rather than live wired to a machine. When, for example, a hopelessly sick patient contracts pneumonia – "the dying man's friend" – it is not only misdirected zeal for the doctor to try to cure him, but also meddlesome medicine.

What is symptomatic treatment?

Treating the symptoms and not the disease. Symptomatic treatment is also called terminal treatment, because it occurs during the terminal stage of an illness. In dying patients, the terminal stage usually lasts no more than six weeks.

Once cancer has become widespread and curative treatment is no longer effective, the doctor must treat the symptoms of the disease. Since widespread cancer is a general disease, affecting more than one organ or area of the body, most dying patients experience discomfort from various symptoms. Some of the most common are: pain, nausea, vomiting, constipation, shortness of breath, loss of appetite, and weakness (see pp. 169–172). If the doctor is to treat and relieve these symptoms, he must be familiar with the palliative use of drugs, surgery, radiotherapy, and chemotherapy.

The transition from curative to symptomatic treatment occurs (or should occur) when the doctor indicates that nothing more can be done to cure the patient. The doctor must then think of symptoms as disease and employ every measure to relieve the dying patient's suffering. Surely one of the tests of a competent doctor ought to be his ability to palliate the symptoms of a disease when he cannot cure it. As Francis Bacon remarked in *The New Atlantis*:

> I esteem it the office of a physician not only to restore health, but to mitigate pain and dolors; and not only when such mitigation may conduce to recovery, but when it may serve to make a fair and easy passage.

Palliation can eliminate the suffering of most cancer patients, and can thus extend to most a comfortable death.

What is meant by palliative treatment?

Palliative treatment is that part of symptomatic treatment that seeks to relieve physical discomfort. The word palliative means to make less terrible, serious, or painful. Palliative treatment relieves and makes less terrible the pain of disease, without curing the disease. Palliation may take the form of drugs, in which pain-killing medicines are given at regular intervals; or surgery, in which nerves are cut and obstructions removed; or radiotherapy, in which a cancer is irradiated to relieve a feeling of pressure or suffocation; or chemotherapy, in which chemicals are given to relieve the weakness and breathlessness caused by some cancers (see pp. 165–172).

Shouldn't unproven treatments be used in the hope that they might work?

No. Unproven treatments are unproven not because they have not been tried, but because they have failed to pass tests imposed by the government to protect the public against dangerous and ineffective remedies (see pp. 206–209). Although it can be argued that the dying patient has nothing to lose by trying any kind of remedy, it should be pointed out that unproven treatments are often painful, poisonous, preposterous (for example, coffee enemas), and expensive.

No doubt because conventional cancer treatment in the United States can be so expensive as to beggar a family, patients are sometimes attracted to treatments that promise a cure at low cost. But in fact nowhere in the world has a miracle cure for cancer been discovered. To think otherwise is to engage in self-deception and false hope.

At best, unproven treatments have no effect; at worst, they mislead and kill. When the dying patient is willing, out of desperation, to embrace any diet, any device, he wastes his precious time in futilely seeking a cure that does not exist. He would receive more joy from spending his remaining days with people he loves than from trying to extract sunbeams from apricot seeds.

Isn't symptomatic treatment an admission of failure?

No. Symptomatic or palliative treatment is merely treatment of a different kind. Because of the great discoveries and numerous successes of modern medicine, most people think that all illnesses are curable. But some illnesses are not. Terminal cancer, for example, cannot be cured, although its symptoms can be controlled. A person might observe that if symptoms are adequately controlled, then for all intents and purposes the symptoms – if not the disease – are cured. True. The difficulty is to keep the symptoms adequately *and continuously* controlled so that the patient never notices them. Therein lies the challenge of symptomatic or palliative treatment.

"The greatest evil," wrote St. Augustine, "is physical pain." When a doctor cannot cure disease, he can express both his skill and his benevolence by alleviating the pain of the dying patient.

Should the doctor tell the dying patient that he is dying?

Yes, if the patient indicates that he wants to know. Truth, when requested, should never be denied. The difficulty is that some patients do not indicate whether they want to know. The doctor may then have to draw out the patient with leading questions or interpret the patient's silence.

But in most cases the patient wants to know, and if given the opportunity will, in one way or another, ask the doctor to tell him the truth. How the doctor reveals the truth is important. An abrupt statement is cruel and may be rejected by the patient because he finds it brutal or frightening. On the other hand, when the patient is told the truth gently and made to understand that he must know what is wrong with him if he is to cooperate in his own treatment, he will often behave bravely and even thank the doctor for his candor.

To lie to a patient is always wrong. Even when the patient does not want to hear the whole truth, he does not want to hear lies. Doctors are mistaken if they think that lying or withholding the truth protects the patient. A lack of candor leaves the patient prey to his worst fears and condemns him to suffer alone.

How does the patient feel when he is denied the opportunity to ask about his condition?

When the patient is effectively discouraged from asking about his condition, either because he has been given false hopes or because his family does not want him to know, he feels isolated. His doctor has kept from him the most important matter in his life: his life. The patient, anxious to know if his time is running out, or if he should settle his family and business affairs, is left without an answer. The doctor's silence victimizes him.

Unable to decide whether or not to plan, the patient seeks confirmation about his condition from others: nurses, orderlies, social workers, family, friends. But they, lacking the authority to tell him the truth, should they know it, can only advise him to speak to his doctor. Out of frustration, the patient finally grows angry and resentful or, even worse, silent.

Churches and synagogues are particularly critical of doctors (and families) who do not tell the patient the truth or who dissuade him from asking about his condition. Clergymen argue that the patient must know if he has a terminal illness so that he can prepare spiritually for his death, and so that they can be present to ease the patient's anxieties and fears.

What is the best way for the doctor to raise the question of dying?

By assessing how much the patient knows and how much he wishes to know. If the patient makes clear that he does not want to discuss the subject, the doctor ought not bring it up unless the patient does. Some people are not prepared to talk about death until their bodies have begun to fail. Other people are frightened or reticent. With a little encouragement, however, most people are glad to talk – if the doctor is willing, or has the time, to listen.

The doctor can, by asking questions, gently lead the patient to the vital issue. When a patient is asked, for example, about his symptoms or his fears, he will often begin to talk about dying, perhaps first in general terms, but then with respect to himself.

In most cases, it is the patient who indicates, by the questions he asks, that he is ready to speak. Such questions as the following usually indicate that the patient wants to talk to the doctor about future prospects: "What are my chances of being cured?" "Can you help me?" "Should I seek a second opinion?" "Will I have pain?" "Should I make a will?"

But even when a patient is silent, he may nevertheless wish to speak. Although very few doctors have the time to wait until a reticent patient is prepared to ask about death, most institutions have nurses, social workers, and chaplains available to sit with the patient and listen – until he is ready to express his fears.

Of all the means to inform the dying patient about his condition, none is more successful than *listening* to what the patient has to say. When given the chance to speak, the patient more often than not requests that he be told the truth or volunteers that he knows he is dying. Most doctors, then, would be well advised to ask themselves, "What do I let my patients tell me?"

Why do some doctors withhold the truth from their patients?

Although some patients want to know the truth about their condition, most doctors do not want to tell them. According to various studies, 77 to 87 percent of terminal patients favored knowing the truth and 69 to 90 percent of doctors favored avoiding the truth. The reasons for this discrepancy are not difficult to understand.

No one wants to play the angel of death. The Greeks not infrequently killed the messenger who brought bad news, or simply ignored him, as they did Cassandra when she warned of impending danger. Jonah chose to run away rather than deliver to the Ninevites God's dire message. The bearer of bad news, whether Greek messenger or modern-day doctor, is not gladly received. Little wonder, then, that doctors avoid telling a patient that he is under sentence of death.

In their own defense, doctors contend that some patients cannot accept the truth, some never want to know the truth, and some much prefer half-truths and evasion to candor. Hence a great many doctors, either because they lack the courage or the words, simply cannot bring themselves to tell a patient that his disease is incurable and that he is going to die. Particularly when the patient is young and has small children, they try to leave him with some sense of hope – for a future cure or remission.

The impulse to avoid bad news is, to some degree, shared by the patient. In one study, when patients were asked whether they would want to know if they had a terminal illness, a majority said yes. But when asked if they thought other patients with terminal illness ought to be told, a majority said no.

Most people, it would appear, think that they have the courage to face the truth, but that others do not. Doctors, not surprisingly, feel the same way.

Should the patient's family be told?

Yes. Even when doctors disagree on whether to tell the patient that he is dying, they agree that the family should be told. Ideally, both patient and family ought to be informed. The difficulty is whether to tell the patient or the family first. A number of doctors prefer to tell the family before they tell the patient. This decision, although understandable (because the family helps break the news to the patient), undermines the traditional doctor-patient relationship, in which the doctor discloses information only at the patient's direction.

Families receive the news no differently from patients. Some respond courageously, some hysterically, some evasively, some angrily, and so on. Like patients, families often need time to adjust to the news. Some relatives even insist that the doctor keep the truth from the patient. At such times, the doctor is placed in the delicate position of having to choose between the candor he owes the patient and the blame he may receive if the patient takes the news badly. The accusation "See what comes of telling the truth!" has bedeviled more than one doctor in a lifetime.

Probably the best solution is for the doctor to tell the patient first and let the patient inform the family. In that way, the patient will not resent his family for having kept him in ignorance.

How do most people react when they are told that they have a terminal illness?

According to Dr. Elisabeth Kübler-Ross, a specialist in the study of death and dying, most people pass through five stages.

1 Denial. The patient refuses to believe the doctor's report of the laboratory tests. "It can't be me," he says. "You've made a mistake. Your tests are in error."

2 Anger. The patient rages against his premature death. "Why me?" he asks. "What did I do to deserve this fate?"

3 Bargaining. The patient tries to strike a bargain with some heavenly power. "Dear Lord," he pleads, "just cure me and I'll never misbehave again. I promise. Anything you ask of me, I'll do."

4 Depression. The patient loses interest in himself and others. "I'm dying," he says. "But who cares? Nothing matters any more."

5 Acceptance or resignation. The patient is resigned to dying and has made his peace with himself and others. "We all die," he observes, "some sooner, some later. So I'll just make the most of what little time is left me." If the period of dying is to be valuable, the acceptance must be more than passive surrender; the acceptance must be vital and active.

It should be observed that even though the patient moves from denial to acceptance, he never loses hope that some cure, some treatment, will be found to save him. Such hope is life-sustaining and should never be discouraged.

Note: The families of dying patients often go through the same five stages before they can accept the idea of a loved one's death.

Should the dying patient be given hope?

Hope of recovery ends when curative treatment is discontinued. Although most dying patients cling to the hope that a miraculous cure will be found in time to save them, doctors should not encourage this kind of thinking. When a patient enters the terminal phase of cancer, he cannot fight the disease or try to hold it at bay without adding to his own depression.

Some doctors encourage the dying patient to hope, because they believe that it is easier to deal with a patient who expects to recover than with one who is persuaded he is going to die. Even if this belief were true, and it is probably not, false encouragement has no place in the care of the terminally ill. The patient who is initially deceived can become resentful and sometimes paranoid when he discovers that he is not going to be cured. The doctor and the patient's family then find themselves having to deal with an angry, uncooperative patient.

Hope is justified when confined to small things that the patient may indeed be able to accomplish. If, for example, hope means seeing an old friend next week, taking a short walk, watching a football match on television, then the patient may in all fairness be given hope.

How does knowing the truth enable the patient to select his own treatment?

Once the patient knows the nature of his disease and the treatments available to him, he must ask himself some very important questions. For example: "Am I willing to prolong my life at any cost? If not, at what cost?" "To live an additional six weeks of life, am I willing to suffer serious side effects from treatment?" "Will the quality of my remaining life be better or worse without the treatment?"

The patient must then determine his objectives and tell the doctor what they are. If the patient is silent, the doctor, who is trained to keep patients alive as long as possible, will do what he thinks best. But the doctor's objectives may not suit the patient. A craftsman, for instance, may tell the doctor that he does not want chemotherapy if it will numb his hands. A writer may refuse pain-killing drugs if they cause mental confusion. In every instance, it is for the patient to decide what is most important to him – given what is achievable – and to tell the doctor. Most doctors, it should be pointed out, welcome the chance to treat a dying patient as the patient wants.

But such an ideal relationship cannot be achieved unless the patient knows from the outset the truth about himself and his disease.

How does terminal cancer alter a patient's view of the world?

By making a few patients morose and reclusive, and causing most others to become passionately involved in living. Suddenly old arguments no longer matter and occupations that had seemed important pale into insignificance. Frequently, the transforming knowledge of cancer gives the patient a new view of reality. What was once of major concern becomes of minor concern, or of no concern, and vice versa. Human relationships take on added meaning; each day is valued for its length and quality and variety; every detail is noticed, the veins in the tree leaf, the red bud, the slant of light. In fact, the physical world, the seasons of the year, the duration of a day all become vitally interesting. When each day is treated as the last, a lifetime of feeling is compressed into a short space of time. Everything is more intense: loving, looking, touching, tasting, enjoying. Every sense is heightened, every moment appreciated.

What are some of the consequences of not knowing?

When the patient is not told that he is going to die, he is placed by his doctor at a terrible disadvantage. For one thing, the patient cannot make the most of the little time that remains. For another, he sees no reason to conclude his business affairs, to look after his will, to plan religious matters.

The patient may even embark on a new business venture or contract to undertake a difficult project. When his declining health prevents him from pursuing these plans, he often seeks additional treatments and incurs further expense. Fully expecting to recover, he cannot understand why his body does not respond to treatment. He questions the doctor; he asks the nurses; he interrogates his family and friends. What began as a kindness – a desire to protect the patient from the truth – becomes a conspiracy of silence, implicating not only the patient's doctor, but also the other staff doctors and nurses, as well as the patient's family and friends.

Do all dying patients want to know the truth?

No. Some patients make their preferences very clear to the doctor: they do not want to be told that they will not recover. Rather they want to live with the belief that they will be cured, or with some other fantasy of their own creation. A few patients are too frightened or defensive to know whether they want to know. If the doctor is uncertain about how a person feels, he can start by giving gentle hints or by inviting a response to leading questions.

Normally the doctor can learn a great deal about the patient's state of mind from the questions the patient asks and the wishes he expresses. If, for example, the patient insists that he is going to buy a new car or remodel his house after he leaves the hospital, then he is telling the doctor that he does not want to be told about his condition.

To force the truth upon a patient is cruel and may cause hysteria and bitterness. The doctor must, after all, keep in mind that his major responsibility is to care for the patient, not to reveal the truth at any cost. If the patient wishes to believe that the world is flat and that the moon is made of cheese, he must have his reasons. For the doctor to insist that fantasy give way to truth is to ask the dying patient to substitute the knowledge of certain death for the poetry of dreams.

According to Dr. Cicely Saunders, founder of the famous St. Christopher's Hospice in London, it is by no means essential that every dying patient be told that he is dying.

How does the patient know that he is dying when he has not been told?

Even when he has not been told, the patient often knows that he is dying. A number of clues lead him to this conclusion: (i) his health does not improve; (ii) old symptoms become more serious; (iii) new symptoms arise without explanation; (iv) his body does not function properly;

(v) he feels exhausted for no reason; (vi) he suffers a radical loss of weight; (vii) he interprets the medical staff's gestures, looks, silences; (viii) he overhears the doctor or the nurse; (ix) he remembers the symptoms of terminal illness in family members and friends; (x) he reads the bed chart; (xi) relatives who know either hint at his condition or tell him.

Whether the patient learns quickly or slowly is immaterial. Once he knows, he usually wants to pursue the subject with his doctor as soon as possible. It is when a patient has discovered the truth about himself that he is most vulnerable – and most needs the doctor to sit and listen. Even if the doctor hears only silence, the patient may be saying a great deal.

Do some patients deny knowing?

After requesting the truth and receiving it, some patients deny knowing. After receiving the truth and acknowledging it, some patients deny knowing. After complaining that the truth is being kept from them and receiving it, some patients deny knowing. And after discovering the truth for themselves, some patients deny knowing.

Either because the prospect of death cannot be faced day after day, or because they would rather look on the bright side of things, some patients willfully deny the truth. Denial may take the form of the patient's threatening to seek a new doctor and treatment if the doctor persists in telling the patient what he does not want to hear; or it may take the form of the patient's one day pretending that he does not know and the next day admitting that he does know; or it may take the form of the patient's constructing an elaborate fantasy about himself and his disease, and inviting other patients to share in his fantasy.

Denying the truth or not wanting to know the truth serves a similar function: each protects the mind from the frightening visage of death and enables the patient to fashion the world as he would have it.

How many patients acknowledge that they are dying?

According to one study, at least half of all dying patients know that they are dying. The most candid responses usually come from the elderly and the most guarded from patients under sixty-five. The percentages are as follows.

At least 50 percent acknowledge that they know.

25 percent do not acknowledge that they know and cannot speak about the subject without distress.

25 percent do not even speak about the subject.

Notwithstanding these percentages, some doctors argue that very few patients know, while other doctors argue that most patients know. Perhaps the only way to settle the question is for the doctor to take the time to listen to the patient. The more the patient is encouraged to speak, the more he will be willing to share his personal doubts and fears.

Which types of people are most likely to speak about dying?

The elderly and people with small children. The elderly often have the impulse to sum up their lives and talk about their place in the world. People with small children want to discuss the consequences of their death on those who are left behind.

The elderly are, ironically, the group whom doctors most often wish to protect from the truth. Yet the elderly are the ones who generally talk most easily about death, perhaps because they are often content to see the long drawn-out process of life come to an end.

Do social and educational differences affect a patient's willingness to speak about dying?

Where a person went to school and for how many years, his religious views, church membership, social background, occupation – none of these things seems to matter. What matter are age and hardship. The elderly are willing to speak about their dying, and so too are parents of small children and people who have a great many dependents.

Is suicide or mercy killing (euthanasia) common among cancer patients?

No. Although patients frequently talk about taking their lives, they rarely do so. In one study of Veterans' Hospitals, it was found that those people most likely to commit suicide were old men with cancer of the throat, young men with Hodgkin's disease or leukemia, and men of any age suffering from severe anxiety, having little or no tolerance for pain, and enjoying no emotional support from family or friends.

So long as a dying patient is relatively free from pain, he is not drawn to suicide or euthanasia. Terrible pain invites thoughts of both. But with the numerous palliative treatments currently available, such suffering is unnecessary and unconscionable.

For reasons that are not wholly clear, society has tended to condemn suicide and condone euthanasia, even though they are similar. Until 1824, for example, the person who committed suicide in England was buried at a crossroads, or in other unhallowed ground, with a stake through his heart. But the person who asked that a lethal dose of drugs be administered to end his misery was pitied. Today suicide is condoned, and euthanasia is illegal.

The major questions that opponents of euthanasia ask are: who will perform it and under what conditions? Observing that patients who are properly treated rarely wish to die, opponents of both suicide and euthanasia insist that the following questions must be asked. Would this person wish to end his life if he were not depressed; he did not feel unwanted; he did not regard himself as a burden to his loved ones; he did not have pain; he did not have to suffer tubes and tents and hoses and injections and respirators and resuscitators; he were not afraid of a long and miserable death?

Questions of this sort ought to provide the doctor with an explanation for the patient's wanting to end his life. And since none of the above conditions need afflict the patient, it is up to the doctor to try to see that they do not.

What kinds of pain do the dying suffer?

> *I ask for a natural death.*
> *no teeth on the ground,*
> *no blood about the place . . .*
> *It's not death I fear,*
> *but unspecified, unlimited pain*
>
> Robert Lowell, "Death of a Critic"

Pain in the terminally ill is often treated under different headings: physical pain, emotional pain, social pain, and mental or spiritual pain.

Physical pain may be caused by the primary tumor, if it affects a vital organ, or by the consequences of widespread cancer: for example, bone metastasis, infection, bloodclots, constipation, shortness of breath, bedsores, headaches, and the like.

Emotional pain may be caused by fear of death or physical pain, by anxiety about the patient's steadily declining physical condition, by depression from the loneliness and isolation that a serious disease often imposes.

Social pain may be caused by the anticipated loss of family, friends, job, and home, by the loss of mobility and independence, by the re-linquishing of responsibility for the care of loved ones (wife, children, parents), by the leaving of work undone and a life unfulfilled.

Mental or spiritual pain may be caused by the apparent meaning-lessness of life and death, by the uncertainty of an afterlife, by the guilt of not believing or not believing well enough, by the question of whether a person has lived a good and useful life, by the inability to express dread and terror.

Pain, then, can affect the mind as well as the body. When severe, it can so obsess the patient that he thinks of nothing else, to the exclusion of other people and the events around him. Chronic pain, because it is senseless and continuous, may even undermine a patient's sanity, until he thinks he will go mad unless the pain is relieved. In such extreme cases, the pain is made worse by the patient's remembering the pain he had in the past, brooding about the pain he has in the present, and anticipating the pain he will have in the future. The fact is that terminal cancer patients are usually more concerned about pain than about dying.

Do all patients with terminal cancer experience physical pain?

No. According to various studies, as many as 50 percent of all cancer patients report no pain, even in their last days. Of the other half, 10 percent report occasional pain, and 40 percent report chronic pain, especially during the last six weeks of their illness.

Who suffer less pain: the elderly or the young?

The elderly seem to suffer less pain than the young. According to one study, as a person grows older his willingness or ability to withstand pain increases.

UNDER FIFTY 45 percent experienced considerable pain

FIFTY TO SEVENTY 32 percent experienced considerable pain

OVER SEVENTY 10 percent experienced considerable pain

The young suffer more than the elderly for at least two reasons. First, a young person is physically strong enough to fight the disease for a long time. But the longer the fight, the longer the pain. Second, a young person suffers mentally because often he is leaving behind a dependent family and a promising career. To forestall these losses, he resists psychologically and thus causes himself additional anguish and pain.

The elderly, on the other hand, are often resigned. They have lived their lives and are prepared to step aside to make room for the next generation.

What is the difference between acute pain and chronic pain?

An acute pain is one that is brief and severe: for example, a migraine headache, an injury to the testicles, a toothache, a sharp cut, a bad bruise, a postoperative throb. After a period of time or treatment, the pain goes away.

A chronic pain is one that is long and continued, but not necessarily severe. In terminal cancer patients with chronic pain, the pain is usually severe and, unless treated, will worsen rather than improve.

Can pain be prevented?

Yes, in most patients. Once the doctor has diagnosed the type and degree of pain, he can arrange for the patient to receive specific doses of drugs at regular intervals to prevent the pain from recurring. The prevention of pain is critical, because when pain is absent so too are misery and wretchedness. Doctors frequently find that as soon as a patient's pain disappears, a great many of the patient's other symptoms also disappear.

Even in the most serious cases, where pain may not be completely banished, it can be controlled. With the numerous treatments now available, no patient ever need suffer unrelenting physical pain.

It cannot be emphasized enough that most people fear pain more than dying. And since fear causes tension, a major source of pain in cancer patients, the doctor, by controlling pain, is able to break the cruel cycle of fear-pain-fear.

Can preventing pain lengthen a patient's life?

Yes. Pain weakens the body so that it cannot resist disease. When pain is absent, the body may withstand disease for months or even years.

What is an analgesic?

A remedy that relieves or removes pain. Doctors often call pain-killing drugs analgesics.

How is pain normally treated?

With drugs, administered orally or by injection. In the early stages of pain, aspirin, when used by itself or in combination with other drugs, is an effective painkiller. In the United States, late-stage pain is treated with morphine because heroin is banned. In England, diamorphine (heroin) is used with good results.

Which drug is more effective, morphine or diamorphine?

Recent field tests indicate that the drugs are equally effective. But in tests performed during the 1950s and 60s, diamorphine seemed to be more effective than morphine for the following reasons.

Diamorphine (i) causes less nausea and vomiting; (ii) creates appetite in patients who do not want to eat; (iii) is less constipating; (iv) has an exhilarating effect, while morphine has a depressing effect; (v) inspires patients to be alert and cooperative; (vi) is an effective anti-cough agent; (vii) relieves the anxiety of patients who are having trouble breathing.

The disadvantages of Diamorphine are as follows. Diamorphine is very addictive; and because it is easily tolerated, the dosage must be constantly increased.

How early in the disease should pain-relieving drugs be started?

As soon as the patient experiences pain. Since the memory of pain can be as painful as pain itself, it is important for the doctor quickly and decisively to prescribe a regular schedule of drugs. The sooner the patient loses his fear of pain, the easier his dying will be.

What is the right dosage?

The dosage that gives a patient the most relief for the longest period of time. The doctor will normally start with a small amount, which is gradually increased until the patient reports that he is out of pain.

How often should pain-relieving drugs be given?

As often as necessary. But no patient wants to spend his last days summoning the doctor to relieve his pain. The best procedure is for the doctor to determine the dosage a patient requires for the prevention of pain and to administer that dosage at regular intervals, normally every four hours. When drugs are well managed, the next dose is given before the effect of the previous one has worn off, so the patient is never aware of the need for another dose. A regular schedule makes it possible for the doctor to give the patient small doses and to avoid heavy sedation, which makes the patient feel "dopey" and sometimes causes changes in personality.

What does PRN mean?

Pro re nata: "for an occasion as it arises." The initials PRN, as used in hospitals, mean: drugs or medicines should be taken only as required, needed, or requested.

Although it is common practice for a doctor to administer pain-relieving drugs when a patient feels discomfort, PRN serves no purpose in the treatment of chronic pain. Whatever the cause, chronic pain requires preventive treatment, not reactive treatment.

May the amount of pain-relieving drugs be increased liberally?

Yes, if the schedule for assigning drugs remains unaltered. Drugs, although often abused, have a beneficial purpose. They can relieve pain and suffering, particularly among the dying. The use of drugs should not be regarded as a measure of moral depravity.

What if the dying patient becomes addicted to drugs?

When drugs are given on a regular schedule, the patient does not develop a psychological addiction to them. Patients develop a craving for drugs when they have to endure pain before they can have relief. As long as pain is prevented by the administration of drugs at regular intervals, patients show no sign of psychological dependency.

It may be argued, of course, that taking drugs at regular intervals is evidence of physical addiction. But such an argument invites the comment, "So what?" Although it may be true that doctors merely substitute one disease for another – drug addiction for pain – ask any dying patient which disease he would prefer.

If drugs cannot control pain, what else is there?

Because pain is psychological as well as physical, the patient must be diverted from thinking about his pain. Worry increases pain. Diversion diminishes pain. Since large doses of drugs tend to make the patient "dopey," group activities and therapy are much to be preferred. Patients feel better when they are occupied playing games, listening to the radio, watching television, talking to friends, reading, writing, and so on. Sigmund Freud, who for eighteen years experienced terrible pain from cancer of the jaw, would not take drugs, but diverted himself with his writing.

Is alcohol an effective painkiller?

Yes. Alcohol not only gives pleasure, but also promotes conversation, which is an effective diversion. A drink shared with relatives or friends may produce happier results than any other medication.

Whiskey or brandy in a hot drink before the patient goes to bed makes an excellent sedative. A glass or two of sherry in the midafternoon can lift flagging spirits. And beer or wine for lunch or dinner is rarely ever declined.

If all else fails . . . ?

If drugs, diversions, and psychological counseling prove ineffective in reducing pain, the doctor has at his disposal surgery to relieve pressure, to clear an obstruction, to repair fractures, to cut nerves; radiotherapy to relieve bone pain, or to shrink a large tumor that impinges on a nerve or some other sensitive area of the body; chemotherapy to poison cancerous cells; intense heat or cold to dry up a tumor; and even hypnosis.

On rare occasions, nerve surgery (neurosurgery) may be used to treat very specific areas of pain. To understand how neurosurgery works, the reader must know that physical pain is conveyed through the nerves, a complex network of fibers extending throughout the body. Nerves, which can be likened to telephone wires, transmit messages from all parts of the body through the spine to the brain. At their most distant point from the spine, the fibers are single strands. As they approach the spine they come together in branches that unite within the spine to form nerve tracts. These tracts, which travel to the brain, comprise the spinal cord.

The most common neurosurgical procedures are as follows:

DORSAL RHIZOTOMY: the neurosurgeon cuts the large nerve that serves the affected area.

CORDOTOMY: the neurosurgeon inserts an electric needle into the spinal cord and congeals the nerve tract that carries fibers from the affected area through the spine to the brain.

TRACTOTOMY: the neurosurgeon interrupts the nerve fibers in the area of the brainstem, well above the spinal cord. This procedure is particularly suited to shoulder and neck pain, which cannot be treated at a level lower than the brainstem.

THALAMOTOMY: the neurosurgeon interrupts the nerve fibers high in the brain. This procedure is similar to a prefrontal lobotomy and is rarely used because it radically alters the patient's personality.

ELECTROSTIMULATION: the neurosurgeon inserts an electric needle into the spinal cord and stimulates the nerve fibers, a procedure that tends to make the nerves resist pain.

Nerve blocks may also be used to relieve pain among a few patients. An anaesthesiologist (a specially trained doctor or nurse who administers anaesthetics) can produce local nerve blocks that are either permanent or nonpermanent by expertly inserting a needle with pain-relieving substances into a specific area of the body. The different types of blocks are called:

NERVE BLOCK: the anaesthesiologist blocks the nerve that lies between the painful area and the spinal cord.

EPIDURAL BLOCK: the anaesthesiologist blocks an area near the spinal cord and thus "deadens" the nerves just before they enter the spinal cord.

AUTONOMIC PLEXUS BLOCK: the anaesthesiologist blocks an area near an internal organ where the small nerve fibers that supply the organ come together. This kind of block is performed specifically for carcinoma of the pancreas.

Because neurosurgery and nerve blocks may cause permanent paralysis, doctors often discourage their use.

In addition to general pain, what are some other common symptoms of terminal illness, their causes, and their treatments?

Although it might be useful to list the symptoms according to how often they occur, such precise statistical information is not available. The symptoms have, instead, been listed alphabetically with a partial list of causes and treatments.

Note: Patients are advised not to diagnose or treat themselves.

SYMPTOMS	CAUSES	TREATMENT
Anorexia (loss of appetite)	Advanced cancer, intestinal obstruction from a tumor, lack of food, dehydration	Difficult to treat
Bedsores	Confinement in bed, lack of movement	Better prevented than treated. Frequent movement of patient; special sheets or an inflatable mattress; in serious cases, skin grafts
Bone fractures	Tumor in the bone, confinement to bed, depletion of protein	Radiotherapy to the bone, sometimes followed by splinting, pinning, bone glue. Also canes, walkers, crutches, wheelchairs

Catheter irritation	Mild chronic infection from bacteria that alight on the catheter	Antibiotics
Constipation	Dehydration, lack of bulky food, use of analgesics (especially morphine), high blood calcium levels, loss of muscle tone in the intestine, obstruction of the anus or rectum by a tumor	Diet of fluids and bulky foods (bran), stool softeners, mild laxatives, enemas, suppositories, radiotherapy to shrink tumor
Cough	Infection, dehydration, dryness caused by radiotherapy, tumor in the lung or pleura (covering of the lung)	Antibiotics, codeine and other cough suppressants, humidifier, diet of fluids, radiotherapy or chemotherapy to shrink tumor
Cracked lips	Dehydration, lack of saliva, loss of firmness in the tissue, cold sores	Lip pomades, vaseline, hand lotion
Diarrhea	Chemotherapy, infection, prolonged constipation	Medication, diet of rice and bulky foods
Dry mouth	Radiotherapy, chemotherapy, dehydration	Frequent sips of water, pineapple chunks, soft candies
Dysphagia (difficulty in swallowing)	Dry mouth, obstruction of the throat by a tumor, pressure from a tumor on the nerves of the brain	Local anaesthetic, iced drinks, fizzy (carbonated) drinks, radiotherapy to shrink tumor

Dyspnea (shortness of breath and sensation of suffocation)	Heart failure, fluid in or around the lungs, infection, tumor in the lung	Digitalis, diuretics, removal of fluid through a tube, antibiotics, analgesics, radiotherapy to shrink tumor
Fatigue	Anemia, heart failure, loss of weight, dehydration	Correction of anemia, improvement of diet, increased fluids
Fluid accumulation, particularly in the chest and abdomen	Cancer in the lining of the chest and abdomen	Diuretics, removal of fluid through a tube and sometimes installation of an agent to prevent reaccumulation
Headaches	Anxiety, tension, tumor in the brain	Analgesics, tranquilizers, steroids, radiotherapy to shrink tumor
Hemoptysis (spitting blood)	Tumor in the lung, heart failure, blood clots	Radiotherapy to shrink tumor, anticoagulants, antibiotics, cough suppressants
Hiccups	Normal causes, pressure from a tumor on the diaphragm or phrenic nerve, which controls movement of the diaphragm	Tranquilizers, radiotherapy or chemotherapy to shrink tumor
Hoarseness	Dry throat, cancer in the throat, tumor affecting the vocal cords or the nerves	Gargles, increased fluids, radiotherapy or chemotherapy to shrink tumor

Incipient incontinence (uncontrolled urination and defecation)	Infection, impairment of nerves serving the bladder, obstruction of urinary canal	Antibiotics, catheterization
Insomnia (sleeplessness)	Anxiety, pain	Sedatives, hot drinks, alcohol, analgesics
Itching	Allergic reaction to drugs, jaundice, tumor in the skin	Antihistamines, soaps, radiotherapy or chemotherapy to shrink tumor
Mental distress, including anxiety, depression, confusion, and loss of memory	Pain, fear of death, tumor in the brain	Analgesics, tranquilizers, radiotherapy to shrink tumor, steroids
Nausea	Chemotherapy or radiotherapy; malfunctioning liver, kidneys, or intestine; tumor	Anti-nausea medicines, marijuana (under study), changes in diet, radiotherapy to shrink tumor
Partial paralysis	Tumor in the brain, pressure on the spinal cord	Radiotherapy or surgery to treat tumor, steroids
Thirstiness	Dehydration; occasionally, tumor in the pituitary gland	Increased fluids, radiotherapy to shrink tumor
Vomiting	Chemotherapy, malfunctioning liver or kidneys, obstruction of the intestine by a tumor, constipation	Anti-nausea medicines, marijuana (under study), changes in diet, radiotherapy to shrink tumor, relief of constipation
Weakness, in general	Innumerable causes, both physical and psychological	Improvement of diet, change in medication

At what point does the terminal stage begin?

The point at which the doctor says there is nothing more that he can do to cure the patient; or the point at which a hospital official informs a member of the patient's family that everything that could be done has been done, and that now the patient must be helped to die.

It is also at this point that the dispensers of unproven remedies show up to tell the dying patient that the terminal point has not been reached and that they can cure him. Capitalizing on the despair of the patient and his family, they thrive on false hopes, worthless treatments, and sham medicines.

Where do most people in the United States die?

In nursing homes or hospitals, although at the turn of the century most of them died at home.

Where do most people in Britain die?

Approximately half the people in Britain die at home. The other half die in hospitals, homes for the aged, nursing homes, hospices, and the like.

Which cancer patients should be admitted to a hospital?

Those patients:
   who need special medical attention and facilities,
   who are close to dying,
   who, in view of the above, can afford the expense of a hospital.
Some patients who wish to prolong their lives as long as possible cannot be cared for at home. To remain alive, they require special machinery and technical aids, like a respirator or a cardiac resuscitator, which cannot be had outside a hospital.

Although most families who care for the terminally ill at home are remarkably brave, they and the patient usually prefer to have the patient die in a hospital or a hospice. The trauma of a death not only in the family, but also in the house is often too much for the family to endure. Hospitals or hospices are better able than private homes to see a patient through his final hours and to help the family through the

174 THE CANCER REFERENCE BOOK

period immediately following death.

Hospitals, however, are expensive, especially those employed to keep a patient alive with sophisticated technical equipment. Costs can run as high as $1,000 a day, so that even a short hospital stay can impoverish a family, unless there is adequate insurance. The sad truth is that people on a modest income cannot afford the hospital care available to the affluent, a truth that promotes guilt among the poor and widespread criticism of the medical profession.

Can a person buy cancer insurance?

Yes. In fact, cancer insurance is selling in the United States at the rate of about 2 million policies a year; and the company most responsible for these sales is said to be the fastest growing insurance company in the world. The reason people buy cancer insurance is that, per patient, the total medical cost for treating cancers other than cancer of the skin ranges from $20,000 for cancer of the colon to $100,000 for cancer of the breast. But whether cancer insurance provides adequate financial protection is open to question.

What does cancer insurance pay for?

All cancer insurance will, to one degree or another, pay for hospital bills, doctor bills that are hospital-related, surgery, and radiotherapy for the treatment of cancer. Some insurance companies will pay a percentage of *all* legitimate expenses, less a deductible amount. For example, a person will pay the first $1,000, and the insurance company will pay 50 percent of the next $1,500 and 80 percent of the remainder.

In most cancer insurance, hospital coverage is inadequate for a person who stays less than ninety days. The average hospital stay for a cancer patient is sixteen days at a total cost of about $400 a day ($6,400). Cancer insurance will pay less than one-third of the $6,400.

For a stay of forty days, the cost is about $16,000. Very few policies will pay more than one-third of the $16,000; most pay less.

And yet, for a person who stays longer than ninety days, a majority of cancer policies will pay all, or nearly all, of the hospital bills.

Doctor bills may or may not be covered. Some cancer insurance will not cover these bills unless a patient is in the hospital. Some will not cover the complications of cancer: for example, the surgical implantation of a pin in a bone to help a person suffering from cancer of the bone. Some will not cover illness caused by cancer treatment: for example, treatment for pneumonia in a patient with leukemia.

Time limits in cancer insurance are often unreasonable. One insurance company stops payments three years after a cancer is first diagnosed and, if cancer is diagnosed within 120 days after purchase of the policy, makes no payments for two years.

Premiums for cancer insurance are subject at any time to increase, unless the policy-holder already has cancer.

What states permit the sale of cancer insurance?

Cancer insurance may be sold in forty-seven states. It is banned in Connecticut and severely restricted in New York and New Jersey because these states regulate the sale of "dread-disease" policies – insurance policies limited to specific diseases. Cancer insurance is currently the chief example in the United States of "dread-disease" policies. Polio insurance, a similar kind of "dread-disease" policy, was actively marketed in the 1940s and early 50s.

Are there alternatives to cancer insurance?

A comprehensive health insurance (CHI) policy can include a rider, for an additional $100 a year, for "excess major medical" coverage that will pay 80 percent of all medical bills exceeding $10,000. (The $10,000 is covered in whole or part by the original CHI policy.) The initial cost of a CHI policy and rider, though greater than cancer insurance, is offset by the additional protection a person receives. A CHI policy and rider provide ten times more financial protection than cancer insurance because they are ten times as comprehensive. Since cancer accounts in a lifetime for only about 10 percent of all medical expenses, a CHI policy or its equivalent is, in the view of most experts, far more beneficial than cancer insurance, which has been likened to flight insurance purchased out of an airport vending machine.

Do patients with terminal cancer receive better care at home or in a hospital?

At home. Some patients, of course, cannot be cared for at home because of the seriousness of their terminal symptoms. But if the patient does not require special treatment that can be found only in a hospital, he tends to receive better care at home. Reason: most patients prefer to be cared for at home and families that want to keep the patient at home usually go to extraordinary lengths to assist him.

At home, the patient is able to maintain his independence – at least the independence that would be lost in a hospital – and to remain a part of the family unit. The patient can, to some degree, participate in the family's activities and assume some of its responsibilities. He can, for example, look after the children or grandchildren, set the table, wash the dishes, advise the family, and take part in its decisions. In addition, the patient may give unity to a family, if the members rally round and find in his dying meaning and purpose.

But being cared for at home also has its drawbacks. After initially showing the patient great attention, the family can grow tired of the continuous care required by the patient, who is always there. The patient, in turn, can find the frequent encouragement he receives to be stale and insincere. Since few homes are equipped to provide the technical assistance that some patients probably ought to have, the families sometimes feel guilty for not being able to provide such assistance.

In general, though, home care is preferable to hospital care because of the personal attention the patient enjoys.

What sort of hospital can care for the dying patient?

If the patient is admitted to a hospital in order to prolong his life, the hospital must be equipped with life-support systems.

If the patient is admitted to a hospital in order to die, most any hospital will be willing to care for him.

What sort of ward?

Doctors differ on this question. Some believe that hospitals ought to maintain a separate ward for dying patients; others believe that hospitals ought to maintain mixed wards, in which dying patients and other patients, young and old, terminal and non-terminal, can mingle.

One thing is certain: if hospitals included among their many services a hospice (see pp. 177–181), the terminally ill patient would feel less like an intruder among the hopeful convalescents.

Why do some doctors abandon the dying patient?

Doctors are trained to save lives. All too often, doctors gauge their worth by how many lives they save, by how many people they rescue and keep alive. A doctor's medical school training and the patients he treats all tell him that death is a failure. So when a patient, after the doctor's best efforts, does not improve, the doctor hurries past the patient's bed or, even worse, never sees the patient again.

Conventional medicine, with all its great advances, has virtually one purpose: curative treatment. But the dying patient requires a different kind of treatment from curative. He requires symptomatic treatment – palliation. Yet some doctors seem unequipped or untrained to treat the dying patient. They know how to work with the curable, not the incurable; with the hope of recovery, not with the certainty of death. When confronted by the dying patient, a medical failure, they are unable to shift from curative to symptomatic treatment, and they withdraw, isolating the patient.

Are there special places for the care of the dying?

Yes, hospices. In the United States, where the hospice movement has just begun to grow, hospices care for the dying patient during his last few weeks of life. In England, where the hospice movement is widespread, hospices often care for the dying patient during the entire course of his terminal illness.

What are the origins of hospices?

As far back as the Greeks, 2,500 years ago, places of healing were available to the sick and weary, but not to the dying. The terminally ill who did not die at home died in the open, along the road, or in a wood, a field, or on a hillside. The first record of a house for the dying occurs during the reign of the Roman Emperor Julian the Apostate in A.D. 361–63. The house was owned by a wealthy Roman woman who was apparently a convert to Christianity and, for charity's sake, opened her house to the poor, the sick, and the dying. Her name was Fabiola.

In 1070, a group of merchants from Amalfi bought the site that was thought to be the Latin Hospice founded in Jerusalem by Charlemagne. A hospital under the Benedictine rule was built there for Christian pilgrims. The word hospice, derived from the Latin word for guest and related to the word hospital, is associated with the twelfth century activities of the Knights Hospitallers of the Order of St. John of Jerusalem, a group devoted to the care of not only Christian pilgrims and crusaders, but also the weary, the ailing, and the dying traveler.

By the nineteenth century, the word hospice designated a place where Roman Catholic nuns cared for the dying.

What is a modern hospice?

And a man shall be as an hiding place from the wind, and a covert from the tempest; as rivers of water in a dry place, as the shadow of a great rock in a weary land.

Isaiah 32:2

Unlike the religious houses and way stations of the Middle Ages, where the sick, the exhausted, and the dying were replenished and refreshed, the modern hospice does more than bathe the feet of the weary and attend to the souls of the dying. Although frequently named after a saint and often run by a religious order, the modern hospice is a nondenominational place of care, housed and operated independently, or in a hospital, or in a nursing home.

Providing a sanctuary for people passing through life's last station, the hospice not only serves patients under its own roof, but also sends trained staff to private homes. Available every hour of every day of the week, hospice staff – doctors, nurses, social workers, and chaplains – render palliative and supportive care to the dying patient and his family. If the patient wishes to retain his own doctor, he is permitted to do so; if he wishes one from the hospice, he is assigned one. In the event the patient requires nursing assistance, either at home or in the hospice, such assistance is arranged.

The modern hospice movement, which began in England and spread to the United States, answers to a particular need in the community: the need for a place where a person can die without pain, free from distress, comforted, and cared for. Because terminal illness tends to separate people at a time when they most need one another, hospices define the unit of care, before and after death, as the dying patient and his family. After death, the hospice staff treat the bereaved family by making home visits and offering psychological counseling for up to two years.

What types of treatment do hospices engage in?

Symptomatic treatment and psychological counseling. Hospices make no attempt to cure the patient or to prolong life. The terminally ill patient comes to a hospice to find relief from his terminal symptoms, and to die. The assumption is not that the patient is suffering from incurable cancer, but that he is suffering from the diseases that result from incurable cancer: pain, nausea, vomiting, constipation, shortness of breath, loss of appetite, and so on. These diseases are controlled by the administration of drugs and other means so that the patient can die comfortably, free of tubes and catheters. When pain and suffering are controlled, the patient usually finds that the life remaining to him is worth living.

Psychological counseling includes not only the patient, but also his family. Both are made ready for the trauma of death. Hospice staff listen to the patient and his family to determine the nature of their pain and suffering. Unlike hospitals, where the dying patient has frequently to endure pain before he is given pain-killing drugs, hospices analyze the dying patient's situation and prescribe a program of care that will enable him to remain himself, as much as possible, to the end. The same attention to detail is lavished on the family – because in minor matters are often found the clues to major concerns.

In hospices, what is the unit of care?

As mentioned above, the unit of care is the dying patient and his family. Because terminal illness affects every member of a family, every member must be extended terminal care. Since the survivors, as well as the dying patient, experience profound depression and loneliness, they are as much in need of emotional support as the patient. By preparing the patient and his family beforehand for death, the hospice makes it possible for both to share without fear the remaining time. During the period of mourning, the bereaved are left with the fond memory of a family united together until the end.

In hospices, what is the unit of treatment?

In addition to the dying patient and his family, both of whom can help one another through the period of dying, the unit of treatment normally includes:

1 DOCTORS who are specialists in geriatrics, that is, the problems of the old and the dying; who are skilled in the control of pain and other symptomatic or palliative treatments; who are proficient in psychological counseling.

2 NURSES trained in every specialty.

3 SOCIAL WORKERS trained in medical social work and psychiatric social work.

4 CHAPLAINS who are nondenominational or, if the patient wishes, denominational.

5 THERAPISTS trained in physiotherapy and occupational therapy.

6 VOLUNTEERS and other health care staff.

Different hospices, of course, may have more or less staff; but the composition is essentially the same.

In hospices, what are the major principles of terminal care?

Cooperation and confidence. The care of the dying should not be, and cannot be, the work of one person. A hospice implies a community of shared labors. It is no place for heroic solo performances. The group and not the individual must administer to the patient and his family. If the hospice is to work effectively, cooperation and communication are vital.

Confidence born of competence must be apparent if the patient and his family are to trust the hospice staff. For example, the doctors must have a thorough knowledge of drugs and symptomatic treatment; nurses must know how to deal with the aged; social workers must know when to listen and when to advise. Everything that can be done, should be done.

A hospice, in short, requires teamwork and sureness; anything less contributes to the legions of dissatisfied dead.

Are hospices appropriate for pre-terminal patients?

Yes, if they are available, as they are in England. The pre-terminal period is usually defined as the period of illness prior to the last six weeks of life. During this time, severe pain, according to one study in England, was experienced more often by those people being cared for at home than by those being cared for in institutions.

HOME CARE 29 percent reported severe pre-terminal pain
HOSPITAL CARE 20 percent reported severe pre-terminal pain
HOSPICE CARE 8 percent reported severe pre-terminal pain
Not surprisingly, what these figures indicate is that hospices are best equipped to treat pain in pre-terminal patients. Reason: hospices, among other things, are pain clinics, specializing in palliative treatment.

At present, can all dying patients be adequately cared for?

No. In the United States, the subject of death and dying is only just now receiving attention. In England, where the subject has for years been widely discussed, the result is an active hospice movement.

Most hospitals, nursing homes, and homes for the aged are ill-equipped to care for the dying. Hospitals are primarily interested in obtaining cures and prolonging life. Very few hospitals have room to house the dying; most wards are for the curable. Nursing homes and homes for the aged are usually places for the sick and elderly "to do time" until they die. They are, in effect, not way stations, but waiting stations.

Until Americans are willing to treat the sick and elderly with the dignity and respect that they deserve, Americans will, in great numbers, die deserted and distressed.

Why do some people die easily and others not?

If a person is free from pain, he usually dies as he has lived. Those who are frightened of life are frightened of death. Those who die easily realize that death, like birth, is a part of life, and that death is merely the conclusion of a natural cycle.

The elderly, as mentioned above, die more easily than the young. When a person feels that he has lived his portion, he dies content. But when a person is denied his biblical three score years and ten, he feels cheated.

For a great many elderly people, living becomes a wearying and exhausting process. By the time they reach old age, life has grown burdensome and stale. Some of them, having outlived family and friends, are like Mr. Flood, in E.A. Robinson's poem "Mr. Flood's Party," who toasts the memory of friends since gone.

"For auld lang syne." The weary throat gave out;
The last word wavered, and the song was done.
He raised again the jug regretfully
And shook his head, and was again alone.
There was not much that was ahead of him,
And there was nothing in the town below—
Where strangers would have shut the many doors
That many friends had opened long ago.

Without friends and a future, the elderly are often resigned to death.

The person who has lived a full and active life usually dies without regret. He can look back at his life and see its richness, and know that he has lived well. When the Italian painter Amedeo Modigliani died at thirty-six, he is reported to have said that he was satisfied because he had in his thirty-six years compressed ninety.

The religious person who feels secure about his place in an afterlife often dies easily. The insecure believer, on the other hand, often dies uneasily, because the same insecurity that motivated his faith prevents his final acceptance.

Patients die easily when they know the truth about their terminal illness, and have known for some time. A lengthy period in which to digest the truth enables people to come to terms with their own death.

Some patients who have enjoyed to the end their family's love find in dying a positive experience, a time of great intimacy and leave-taking. Some even regard death as a new experience, not to be feared, but to be treated with wonder, like the novelist Henry James, who at the approach of death remarked, "So here it is at last, the Distinguished Thing."

Do the religious die more easily than the nonreligious?

No. The devout believer and the devout nonbeliever die more easily than the halfhearted believer. Conviction, one way or the other, seems to provide solace; the religious person and the atheist are equally fortified against doubt.

Although religion offers comfort and hope to the dying, the dying person is not always able to find in religion the peace and assurance he seeks. Anxiety about death is a natural reaction, perhaps bred into the race when for thousands of years men had to survive in the wilds. To overcome that anxiety is neither natural nor easy. Many people are attracted to religion because of the promise of a life after death. But the very anxiety about death that first attracted them to religion is often still present when they die.

Moreover, some religions make a life after death conditional on a person's behavior. Those who die feeling unworthy are unlikely to feel confident about being admitted to the kingdom of heaven.

In fact, very few people actually believe that death is a transition to a fuller, better heavenly life. Rather most believe that death is a ceasing to be, oblivion, nothingness; in short, the absence of someone who was there before.

Do the rich die more easily than the poor?

No. A patient's social and educational background may affect the way he describes his feelings, but normally the rich and the poor, the educated and the uneducated, share the same anxieties and worry about the same things.

The presence or absence of anxiety seems to be related to age and religious belief. The elderly and the devout believer, including the devout nonbeliever, experience the least anxiety.

Do some patients resist to the end?

Yes. Even though they know they are dying, some patients will not give up the fight to live. They struggle until the end. A passionate struggle against death is by no means confined to the young; but it usually involves young adults, particularly those with small children.

People of all ages fight. They insist that the doctor try the newest treatments and that he not prescribe pain-relieving drugs, lest they reduce the patient's resistance to death. When improvement is not forthcoming, they change doctors, travel to foreign countries for exotic treatment at cancer "institutes," buy unproven remedies, and follow faddish diets.

But although destined to fail from the outset, the struggle to live must be admired. Struggle invites hope, and without hope the dying patient has nothing.

What fears are most often expressed by the dying patient?

Most dying patients fear mutilation and pain, and fear for the welfare of their family. Other fears, in no particular order, are:

Ceasing to be

Having to give up a pleasurable life

Having to leave a profitable business or profession

Leaving unsettled an estate, or will, or insurance

Causing the survivors great medical expense

Losing every relationship in life

Facing the unknown

Leaving behind unfinished work

Becoming dependent on others

Losing control of the body and possibly even the mind

Becoming a nuisance to others

Leaving life before having enjoyed it

Parting with family and friends

Dying alone, without family or friends nearby

Coping with a diseased body

Appearing undignified because of the ravages of the disease

Behaving badly as death approaches

Being the last witness, the last link, to a particular event, or society, or person

Relinquishing a body or a personality that gave and received pleasure

Losing the future and not being able to witness what is yet to come

Facing the possibility of an afterlife

Being judged after death and held accountable

Having no time to apologize for past arguments and to reconcile differences

Having been an indifferent churchgoer or a nonbeliever

Dying over a long period of time.

Why do some people feel guilt for having cancer?

Some cancer patients regard the disease as a sign of God's displeasure, or as a punishment for real or imagined sins, such as infidelity or high living. Unable to understand why they should have the disease, they blame themselves. Some cancer patients feel guilty about leaving behind family who depend on them for support, or unfinished work that they and perhaps others regard as important. Some cancer patients suffer guilt because of the loss of self-respect that often accompanies dependency, incontinence, body odors, oozing wounds.

In addition, parents of children with cancer feel enormous guilt, because they hold themselves responsible for somehow passing on to their children the disease.

How can the sorrow of the dying patient be relieved?

May I never see in the patient anything else but a fellow creature in pain.

Maimonides, "Physician's Prayer"

Human contact is the most potent medicine of all. Drugs can, of course, keep pain and loneliness from surfacing; but no medicine has power to work the wonders of a single caring person.

The dying patient does not want to be thought of as being "half-dead" or as "having one foot in the grave." He wants to receive the same respect accorded the healthy person. Having every day to face the prospect of his own death, the dying patient requires, and ought to have, some person regularly at his bedside whose presence, in effect, says "Behold the man!" The dying patient, in other words, wants other people to know that his sickness has not diminished him as a human being.

When visiting the dying patient, visitors might remember the following.

1 Visit often and do not, at some point, abandon the patient.

2 Inform the patient ahead of time if a visit has to be canceled.

3 Talk to the patient about subjects that interest him.

4 Engage the patient in any social or creative activities that he is capable of performing: for example, a walk, a card game, a movie, a painting class, a book discussion.

5 Be understanding and try to sense what the patient is undergoing.

6 Touch the patient to let him "feel" the presence of someone next to him; for example, put an arm around his shoulders, hold his hand.

7 Sit on a chair next to the bed, or sit on the bed, to show closeness and affection.

8 Let the patient know that he will not die alone. Assure him that

someone will be there to say good-bye and to bear witness to his passing.

Remember that it is the visitor's attempt to understand the patient rather than the success or failure that finally matters. As Gerasim observes in Tolstoy's *The Death of Ivan Ilych*, " 'We shall all of us die, so why should I grudge a little trouble?' – expressing the fact that he did not think his work burdensome, because he was doing it for a dying man and hoped someone would do the same for him when his time came."

Do dying patients suffer a loss of independence?

Yes. Every physical and mental capacity that is lost erodes the patient's independence. The fastidious suffer the embarrassment of incontinence; the reflective suffer the decline of mental ability; the athletic suffer the frustration of weakness. And most everyone suffers the loss of home, family, children, and routine.

For those who are in hospitals or nursing homes, there is the loss of the familiar. Gone are the sounds and smells of a once normal life, the clacking lawnmower, the groaning bus, the barking dogs, the scent of lilacs, fresh paint, the salt air. Gone too is the freedom to pursue old habits and idiosyncrasies. Because hospitals and nursing homes must maintain schedules and discipline, patients in these institutions must conform to rules and observe a certain degree of regimentation. So old ways and familiar routines, by which people often express their individuality, have to be relinquished. For example, a woman who had taken vitamin pills every morning, because she believed that they kept her looking young, was told by the ward doctor in a large hospital that since he had not prescribed them, the vitamin pills had to be stopped. A man who liked to wear a smoking jacket while reading in bed was told by the official in his nursing home that white hospital gowns were the standard uniform, not smoking jackets.

Large, impersonal institutions would do well to learn from hospices and encourage a patient to treat his bed and the area around it as his own. Books, knickknacks, wall decorations, photographs, and mementoes should, within reason, be allowed the patient. Nightgowns, hair curlers, earrings, and necklaces enable the female patient to define herself. Razor, shaving cream, comb, and brush may be the items that a man needs to feel comfortable. Favorite foods, whenever possible, should be served. Patients ought not be prevented from bathing themselves, an activity that most people regard as personal. In short, doctors and hospital staff must respect individual foibles, because they are often the personal symbols of independence, and one of the means by which dying patients try to overcome decay and death.

Does the dying patient gain relief from psychotherapy or group therapy?

Psychotherapy can benefit the patient who, upon learning that he has a terminal illness, experiences severe mental depression, or hysterical episodes, or such great anxiety that he cannot carry on from day to day. Working with the therapist, the patient may come to realize that the pleasurable habit of living comes to an end sooner or later, and that part of living is preparing for death.

Group therapy can benefit both outpatients and those who are hospitalized with terminal cancer. The old saying that there is strength in numbers is particularly true of group therapy sessions for cancer patients. Many a patient has discovered himself in these sessions – and gained from others the strength to die easily. By observing how other people live with cancer, the patient learns to live with his own disease. It is one thing to complain about the loss of life to a healthy doctor or nurse, and quite another thing to complain to other cancer patients. The frequent demonstrations in group therapy sessions of good humor, courage, and helpful advice disarm the patient who is inclined to self-pity.

Why does the dying patient often resent having his life prolonged?

The physical deterioration that accompanies terminal illness does not progress in a constant, orderly manner. The body fails irregularly. From one day to the next, the patient never knows if his condition is going to be better or worse or the same. To plan for the future is difficult if not impossible, because even the most modest plan may be upset by a "turn for the worse." In a perpetual state of limbo, the dying patient is a plaything of the gods; he is subject to daily and even hourly changes of fortune.

In such an uncertain state, the patient is afraid not only to plan, but also to act. He fears that any action on his part will intensify the disease. Caught between the desire to make as much as possible of his remaining life and the fear of doing so, he blames his doctor for his condition and grows impatient with his family. As time drags on, saying good-bye becomes repetitious and he wishes for the period of waiting to end. Dying has gone on too long and living has become burdensome.

Why do family and friends sometimes abandon the dying patient?

Different people have different excuses, but the reasons most often given by family and friends are that they (i) cannot bear to be in the presence of sickness and sadness; (ii) think it best to anticipate the absence of a loved one by being absent themselves; (iii) believe it will be easier for the patient to die if family and friends have, by the end, absented themselves; (iv) cannot afford the time because they have to look after their children and homes, and have to engage in various social and professional activities; (v) feel that their health is resented by the patient; (vi) are embarrassed to think that they will go on living after the loved one has died; (vii) are hurt and angry that the loved one is deserting them.

Although these reasons are by no means frivolous, it cannot be too often repeated that dying isolates a person and that the dying patient, more than at any other time in his life, needs companionship, conversation, communion, and all the other loving arts.

Why is the dying patient sometimes resented by his family?

Because he may diminish their time, their energy, their resources, and their future.

The dying patient, particularly if treated at home, requires constant attention. Someone must look after his medical needs, talk to him, check on him, sit with him. After a while, the other members of the family may feel neglected, may feel that the patient is taking up too much time. Because the patient's requirements draw attention away from the family, it is not unusual for the children to complain that they are being ignored and for the wife to wonder about her own needs.

When the patient is not covered by national health insurance, as he is in England, he must pay for his own medical bills. In the event that he is insufficiently insured or has no insurance, the cost of dying can bankrupt a family. The dying patient may then be resented because the surviving members of the family will be left with enormous debts.

Furthermore, the family members may well have entrusted to the patient their hope for a vibrant future. But if they see in his dying an erosion of their hope, if his death means the promise of their lives will be unfulfilled, then it is neither unlikely nor unforgivable that they will be resentful.

Why does the dying patient sometimes abandon his family and friends?

Notwithstanding the patient's need to be supported by family and friends, he occasionally drives them away, for some of the following reasons: (i) he does not want those he cares about to suffer his dying; (ii) he does not want to be the object of pity; (iii) he does not want people to pretend to be cheerful when the occasion does not warrant; (iv) he feels that among his family and friends he has lost his sense of belonging; (v) he thinks that his family can get by without him, and therefore he is hurt; (vi) he feels diminished as a human being because of his declining physical abilities; (vii) he does not want others to see him as sick and weak, and as having lost control of his body.

The loss of self-esteem that can result from serious illness may be difficult to combat; but if the patient is made to feel that he is a vital part of his family and his network of friends, the patient's desire to withdraw may diminish.

Who should be with the dying patient at the end?

If at all possible, the dying patient should be attended by someone very close to him: his wife, a child, a parent, a relative, a friend. But when family and friends are not available, the hospital or hospice staff should select a person with whom the dying patient feels comfortable.

The important point – and a point that bears repeating over and over again – is that the patient should not die unattended. Death is fearful enough without the patient's having to suffer it alone.

Moreover, for some innate reason people feel it important not to die without a witness, perhaps because they fear that to die unwitnessed is to be forgotten. During the Holocaust, innumerable people, young and old, asked with their last words that their deaths be remembered. So important is this request to the dying person that whether spoken or not it ought never to be neglected.

What happens just before death?

Although no two people die in exactly the same way, the dying patient can be described in the following manner.

He is usually bedridden, preferring to lie on his side rather than in any other position. His head is propped up with pillows. He is restless and dislikes having anything rub against his skin, so he frequently moves about trying to shed his hospital gown or pajamas or blanket. Afraid of the dark, he wants to have the light on during the night.

As his circulation begins to fail, his extremities – arms, legs, fingers, toes – become cold and clammy, while the rest of his body becomes sweaty. Constant rubbing and sponging are required to keep the circulation moving and the body dry. Often thirsty, he must be given frequent sips of water, preferably ice water. Because his mouth is dry and his lips cracked, he rolls his tongue and wets his lips. He tends to emit a gurgling sound from his throat ("the death rattle") because of mucus and phlegm in the windpipe. Deafness overtakes him late, so family and friends should not speak idly by his bedside.

At the very end, the patient is usually unconscious and exhibits no signs of discomfort or pain. The body, seeming to know when to withdraw from the struggle, resigns peacefully. What follows? The question has for thousands of years been the subject of theology and philosophy and has inspired both fear and faith. As Socrates remarked:

> *No one knows whether death, which men in their fear apprehend to be the greatest evil, may not be the greatest good.*

> Plato, *Apology*

How does the death of a loved one affect the survivors?

> *But O the heavy change, now thou art gone,*
> *Now thou art gone, and never must return!*

> John Milton, "Lycidas"

After the death of a loved one, the survivors grieve for the absent person. In extreme cases, grief can lead to physical or mental illness and even death.

The elderly suffer the worst effects of grief. Their distress is often physical and, especially among women, may result in death. Widows, in the first year after the death of their husbands, run a 40 percent greater risk of dying than longstanding widows of a similar age. In fact, both widows and widowers, during the first year of mourning, suffer a higher than normal rate of death.

Adult survivors also have an increased rate of suicide, alcoholism, and depression. Children who have lost a parent have an increased rate of delinquency and mental instability.

If a lesson is to be learned from these facts and figures, it is that for at least one year after a loved one has died, the survivors require care and attention.

Why shouldn't the dying patient and his family rage against his death?

> *Do not go gentle into that good night.*
> *Rage, rage against the dying of the light.*
>
>   Dylan Thomas, "Do Not Go Gentle"

Rage can be constructive. It is a profound expression of feeling, better said than stifled. But as with most emotional outbursts, once rage has taken the form of utterance, repetition has little value.

Dying, like living, has its own rhythm and style. To live and die intensely may be suitable for painters and poets, but for most people resignation, after initial disbelief and anger, provides a time for the mind to be transformed, for the world to narrow, and for desire to end. The period of dying seems tolerable to most patients if it is used well – if it gives the dying person a chance to put things in order. Order does not emerge from rage; it emerges from resignation, which can be productive if it is not a surrender to despair.

Patients must be told that they are justified in letting go, and that the period of dying should be regarded as a chance to say goodbye properly and affectionately. They must be told that dying is part of living – that it may, in fact, be the part of living that makes life serious. In some paradoxical way, death is an assurance that life means something – either because death is an introduction to an afterlife, or because death imposes meaning and value on the life that will be lost.

Can death be creative?

Yes. Because death is a conclusion, a summing up, people often choose to end their lives with a particularly generous act. Brave behavior, for example, is not unusual in people facing death: consider the incurable patients who have volunteered to be used as "guinea pigs" for medical experiments; or the dying concentration-camp inmates who gave their scanty rations to the camp children; or the dying parents who have, throughout history, disowned their children in order to provide adoptive parents for them. The number of people is limitless who have bravely died as a result of their courage or their charity.

In primitive societies, the way in which a person died was often a matter of prescribed ritual. The act of death was greatly honored by the community, and to show his respect for his family and neighbors the dying person conformed with dignity to the death ritual. In modern societies, death is no longer regarded as a responsibility the individual owes the community. So people now die according to their own values.

Nevertheless, a great many people manage to invest death with meaning and turn sorrow into triumph. The person, for instance, who donates his eyes or kidneys to a hospital is achieving an immortality of sorts. The person who leaves his art collection to the country is forever enriching his countrymen. The person who merely says "I'm sorry for the unhappiness that I may have caused you," or "Forgive me my anger," creates himself anew in the most catholic and most profound way possible – that is, by confessing away his old life and creating, if not a new life, a memory that others will have of him as a loving, forgiving individual.

5 Unproven Methods of Treatment

"Simplify, simplify," Thoreau urged. In all ages, people have dreamed of a single key to unlock the mysteries of life. The appeal is universal. To find the clue in a simple phrase, a magic potion, a miraculous place has led people to the gospels to discover the Word; to the jungles of Florida to partake of the fountain of youth; to the isles of Greece to recover Atlantis under the sea. But no search has been more profound or more singular than the age-old search for an end to pain and pestilence.

In the hope of finding one remedy, one cure-all for every illness, both sufferer and scientist have, at one time or another, invoked the assistance of heaven, gone on crusade for a piece of the true Cross, gathered holy relics, unearthed the plants of the forest and the roots of the jungle, mixed one chemical with another, and harnessed the rays of the sun – but all to no avail. Paradise and panacea elude mankind yet.

Only the dream persists. Like small boats against the current, people beat onward seeking a single cure, a simple potion that will deliver them from all their ills and return the world to that Adamic garden where once perfection reigned. And so, faced with the despair of disease, the helpless and the hopeless turn to the weavers of dream: the faith healers and the herbalists, the potion-peddlers and the diet-dispensers, the salesmen of silver bullets and the merchants of unproven methods.

Why do people turn to unproven methods of treatment?

Because either from fear or distrust, they have no respect for proven treatments and seek, if not a miraculous cure, at least one that is painless and inexpensive. People who turn to unproven treatments are often found to be:

UNEDUCATED Some people do not know the difference between a medical doctor – that is, an M.D. – and a person who calls himself "doctor," usually as a result of a mail-order degree that contains the word doctor, but not the word medical. Many people are unaware of the differences between proven methods of treatment and unproven, between effective therapy and ineffective. And most people have no idea of what cancer is, how it spreads, or how it may be treated. Victimized by an incomprehensible disease, they become frightened and seek simple explanations and easy remedies. When a cancer patient is told, for example, that his disease results from a poor diet and that a healthy one will cure him, he can appreciate this explanation – even if it is wrong. Medicine, like most professions, has its own jargon, a language that in great part keeps the public ignorant of how doctors combat disease. Little wonder, then, that some people find it easier to believe what is understandable than what is obscure, even though the one may be wrong and the other right.

POOR Except in countries, like England, with a national health service, medical care is very expensive. A surprising number of people have no medical insurance of any kind, and little or no access to free clinical treatment. To become seriously ill with cancer and to seek conventional treatment is, for these people, to incur great expense. So they seek low-cost remedies, like herbs, lotions, and fruit juices, which they can afford financially, but not physically. It is unfortunate that the phrase "You get what you pay for" is true in medicine.

DESPERATE Once a patient has been told that he has terminal cancer, he feels that he has nothing to lose by trying unconventional treatments. Like most people under sentence of death, he will frequently seek any means to stay alive. After all, the hope always exists that some magic formula, some silver bullet, may be found to kill the cancer.

HOPELESS All too often, the patient with terminal cancer is abandoned by his doctor who, unable to cure him, retreats in embarrassment. The patient, finding no hope in the words "terminal" and "incurable," becomes easy prey to the person who promises a possible cure, an end to pain, a longer life. Suddenly in place of neglect and despair, which were all the patient had, he finds encouragement and hope. Needless to say, a hopeful word has persuaded more than one patient to try unproven methods.

SKEPTICAL Some patients are never satisfied that they are receiving adequate treatment. Unless they try every method, every remedy, they are not content. To be sure that they have not missed anything, they will frequently undergo different therapies at the same time. While being treated with X-rays, for example, they may also be following a vegetable diet – just in case. If the patient's health does not improve, the proponents of unproven methods often contend that their remedies failed because of the mixture of therapies.

IMPATIENT Unlike an infection that may be cured quickly with an antibiotic, cancer usually takes a long time to cure. Even before the actual treatment begins, the patient must wait for the biopsy, the X-rays, the diagnosis, and the plan of treatment. Then comes the long wait for the surgery, radiotherapy, or chemotherapy to prove effective. Some people grow impatient and want, if not an instant cure, a quick one. So they look for healers who promise dramatic results with "miraculous" drugs, diets, or devices.

FEARFUL Conventional treatments may have serious consequences. The loss of a breast, for example, or a leg or a larynx is distressing not only physically, but also psychologically. Well aware of this distress, the salesmen for "natural" remedies emphasize that surgery cuts, X-rays burn, and chemotherapy poisons. Probably the greatest single reason that patients subscribe to unproven methods is the fear of pain and disfigurement.

DISILLUSIONED WITH SCIENCE As the renewed interest in astrology, magic, and meditation demonstrates, people no longer regard science as the cure-all for their problems. Neither the computer nor cortisone has ushered in the brave new world. Unimpressed by recent scientific advances that they cannot understand, most people think that science has become too complex. So some of them turn to simpler arts: faith healing instead of surgery, creative visualization instead of X-rays, herbs instead of chemicals.

SUSPICIOUS OF DOCTORS AND DRUGS The language of cancer can be both menacing and foreign, the equipment strange and intimidating, the drugs mysterious and frightening. When a doctor neglects to explain to the patient the nature of his disease and the course of his treatment, the patient becomes suspicious. His faith in the doctor is undermined, his confidence in the treatment eroded. He wonders what terrors are masked by words like sarcoma and carcinoma, and fears that drugs may be only a soft word for poison. His faith undermined, he longs for a remedy that he can understand. So he succumbs to the lure of words like, "natural cures," "health foods," and "diet therapy."

ANGRY The patient with terminal cancer has cause to be angry. He cannot understand his affliction, his death sentence, his doctor's inability to cure him. Why, he asks himself, has his body betrayed him; why do his friends and family shun him, his doctors avoid him? Unable to answer these questions, he angrily rejects the treatment that has failed him and sets out in quest of a miraculous cure.

FADDISH The world is never short of faddists pursuing the perfect formula for youth, health, beauty, a lovely head of hair, long life, sexual appeal, happiness, and, of course, a cure for cancer. These people are romantics, dreamers, who seek to find in nature some fruit of the field, some flower of the forest, that will provide the perfect potion for all their defects, both physical and mental. Man-made medicines are rejected as artificial, synthetic, processed, imitative. Only the natural will do: herbs, seeds, stems, roots, leaves, petals, grains, vegetables, fruits, and the like. Dismissing conventional treatment as unnatural and false, the faddist hopes to find health, if not in a hyacinth bulb, then perhaps in a hickory nut.

SUSCEPTIBLE TO ADVERTISING Most people are susceptible to advertising, if the appeal is right; but people with cancer are particularly inclined to believe what they read. The mere suggestion of hope is often enough to send such people in search of an elusive cure at the end of a rainbow.

What types of unproven methods are there?

Unproven methods usually fall into three categories: diets, drugs, and devices.

DIETS A great many health food stores promote the belief that diet can cure cancer. They sell books on nutrition, as well as foods and appliances (juicers, atomizers, crushers, and mixers) for preparing the recipes found in these books. The recipes include dietary cures for arthritis, eye disease, insomnia, kidney trouble, tuberculosis, and numerous other ailments.

According to one of these books, the way to cure a baby with leukemia, for example, is with a diet composed exclusively of carrot juice. The author writes

It is interesting to note that during the first three months of this baby's life, NO OTHER FOOD was allowed. After three months, however, other foods were added to his diet, including both fruits and vegetables. Did this simple raw juice therapy work? Much to the joy and satisfaction of every one concerned, at the end of one year the blood count was normal. There was no evidence of leukemia! The carrot juice had evidently performed a miracle in restoring the child's diseased bloodstream to a normal healthy condition.

Since the family and the child are not identified, and since no supporting documentation is given, it is next to impossible to check the validity of the "cure."

DRUGS Artfully distinguishing between chemical and natural drugs, the proponents of the latter argue that chemicals poison and nature cures. The argument that natural methods are both effective and non-toxic appeals both to people's desire for a simple cure and to their romantic impulse for a life lived close to nature.

Laetrile, for example, is made from the residue of apricot pits and promoted as a natural drug, vitamin B-17. According to its proponents, laetrile assists the body to fight cancer, which results, they say, from a vitamin deficiency. Their theory, however, has never been proved in laboratory tests.

DEVICES People are endlessly fascinated by charms and gadgets. The "cancer cure" salesman, appealing to this fascination, attracts the patient with an assortment of devices: for example, amulets, necklaces, and bracelets to draw off the cancerous poison that has infected the patient; or a zinc-lined pine box in which the patient sits to absorb "cancer-curing" orgone energy; or a mechanism composed of lights, dials, terminals, switches, and sound effects that fastens to the patient's forehead to detect the presence of cancer.

One particularly incredible device was a box called the oscilloclast. It was supposed to cure cancer by emitting sympathetic vibrations. The patient applied an ointment to his stomach, attached the box to an electrical outlet (but not to himself), and waited for sympathetic vibrations to pass through his stomach and cure him. The initial charge to lease the box (which could not be bought) was $250. The monthly rental fee was $5. The instructions warned the patient never to open the box and look inside.

How do people learn about unproven methods?

Most patients are first introduced to unorthodox cancer therapy in their own community. The formula is familiar: the patient has read, or a friend has heard, or a relative has seen, or someone has tried . . . *something* that everyone should know about.

The avenues of information are virtually limitless. They include:

NEWSPAPERS Controversy makes interesting reading, so newspapers are quick to report exaggerated claims, purported cures, and alleged miracles.

MAGAZINES A number of anti-Establishment magazines, dietary and political, promote the cause of unproven methods.

TELEVISION Special news programs will, on occasion, investigate the extravagant claims of "miracle" drugs and unlicensed health clinics. A program on laetrile, for example, was recently aired.

RADIO The popularity of "talk shows" has spawned radio interviews in which the commentator invites advocates and critics to debate a specific issue, like the value of diet in arresting cancer.

DOCUMENTARY FILMS Private groups, for the purposes of advertising, commission so-called documentary films that show the virtues of their remedy and the vices of those who oppose it.

WORD OF MOUTH Rumor, or the grapevine, is a fertile source of publicity. Like most rumors, those about "cures" for cancer contain few details and much misinformation.

TESTIMONIALS When famous people extol the benefits of a particular product, the public listens. No less a figure than the American novelist Upton Sinclair praised a cancer treatment that proved to be worthless. Too often, people are overawed by the famous and do not stop to ask themselves whether the person in question knows anything about the subject that he is addressing.

ANECDOTES The folklore of medicine abounds in miraculous tales about potions, treatments, and cures. Although often repeated, these tales rarely, if ever, turn out to be accurate. Nevertheless, people love a story, and so these tales are passed from one generation to the next.

COURT CASES Whenever the government goes to court to stop the distribution of a drug or to force the closure of an unlicensed clinic, the community, if not the world, immediately learns about the incident through the vast news coverage it receives.

CLINICS IN MEXICO AND EUROPE To escape prosecution in the United States and in some other countries, cancer clinics have sprung up in Mexico (for example, Tijuana) and Europe (for example, Germany).

These clinics often acquire a Robin Hood reputation for their resistance to authority.

CIRCULARS AND BROCHURES The mailbox is an invaluable source of publicity because, except for postage, it is free. The enormous amount of junk mail that people receive each year is an indication of how easy it is for advertisers to reach the public. Brochures may also be left in any office, circulars posted on any wall, so long as the people distributing them are not asked to stop.

ADVERTISEMENTS Unproven methods are advertised in virtually every kind of printed matter from newspapers to newsletters. Although the publishing code of ethics restrains editors from printing errant nonsense, a great many potions and formulas are advertised under false headings, bearing misleading descriptions.

MAIL ORDER CATALOGUES As easily as a person may receive in the mail flower seeds or a bogus degree, he may receive catalogues describing herbal remedies for bronchitis, dietary relief for backache, and vitamin "cures" for cancer.

HEALTH FOOD STORES In the United States, health food stores seem to be taking the place of the country doctor. Not only can a person buy sunflower seeds and ocean salt in these stores, but he can also find books on "natural cures" and receive advice from the resident "healer."

HEALTH ORGANIZATIONS To promote their remedies, some groups form so-called health organizations, which usually bear impressive names and issue dramatic statements about cures and conspiracies. But in fact these organizations are unlicensed and, in some cases, unlawful.

FREEDOM OF CHOICE GROUPS Convinced that every person ought to be able to choose his own treatment, numerous groups distribute literature and wage political campaigns to guarantee healers the right to sell their product, whether effective or not.

POLITICAL GROUPS The phrase "freedom of choice" never fails to attract extremist political groups. The John Birch Society, for example, has been actively promoting the legalization of laetrile under the guise of defending the public's freedom to choose.

RELIGIOUS GROUPS Fundamentalist sects, particularly those in remote areas of the country, frequently urge their followers to trust in God and the fruit of God's good earth. Herbal remedies, vegetable diets, fruit juices, natural potions and lotions, the laying on of hands, and prayers are advocated with revivalist fervor at tent meetings and healing sessions.

UNLICENSED PRACTITIONERS Not infrequently, the waiting room of the doctor with a mail order degree (and even of some licensed doctors) is a clearinghouse for literature distributed by the proponents of unproven methods. Patients, on occasion, have been directed by these practitioners to try an unorthodox remedy, on the chance that it might work.

POST OFFICES Every time the government displays a notice in a post office warning the public to avoid a certain drug or treatment, people are introduced to that therapy. Curiosity is not limited to cats, as the curiosity excited by a warning notice in a post office amply demonstrates.

What are some of the characteristics of people who promote unproven methods?

To tell the difference between the swindler and the prophet is not always easy. Both peddle dreams, promise to harness the sun. Both are reviled. Yesterday's outcast may be tomorrow's saint. The back street abortionist, for example, was not only the savior of the poor, he was also the real author of legalized abortion. But to defend the unconventional is not to defend the unworthy. Some people cruelly swindle the poor, the sick, the simple, and the hopeless. And to accomplish their swindle, they often resort to the following behavior.

1 They display degrees and titles that have in them the word "doctor." Example: Doctor of Naturopathy, D.N., or Doctor of Metaphysics, D.M. These titles, often acquired through the mail from unaccredited "colleges," are regarded as worthless by both the medical profession and the academic community.

2 They claim to have conducted their research in independent laboratories, because their experiments were too imaginative for well-known laboratories to sponsor.

3 They do not communicate the results of their research in the normal manner: they do not publish papers in scholarly journals and deliver talks at professional meetings.

4 They submit as "proof" of their treatment's effectiveness, not scientific data, but rather anecdotes and testimonials (see p. 198). They cite the names of famous people – politicians, actors, lawyers, athletes – who support their work: famous people, it should be pointed out, who know nothing about medicine or basic research.

5 They speak of treatment and cures in a pseudo-scientific language that includes emotional appeals and psychological jargon. Example: "If you trust in us, you may yet be saved with vitamin treatment and with anger therapy, which will accomplish your unfoldment on this life plane."

6 They do not determine the presence of cancer by means of biopsy, because they say that biopsy spreads the cancer. Instead, they use their own tests and devices. It is therefore impossible to know for certain whether the patient who claims to have been cured of cancer ever had the disease.

7 They often treat the patient with both proven and unproven methods, so that if the patient's health improves, it is virtually impossible to tell which method was effective. Any success, however, is almost always attributed to the unproven method – in order to justify the practitioner's art.

8 They keep inadequate records of their patients' treatments and "cures." If asked by doctors and scientists for permission to evaluate their procedures or methods, they usually refuse. When they do cooperate in a joint study, they invariably reject the findings and accuse the examiners of bias.

9 They rarely disclose the composition of their "secret formulas" or "miracle cures."

10 They are unable to provide more than a few names of patients who have allegedly benefited from their cures. And those few patients are often unavailable to be interviewed or examined.

11 They ridicule current cancer research and go to great lengths to point out the failure of conventional treatments.

12 They often engage in personal criticism of prominent doctors and scientists.

13 They like to compare themselves to the famous doctors and scientists of the past who succeeded by overcoming the prejudice and ignorance of their day.

14 They say that were it not for the envy and greed of the medical Establishment, their cancer "cures" would be widely recognized.

15 They often belong to extreme political groups, on the right or the left, that accuse the government of conspiring with doctors and drug companies to keep a cure for cancer from the people.

How do the practitioners of unproven methods characterize their therapies?

By comparing them with conventional medicine, at the expense of proven treatments.

ANTI-ESTABLISHMENT	ESTABLISHMENT
HOMEOPATHY After a patient contracts a disease, he is given small doses of a drug which, in large doses, would create symptoms similar to those exhibited by his disease.	ALLOPATHY After a patient contracts a disease, he is given a drug that causes symptoms different from those exhibited by his disease.
CAUSES Causes are treated and symptoms are palliated.	SYMPTOMS Symptoms are treated, not the cause of the symptoms.
BODY The entire body is treated, even though only a part of the body is sick.	ORGAN Particular organs and sites are treated, not the whole body.
NATURAL DRUGS Drugs that are produced from animals, vegetables, and minerals are used to treat disease. The patient consumes only natural, healthy substances – like fruits, vegetables, and juices.	CHEMICAL DRUGS Drugs that are produced from chemicals and poisons are used to treat disease. The patient swallows or is injected with chemical substances.
SELF The patient relies on himself for a cure.	DOCTOR The patient relies on the doctor for a cure.
LOW EXPENSE Herbalists and healers do not charge large sums of money.	HIGH EXPENSE Doctors, drugs, and hospitals cost the patient a great deal of money.

The above outline exaggerates the differences between conventional and unconventional therapies. But the practitioners of unproven methods promote such exaggeration, because differences invite comparison.

What are some specific examples of anti-Establishment therapies?

Although bearing different names, the following therapies have this characteristic in common: they all suggest that the way to cure cancer is to rid the body of poison and disorder.

HOLISTIC THERAPY: a fashionable phrase, used by medical doctors, as well as unconventional therapists, to describe treatment not of a specific site, but of the whole organism, including the mind. The word holistic means whole, and holistic therapies aim to strengthen the whole body and restore to it the equilibrium (or health) that is undermined by disease. Treatment includes, among other things, a proper diet, abstinence from tobacco and alcohol, enemas, vitamins, minerals, distilled water, fresh air, and exercise.

METABOLIC THERAPY: a form of holistic treatment that professes to strengthen a cancer patient's immune system by correcting his metabolism – the process by which cells convert food to energy. The assumption is that the immune system cannot protect the body from disease (and kill cancerous cells) unless the body's metabolism, which has been disordered chemically by improper diet and living habits, is restored to health. A healthy metabolism is achieved through diet, hormones, vitamins, minerals, enzymes, enemas, exercise, counseling, and rest.

DETOXIFICATION THERAPY: a phrase that is often used to mean enema, but is also used to mean purification. If the body is to function properly, it must be free of intoxication and constipation, toxins and poisons. The arteries, which are like a vast plumbing unit, need frequently to be flushed; and the organs of elimination – the bowels, kidneys, lungs, liver, and skin – need regularly to be purified. A healthy body is one with a pure bloodstream. A toxic body leads to cancer. To rid his system of noxious chemicals, the patient is advised to follow a special diet, and to take enemas, fresh air (which cleanses the lungs), sunshine, rest, exercise (which increases the circulation), sweat baths, salt glows, and rubdowns every morning with a cold towel.

COLONIC IRRIGATION THERAPY: a pretentious phrase to denote an enema. Colonic refers to colon, and irrigation means enema. Most metabolic and detoxification therapies recommend that "colonic irrigation" be self-administered every few hours, with coffee, or fruit juice, or castor oil.

MASSAGE THERAPY: a form of treatment based on the principle that the flow of energy through a system acts to organize that system. Just as a magnet can bring order to a hodgepodge of metal shavings, a skillfully administered massage, it is assumed, can rearrange disorderly cells. The hands of the masseur ostensibly convey an organizing energy to the patient's body.

RAW OR LIVE JUICE THERAPY: a diet that is often prescribed by natural food advocates as one means to cure cancer. Fresh fruits and vegetables (with perhaps a dash of calf's liver) are to be liquefied in a mixer and taken daily by the gallon. Some cancer patients consume so much vegetable juice that their skin changes color: for example, their palms may turn yellow from a massive diet of carrot juice. One well-known book on live juice therapy prescribes as a cancer cure a mixture of the following juices: carrot, celery, spinach, cabbage, and apple. The juices are to come from plants organically grown, free from toxic insecticides.

FEVER THERAPY: a form of treatment associated with Coley's toxins (see pp. 243–244). Cancer patients who run high fevers (and survive) sometimes experience a temporary remission of their cancer. Thus some people believe that artificially induced fevers, if they do not kill the patient first, may either burn up cancerous cells or activate the immune system.

CREATIVE VISUALIZATION THERAPY: a phrase that describes the practice of some therapists who urge patients to visualize their disease as a concrete, material object. If the patient is suffering from a tumor, for example, he might picture it as a crab with claws. The assumption is that a patient may cure himself by willing his disease to die. But since it is difficult to will the death of an abstraction (for example, pneumonia), the patient is directed to clothe the abstraction in a material form and then to imagine it being attacked and killed. Thus the cancer patient who thinks of his tumor as a crab is able to grasp the nature of his disease and concentrate on its destruction.

Are unproven methods less expensive than proven methods?

Conventional medicine is costly. A cancer patient can expect to spend between $20,000 and $100,000 for a full course of proven treatments. The low price of unconventional medicine accounts, in great part, for its attractiveness. A full course of treatments averages about $2,000.

But the practitioners of unproven treatments are not losing money. One laetrile pill, for example, can be manufactured for only 3 cents, but it costs $2 on the United States market.

The real cost, though, may not be in money, but in life. The longer a patient waits to seek adequate medical treatment, the shorter his life will be. Although unproven methods give hope to the terminally ill, who have nothing to lose, such methods can only delay effective treatment for patients with cancer in the early stages.

Are the practitioners of unproven methods frauds?

It is no easy matter to assess the motives of people engaged in unorthodox therapy. Modern medicine, after all, grew from the witch doctor and the medicine man. The herbalist and the healer, not surprisingly, are still revered in primitive societies, and gaining influence in some modern ones.

Although medical research has moved from home laboratories to multi-million dollar hospitals and universities, equipped with the most sophisticated instruments, a place still exists for the dedicated medical amateur and for the doctor who wishes to pursue new avenues of research and treatment. On more than one occasion, medical doctors have, out of concern for their dying patients, employed unproven methods of treatment.

Nevertheless, the danger persists: until a therapy is tested, it cannot be trusted. Good intentions are not enough. Merely witness the fact that some of the greatest medical frauds of the twentieth century have been well-meaning graduates of medical schools, not charlatans posing as M.D.'s. So the question remains: "Are the practitioners of unproven methods frauds?" Perhaps all that can be said is that, regardless of motive, some are and some are not.

What does "unproven" mean?

It means that a treatment has not met the government's strict standards for testing and thus has not been approved for sale to the public. To receive the government's seal of approval, foods and drugs must undergo rigorous laboratory and clinical tests.

What is the FDA?

The Food and Drug Administration. Established in 1931 as a result of the Agricultural Appropriation Act, the FDA grew out of a movement, at the turn of the century, to protect the public from adulterated foods and fraudulent patent medicines.

A major figure in this movement was Dr. Harvey Wiley. As chief chemist of the U.S. Department of Agriculture (1883–1912), Dr. Wiley organized a famous "poison squad" that tested suspected foods and brought to public attention the many poisonous substances for sale over the counter.

Operating as an agency of the U.S. Department of Health, Education, and Welfare, the FDA tests new drugs and inspects the manufacture and distribution of foods, drugs, and cosmetics, in order to protect the public from harmful, unsanitary, or falsely labeled goods.

What tests must a new drug undergo to be approved?

A new drug is one that has not yet been subjected to rigorous laboratory and clinical tests. Before the government will license a drug for release to the public, the drug must be approved as both *safe and effective.*

A drug is classified as new if (i) the drug contains a new chemical; or (ii) the drug contains a new combination of old ingredients; or (iii) an old drug is proposed for a new use – for example, aspirin is proposed as a remedy for seasickness; or (iv) an old drug is recommended in a new form – for example, a pill is substituted for an ointment or a syrup.

The most rigorous tests involve drugs that contain a new chemical. To gain approval for these drugs, the sponsor (usually the drug manufacturer) must first screen them by running laboratory tests on three types of animals and microscopic tests on, for example, bacteria and viruses – to determine if the drug has *any* beneficial effects. If this screening justifies further testing of the drug, additional animal tests will be conducted. The drug will also be compared with similar drugs to see which is more effective. The additional tests are designed to determine:

1 The degree to which the drug is poisonous (its toxicity) and the long-term effect of the drug on both the animals and their individual organs – for example, brain, eyes, and liver.

2 The probable or possible effect of the drug on human beings, including its side effects.

3 The probable or possible form in which the drug will be administered to human beings. Since tests on animals (called "preclinical

investigations") must be similar to those that will later be performed on human beings (called "clinical investigations"), the tests on animals must suggest: (i) how long the drug should normally be taken; (ii) how safe the drug will be for subjects of a particular age or physical condition – for example, infants, pregnant women, and the elderly; (iii) how effective the drug will be in human beings.

Before a new drug may be tested on human subjects, the sponsor must file with the Food and Drug Administration (the FDA) a "Notice of Claimed Investigational Exemption for a New Drug." This application, called an IND, must contain, among other things, the following information: (i) the descriptive name of the drug, and the chemical name and structure of any new chemical found in the drug; (ii) the components of the drug; (iii) the quantity of each component; (iv) the name and address of any supplier who, in addition to the sponsor, contributed a substance to the preparation of the drug, and a description of that substance; (v) the methods, facilities, and safeguards used to manufacture and pack the new drug; (vi) the results of all preclinical tests and of any clinical tests conducted outside the United States; (vii) the relevant hazards and side effects, as well as a copy of the label and the advertising material that accompany the drug; (viii) the background and scientific credentials of the sponsor; (ix) the names and professional records of all those people testing the drug; (x) the plans for testing the drug in human beings.

The IND application, then, essentially does four things: it describes the contents of the drug and the qualifications of those sponsoring it; it summarizes the results of laboratory tests on animals; it evaluates any tests on human beings that have been conducted outside the United States (note: the U.S. government does not permit preclinical tests on human beings); and it describes the sponsor's future plans for testing the drug clinically in the United States on human subjects.

Clinical investigations or field tests may be defined as the treatment and observation of patients, as distinguished from experiments with drugs in a laboratory. Field tests are divided into three phases: in phase one, doctors determine how toxic a drug is, how quickly the body absorbs and eliminates the drug, and how much of the drug may be safely prescribed; in phase two, they assess, on a limited number of patients, the effectiveness of the drug for a specific disease; in phase three, they test the safety and effectiveness of the drug for a specific disease in a large group of subjects.

If the FDA approves the IND application, clinical or field tests on human beings may begin. Not until the FDA is convinced that the field tests have shown the drug to be safe and effective will the government approve the drug for marketing and public use. In the event that the field tests are not satisfactory, the FDA will withhold approval of the drug. Clinical or field tests on a cancer drug must include the following proofs.

1 Proof that the person has cancer. A biopsy constitutes adequate proof.

2 Proof that the benefits of the drug outweigh its harmful side effects. A drug that cures cancer and, in the process, destroys the patient's brain cells may be effective; but it is also lethal – and therefore worthless.

3 Proof that the new drug is *consistently* safe and effective. People differ not only in size and shape, but also in their ability to tolerate drugs. Unless a drug has a reasonable margin of safety, an amount that helps one person may kill another. To determine that a drug is consistently safe and effective, doctors must conduct field tests on a great many people.

4 Proof that, before or during treatment with the new drug, the patient has not received other treatments that might influence the tests.

5 Proof that the new drug is at least as effective as those already on the market.

6 Proof, by means of autopsy, that the new drug is effective. Since the patients who are used as subjects for cancer tests are the terminally ill, the failure of a drug to save their lives should not be taken as an indication of the drug's worth. An autopsy will reveal what effect, if any, the drug has had on the cancerous cells.

7 Proof that the results obtained during field tests can be reproduced in other field tests conducted elsewhere. A comparison of test results obtained in this country, for example, with those obtained in another country will reduce the chance of error that might result from differences in climate, environment, diet, race, or culture.

8 Proof, obtained from interviews with patients, that the new drug has been effective for more than a brief period. Assessing long-term effectiveness guards against premature optimism and ephemeral results.

Once the sponsor has adequate clinical proof that the drug is both safe and effective, he may submit to the FDA a new drug application (NDA) that includes not only a sample of the drug and its labeling, but also a detailed description of (i) the preclinical animal studies; (ii) the clinical human studies; and (iii) the composition, manufacture, and distribution of the drug.

Although the number of safeguards may seem excessive, the thalidomide tragedy proves that anything less may be inadequate.

What is a "double blind" study?

Let us assume that a new drug is being studied. The sponsors of the drug assemble two groups of patients: one group will receive the drug and one will receive a sugar pill (a placebo). If the first group has better results than the second, the sponsor will conclude that the drug is effective. However, two problems must be overcome: (i) patients who receive the sugar pill may be inclined to feel resentful at being denied the benefit of the drug; and (ii) patients who receive the drug may be inclined to feel hopeful and thus to feel better. To avoid these difficulties, the sponsors make the placebo look exactly like the drug, so that neither group knows which is receiving the placebo. Even the doctors do not know, because patients often improve when their doctors expect them to do so. The phrase double blind, then, refers to the "blindness" of both patients and doctors during the course of the study.

In a single blind study, the doctors, but not the patients, are told which group is receiving the placebo.

What "proof" is there that unproven methods work?

The proof that is usually cited by the practitioners of unproven methods is of two kinds: testimonials and anecdotes.

A *testimonial* is a personal statement in which the patient who underwent the treatment swears to its effectiveness. The statement is often extravagant in its claims and emotional in its language.

In 1968 I was afflicted with cancer. This condition became steadily worse. I spent thousands of dollars on doctors, and prescriptions. My appetite disappeared. I was as skinny as a skeleton. By 1973, the cancer had spread to my back, lungs, and bones – and left me in terrible pain. I was now completely helpless.

I took radiation treatments and drugs until I bought a juicer in October, 1973. I drank from two to three quarts of carrot and celery juice daily. In nine weeks, all of my pain had left. In less than a year, my weight returned to normal and I was free of pain.

Believe it or not, I have no cancer now, and my lungs are getting stronger rapidly.

An *anecdote* is a personal account in which one person swears to the effectiveness of another person's treatment.

Mrs X, a neighbor of mine, was so ill with cancer that she could not drink from a glass and had to be fed carrot juice by the spoonful. Gradually, as her strength returned, she began to drink from a glass. During her recovery, she drank ten gallons of juice per day. No other food was allowed. Today she is perfectly healthy.

Testimonials and anecdotes are especially appealing when they are authored by famous people: movie stars, athletes, politicians, singers, and scientists. But in most instances, these people are wholly unqualified to judge a remedy's safety or effectiveness.

Some testimonials and anecdotes claim that a particular remedy is effective not as a cure, but as a pain-reliever, or as a valuable addition to conventional treatment. These claims are the most difficult to prove, since many patients feel free of pain as a result of the power of suggestion (see pp. 210–211 and 221–222) or as a result of the conventional treatment.

The scientific community regards testimonials and anecdotes as worthless because they are not supported by laboratory analysis and clinical tests.

Are unproven methods effective?

Unproven therapies are usually not effective in the control of cancer. The few that have been tested in government laboratories have been found to be worthless. Whether some of the more recent "alternative" forms of cancer therapy prove beneficial remains to be seen.

What is "the placebo effect"?

A placebo is a harmless substance, like a sugar pill, given to a patient (i) to satisfy his wish to have some form of medication, or (ii) to measure his response to a controlled test in which one group is given the real drug and another group an imitation. When a seriously ill patient receives a placebo and reports that his health has improved, scientists attribute his improvement to "the placebo effect." This effect may be explained as wishful thinking. So profoundly does the patient wish to recover that he believes in the effectiveness of the drug he has been given, even though the drug is worthless. And because he believes, his health may in fact improve – at least temporarily.

Unproven remedies, all too often, are nothing more than placebos. But it is difficult to expose these remedies as worthless because patients, desperately wanting to be well, take them and report an improvement in their health ("the placebo effect"). Some people even defend unproven remedies on the grounds that placebos, although misleading, offer a patient relief and hope. The danger, of course, is that patients who could benefit from conventional treatment may be less inclined to seek it if they are being misled by the placebo effect.

If an unproven remedy is ineffective can it be safe?

Yes. Consider vitamins, for example. They will not cure cancer, but they are safe, in reasonable amounts. Diets of vegetable juice are also safe. But no person ought to delay seeing his doctor about a suspicious symptom because he is consuming vitamins or juices. A remedy may be safe without being effective. One thing has nothing to do with the other.

Are unproven methods safe?

Some are and some are not. Many unorthodox remedies are nothing more than grains, cereals, fruits, and vegetables. Other remedies are less innocent. But all unproven methods are unsafe if they keep people from seeking early and effective treatment. Cancer can be successfully treated in the early stages. But once the patient has spent months on exotic diets, enemas, faith healers, massage, or meditation, the cancer may have spread out of control. The old commercial saying *caveat emptor*, "let the buyer beware," is particularly true of unproven methods of treatment for cancer.

Are unproven methods being given a fair chance?

The practitioners of unproven methods argue that their therapies are not being tested fairly because most of their patients are (i) terminally ill, (ii) weakened by surgery and poisoned by X-rays or chemicals, and (iii) disabled by pain. Nevertheless, the practitioners say that they manage to help or cure a considerable number of people.

The difficulty is, of course, that in the absence of detailed case histories, it is impossible for doctors to know how successful unproven methods have been on late-stage patients. Moreover, it is unreasonable for practitioners to expect that unproven methods should be tested on early-stage patients. Even when recognized cancer institutes develop new methods of treatment, they test these methods primarily on the terminally ill. For the practitioners of unproven methods to want an advantage that doctors themselves are denied is not only naive, but also unfair.

If unproven methods are ineffective. why don't they disappear?

Most of them do. The history of medicine is strewn with the wreckage of discarded theories and treatments. But centuries ago, it was no easy matter to disprove a theory, particularly if the theory was one that people were comfortable with. For example, Galen's theory that cancer was caused by an excess of black bile, and could be treated by purging, was believed for about 1,700 years. And in all that time, the theory and treatment were wrong.

A modern laboratory can, of course, test a theory in a relatively short time. So to escape exposure, unproven methods have become chameleon-like: they acquire a protective coloration to stay ahead of the law and to suit the season. They need only change their aspect, or their name, to adapt to a changing world. Smartly setting their sails to the prevailing scientific opinion, the practitioners of unproven methods frequently alter their claims as new research alters old theories. Thus, remedies once hawked as "cures," for example, are now trumpeted as the last word in cancer prevention and the control of pain.

Don't most diseases have their remedies in nature?

In its infancy, medicine resorted not only to superstition and astrology, but also to plants and herbs. Whether previous ages found relief from rheumatism in the motion of the planets would be difficult to say; but they did find potions for pain in the vegetable system, from which, according to one old book, "flows spontaneously the genuine virtues of medicine diffused universally over the face of the earth, where nothing grows in vain."

The idea that "nothing grows in vain" explains why people have sought remedies in the fields and the forests for the many diseases that have beset them. Certainly from earliest times, people have believed that plants were created by God for man's benefit. But as people moved from the country to the city, they were less likely to go into the fields to gather herbs from which to prepare simple, helpful remedies. The decline in herbal medicine, in fact, corresponds to the rise in importance of doctors and pharmacists. And the development of modern medicine, with its brilliant advances, follows, to some degree, the migration from the land to the city. Once research became dependent upon elaborate equipment, doctors turned away from herbal medicine to pursue research at hospitals or laboratories equipped with electron microscopes, ultra-centrifuges, and the like.

Life, though, has a way of repeating itself. Now that modern laboratories are equipped with up-to-date equipment and research tools, where are scientists seeking new remedies and cures? In the fields and the forests. Consider the following list of plants and their treasures.

PLANT	DRUG	MEDICAL USE
Autumn crocus	Colchicine	Treatment of gout
Belladonna	Atropine	Control of spasms and sweating Dilation of pupils Sedative Treatment of ulcers
Cascara bark	Cascara	Laxative
Cephaëlis acuminata	Ipecac	Antidote for poison
Chondodendron tomentosum	Curare	Muscle relaxant in surgery
Coca leaves	Cocaine	Anaesthetic, particularly for the eye

PLANT	DRUG	MEDICAL USE
Coffee and tea	Caffeine	Stimulant (of the central nervous system)
Ma huang (Chinese herb)	Ephedrine	Decongestant Treatment of asthma
Mexican yam	Precursor of steroid hormones	Hormone therapy
Ordeal bean	Physostigmine	Treatment of glaucoma
Periwinkle	Vinblastine Vincristine	Treatment of cancers, particularly childhood leukemia and Hodgkin's disease
Poppy	Opium	Analgesic (drug for relief of pain)
Purple foxglove or "ladies' fingers"	Digitalis	Diuretic Heart stimulant
Quinine bark	Quinine	Treatment of malaria
Snake root	Reserpine	Tranquilizer Treatment of high blood pressure
Squill	Squill	Treatment of heart disease

"In all things of nature," said Aristotle, "there is something of the marvelous." And, he might have added, of the curative.

Are there remedies for cancer in nature?

"There is no new thing under the sun," said the preacher in *Ecclesiastes*. From ancient days to modern, people have sought in plants and minerals, animals and constellations, a cure for cancer. None has yet been found.

For the purpose of showing how right the preacher was, some ancient and modern remedies are here included.

ANCIENT
Asian stone
Ashes of old shoes
Belladonna
Burnt hair and wool
Cabbage
Charcoal
Coriander
Crabs prepared with
   honey, asses milk, and
   herbs
Daffodils
Dung of dog fed on bones
Enemas
Exercise
Female fern in powdered
   form
Figs
Garlic
Goat's dung
Gold
Green figs
Ground gems
Human sweat mixed with bean
   flour
Hyssop
India ink
Iris
Juniper gum
Lead
Lily
Lime from marble, shells,
   or pebbles
Maiden hair
Mandrake root
Mercury

MODERN
Alfalfa
Apricot seeds
Arsenic powder
Birch ashes in tap water
Buckthorn
Clam extract
Clover blossom tea
Cobwebs saturated with
   arsenic powder
Diamond carbon compound
Dock leaf
Enemas
Extract from the posterior lobe
   of the pituitary gland of cattle
Fever
Florence oil and red precipitate
Fungi grown from a combination
   of yeast, salt, whole meat,
   and stale water
Garlic
Grapes
Ground bones
Horse blood
Hydropathy
Iris leaves
Juniper berries
Llama placenta
Magic-in-mud
Mesmerism
Mistletoe, fir tree mistletoe for
   males and apple tree mistletoe
   for females
Morning urine taken from the
   patient

Mistletoe
Mulberry juice with honey
Nettles
Oak leaves and fruit
Old pitch scraped from ships
Oleander
Onion poultice
Opium
Pickled fish brine
Poppy leaves and flowers
Prayer
Pumice stone
Rhubarb
Seaweed
Silver
Sunflower
Urine
Walnut oil
Water pepper
Zinc

Odors, particularly from onions
   and garlic
Ox bile
Powdered emeralds
Prayer cloth
Pure springs of Malvern
   (England)
Quicksilver
Red clover
Rose leaves
Tear extract
Tension reduction
Turnip juice
Turpentine
Violets
Vitamins
Volcanic hot springs of Carlsbad
   (Czechoslovakia)
White pepper
Zinc

Although these remedies may appear humorous, what they reveal is the frenzy and desperation of most cancer patients. Throughout the ages can be heard the psalm, "O Lord, heal me; for my bones are vexed."

Aren't the Hunzas of Pakistan long-lived, and cancer free, because they eat apricot seeds?

The people of Hunza live in a remote mountain valley of northern Pakistan, near the borders of Russia and China. Noted for their longevity, the Hunzas have a diet rich in dried apricots.

No one knows for sure whether these people are long-lived, since their record-keeping is imperfect. In 1955, a Japanese medical expedition studied the Hunzas and reported that they were susceptible to the same diseases as the rest of mankind, including cancer. The only difference was that the Hunzas seemed to suffer from these illnesses less frequently than other people – a fact that may be explained by their pollution-free environment, or their strenuous physical activity, or their diet, or a combination of causes.

The longevity of the Hunzas, in short, has never been proved, nor has the link between a cancer-free life and a diet rich in dried apricots.

Weren't ancient doctors more successful than modern doctors in treating cancer?

They may seem to have been so, because ancient doctors did not distinguish between tumors that were benign and those that were malignant. Although puzzled by the fact that some tumors responded to treatment and others did not, they never considered that the tumors might be of different kinds. Almost certainly, the "cancers" that ancient doctors cured were mostly benign.

Weren't ancient methods of treating cancer very much like methods used in modern hospitals?

Ancient doctors treated tumors by cutting them out of the body (surgery), by burning them with a hot iron or needle (cautery), or by poisoning them with a caustic substance (the use of escharotics). Modern methods of treatment are surgery, radiotherapy, and chemotherapy (see chapter two), which are often referred to by their critics as the cut, burn, and poison therapies. However similar the ancient and modern treatments may appear, the techniques – and rates of success – are vastly different.

What theories of cancer are used to promote unproven methods?

The most familiar theories are as follows.

ELIMINATION THEORY Since the Middle Ages, people have believed that illness is caused by the introduction of some foreign element into the body. Before the advent of modern medicine, the Devil, for example, was the chief culprit. But with the introduction of the microscope, Lucifer has given way to germs and viruses.

For the medieval doctor it followed that elimination of the Devil was the way to cure a cancer patient. So the doctor, who was often a priest, tried to drive out the Devil with noise, by banging pots and pans; with smoke, by burning green wood; with odors, by hanging a garlic bag around the patient's neck; with purging, by bloodletting; with exorcism, by intoning incantations; and with supernatural intervention, by praying. Although few of these remedies are still used today, the theory remains essentially unchanged.

Modern proponents of elimination theory, instead of casting out the Devil, talk about ridding the body of impurities, toxins, radiation, and chemicals. Cancer, according to these people, may be eliminated from the system if the patient purges his body of poison by means of enemas and proper diet.

SIMILARITY THEORY From ancient days to modern, the belief has persisted that a disease may be cured by a remedy that is similar to the disease. At least 2,500 years ago, some doctors, thinking that cancer was caused by a crab-like or toad-like intruder, applied to tumors crabs or toads in live and powdered form. Remedies of this kind can still be found in provincial places.

Similarity theory also includes the belief that since a cancer cure is priceless, it may be effected by treatment with a priceless remedy, for example, gold or silver ornaments pressed against the tumor, or powdered gem stones swallowed in a liquid substance.

Another aspect of the theory is that nasty diseases call for nasty remedies. Cancer being an ugly disease calls for an ugly remedy, something like cutting, burning, or poisoning.

In addition, there is the belief that since cancer is a mysterious ailment, it can be treated only by mysterious means, that is, by invoking the deity, saints, the Virgin Mary, or a host of angels.

To some degree, similarity theory has its modern equivalent in homeopathy. Homeopathic medicine is based on the belief that diseases may be cured with minute quantities of remedies that would, in massive doses, produce effects *similar* to those of the disease being treated.

INJURY OR IRRITATION THEORY For at least 150 years, children have been warned by their parents not to squeeze pimples or pick scabs, because irritations can cause cancer. The warning is based on the theory that lumps, which often form in the area of an injury or an irritation, are the beginnings of tumors.

Resting on an imperfect understanding of how the body functions, irritation theory states that the body rushes blood to an injured area to cleanse and heal the wound. If the tissue near the wound cannot absorb the blood, a clot may form and become the nucleus of a subsequent tumor.

TROPHOBLAST THEORY Forty years ago, when laetrile was first introduced to the public, the proponents of the drug adopted the theory that cancer was the result of leftover fetal cells, called trophoblasts.

Based on a 1902 thesis of Scottish embryologist John Beard, the trophoblast theory holds that an embryo produces special cells – trophoblast cells – that form the placenta and the umbilical cord. (The placenta is a bag-like organ that nourishes the fetus; and the umbilical cord is a cord-like structure that connects the fetus to the placenta.) When the work of the trophoblasts is completed, the pancreas produces an enzyme called trypsin that prevents the further production of trophoblast cells and kills the existing ones. But if, for some reason, the pancreas fails to eliminate all of the trophoblast cells, the cells will, according to Beard's theory, circulate in both mother and child and attempt to form new growths – cancerous growths.

The proponents of laetrile have since abandoned the trophoblast theory in favor of another: namely, that cancer results from a deficiency of vitamin B-17, an imaginary vitamin.

DEFICIENCY THEORY A deficiency disease results from a diet deficient in certain vitamins or minerals. For example, beriberi is caused by lack of vitamin B-1, scurvy by lack of vitamin C, and rickets by lack of vitamin D. If an insufficient diet can cause disease, it follows that a sufficient one can prevent disease. But not every disease is caused by a deficiency in diet. Some people used to think that Infantile Paralysis could be prevented by a diet rich in vitamin C. They were wrong.

Similarly, those people who argue that cancer is a deficiency disease maintain that cancer can be prevented by the right diet. Some of these people think, for example, that cancer is caused by the absence of vitamin B-17; so they advocate the use of laetrile. Others contend that cancer is caused by the absence of some vital nutrient they cannot identify; so they advise people to protect themselves by observing a diet of natural foods rich in vitamins and minerals.

THYROID THEORY The ancient Greeks called it the shield in the form of a door and regarded it as the organ responsible for growth. But not until this century have doctors adequately understood the function of the thyroid gland. Found in the area of the Adam's apple, the thyroid helps to regulate body growth and metabolism – that is, the sum of all the chemical changes caused by the intake of food. It is partially responsible for height and weight, dwarfism and obesity; it can cause popping eyes and cretinism. Because of its power to regulate growth, the thyroid is thought, by some people, to be implicated in cancer. They argue that lawless cell growth is caused by a malfunctioning thyroid.

According to this theory, cancer can be prevented by a healthy diet, free from alcohol and tobacco, and it can be cured by extracts of thyroid. Although the first suggestion has great value, the second, unfortunately, does not.

SURVEILLANCE THEORY The word surveillance means to watch, or to keep watch over, a person or an object. Surveillance theory derives from a complex thesis by Dr. Lewis Thomas, President of the Memorial Sloan-Kettering Cancer Center in New York (see p. 238). Dr. Thomas speculates that all human beings have circulating in their body, at one time or another, cancerous cells. In people who are healthy, the immune system acts like radar, conducting surveillance of the entire body. If any cancerous cells are detected, an army of white blood cells is dispatched to the scene to destroy them. Thus the immune system in a healthy person is always engaged in a search-and-destroy operation. But in people who are unhealthy, the immune system is like a lamp with a defective bulb. The system cannot illuminate the dark reaches of the body, and so discover and destroy any lurking cancerous cells. One object of cancer therapy, then, must be to restore the immune system to a healthy condition.

Capitalizing on Lewis Thomas' thesis, the proponents of surveillance theory argue that a tumor is not cancer, but rather a serious symptom of cancer. They contend that cancer is a chemical imbalance that causes the body's immune system to fail. This imbalance, and therefore the cancer, can be corrected with a healthy diet – or so they think. Immunologists (doctors who study the immune system) think that more than diet is required to correct a defective immune system.

Is there a psychological link to cancer?

The evidence is inconclusive, but not without interest. As long ago as the second century A.D., the Greek doctor and philosopher Galen is said to have observed that unhappy women were more inclined to develop cancer of the breast than happy, outgoing women. In this century, at least two studies, one in the United States and one in England, suggest that cancer may be found more often in people who suppress their emotions than in people who do not. For this reason, centers for self-healing, directed by practitioners of the mental healing arts, have begun to appear in the United States.

In these centers, cancer patients are instructed to express anger and desire, resentment and aggression. If cancer tends to strike the helpless and the hopeless, then the patient must be tutored to help himself. Passiveness must be overcome, silence dispelled, and insecurity defeated. Since cancer patients often feel abandoned and worthless, centers for the mental healing arts offer companionship to the lonely and encouragement to the despairing. It is no medical secret that patients who fight their disease have a better chance of recovery and a longer life expectancy than patients who refuse to fight.

If cancer indeed seems to strike the inhibited and the distressed, it remains for scientists to determine whether these people were initially inhibited and distressed or whether the disease caused them to be so. It also remains for scientists to discover (and this point may be only a footnote to the larger question) why patients who have been in mental hospitals for long periods of time apparently suffer cancer less often than the general population. Some investigators think, for example, that there is a chemical link between a person's state of mind and his physical well-being. Whether such a link exists, and whether it is chemical, psychosomatic, electrical, genetic, or environmental, remains to be seen. But a strong case can, in any event, be made for the need to conduct further research into the question.

Can the power of the mind cure?

Whether or not the mind can cure the body merely by willing a disease to disappear, or by visualizing its destruction (see p. 204), is uncertain. Undoubtedly many people through the centuries have passionately wanted to recover from an illness – and have nevertheless died from it. On the other hand, history is filled with examples of people who have directed their bodies to perform strange and miraculous feats. Consider, for example, the following: (i) people who are under hypnosis; (ii) people who undergo surgery without anaesthetics and experience no pain; (iii) mystics who stand on one leg, in one place, for thirty years or more; (iv) men and women who wish to share Christ's passion and, as a result, receive the stigmata; (v) men who walk across hot coals and feel no pain and suffer no burns; (vi) women who go through false pregnancies and experience an enlargement of their stomach and, nine months later, labor pains. The power of the mind to influence the body may not "pass all understanding," but it certainly passes much.

P.P. Quimby, an American healer who had an enormous following, attributed his success to his ability to convince the patient that his ailment was a mistake of the mind and not an affliction of the body. The other side of the argument, of course, is that the power of the mind has never been known to cure cancer, cirrhosis of the liver, hardening of the arteries, heart disease, polio, tuberculosis, or a broken bone.

Is there, as critics allege, a conspiracy between the medical Establishment and others to oppose a cure for cancer?

Some people believe that the medical Establishment has conspired with the drug companies and the government to prevent a cure for cancer. They argue that doctors maintain a lucrative practice by treating cancer patients, and that drug companies make enormous profits by selling worthless drugs. A cure for cancer, runs the argument, would put an end to this monopoly.

Although cancer is undoubtedly profitable for doctors – $4 billion annually, $10 million daily – other diseases have also been profitable. Yet scientists were not inhibited from producing vaccines for polio and tuberculosis, insulin for diabetes, and so-called miracle drugs like sulfa, cortisone, and penicillin. If doctors and drug companies had wanted to protect their lucrative business, they would presumably have prevented these discoveries. But they did not. In fact, the opposite is true: they contributed to them.

Furthermore, to argue that doctors have conspired to prevent a cure for cancer, even with all the suffering they have seen, is to forget that many of these doctors have spouses and children who die of the disease. Doctors, biologists, chemists, laboratory technicians, drug manufacturers, and government officials all get cancer. It strains the mind to think that so many people would be willing to forego a cure just to make a profit.

Finally, for this alleged conspiracy to work, it would have to include a large part of the world, since research being conducted in other countries would have to be suppressed. In light of U.S.-Soviet competition, for example, it seems unlikely that Russia would forego the satisfaction of being the first country in the world to discover a cure for cancer.

Why is the medical Establishment reluctant to investigate alleged cures for cancer?

Because they know that the publicity attending such an investigation can dignify what may be a fraud. When medical officials agree to test a treatment for cancer, they give that treatment a notoriety and respect that it would not otherwise have. The public assumes, quite naturally, that professional medical groups do not waste their time on counterfeit cures.

But therein lies the problem. Consider, for a moment, the following pattern. The medical Establishment, not wishing to dignify frauds, refuses to investigate an alleged cure. The practitioners of that "cure" then accuse the medical profession of being biased or, worse, of conspiring to keep from the public a valuable therapy. If the medical Establishment responds to this criticism by investigating the alleged cure, it runs the risk of dignifying what may be a fraud. Hence, the problem is circular.

When unproven methods seem to work, why are doctors skeptical?

For at least two reasons.

1 Frequently patients are told by unlicensed practitioners that they have cancer when they do not. Once having been "cured," they attribute their good health to the unproven therapy. But unless the presence of cancer was confirmed at the outset, doctors have no way of knowing whether the original diagnosis was correct. Needless to say, it is easy to cure a patient of cancer when the patient does not have the disease.

2 A large percentage of patients who in fact have cancer and who try unproven treatments have also undergone conventional treatments, usually radiotherapy and chemotherapy. If such a patient's health improves, it is impossible for doctors to determine which treatment is responsible: the conventional, the unconventional, or a combination of both.

Do doctors oppose unproven treatments out of self-interest?

The argument that doctors do not want their patients to seek unproven treatments because the doctors will lose a lucrative source of money suggests, by implication, that doctors are (i) greedy, (ii) blind to human suffering, and (iii) persuaded that unproven treatments work.

Although some doctors behave as though money were the only reason for entering the medical profession, the great majority of doctors are dedicated to the care and well-being of their patients. Financial reward may, in fact, be a reason for having a medical practice; but to say that doctors dissuade patients from seeking unproven treatment because the doctors wish to benefit from the high cost of medical care is to ignore the example of other countries, where such care is virtually free. Conventional medicine in the United States is expensive; in England, by contrast, it is not. And yet British doctors, who have nothing to gain by so doing, warn their patients against unproven methods of treatment.

If doctors were truly insensitive, they could hardly expect to earn vast sums of money from people whom they ignore. Although it is certainly true that overworked doctors spend too little time with their patients, there is a difference between brevity and blindness. It is one thing to have only a few minutes to spend with a patient, it is quite another to neglect him. The two situations should not be confused.

Finally, if doctors counsel their patients to avoid unproven treatments, it is not because of their fear that those treatments will work. It is rather because of their knowledge that the treatments will fail, thus condemning some patients to deaths that might have been avoided, and subjecting others – the terminally ill – to therapies that are pointless and cruel.

What is the "Committee for Freedom of Choice in Cancer Therapy"?

Opposed to the Food and Drug Administration's requirement that a drug must be both "safe and effective," the Committee for Freedom of Choice in Cancer Therapy is dedicated to eliminating the word effective. Supporters of the Committee, including the John Birch Society, contend that in a free country people should have the right to buy and distribute any product they like, so long as the product is safe. In particular, they argue that the patient and his doctor should have the freedom to choose whatever treatment they think best for the patient – regardless of what the scientific community and the government may think. The Committee maintains that if a treatment is harmless, the government should keep "hands off," particularly since harmless treatments not infrequently give patients temporary relief (the placebo effect). Unlike consumerism, which is designed to protect the public from false claims and worthless products, the freedom of choice movement says that government already interferes too much in people's lives.

Critics of the Committee contend that laws are passed to protect consumers from drugs that are worthless, as well as dangerous, because a worthless drug may keep a patient from seeking effective treatment. The critics insist that it is the responsibility of government to protect people from fraud, whatever form the deception takes: bogus stocks, counterfeit money, forged paintings, or spurious real estate. Freedom of choice, these critics point out, is an emotional phrase intended to disguise the fact that people are quite properly prohibited not only from selling worthless drugs, but also from doing numerous other things, like driving an automobile beyond the speed limit, or discharging a gun in public, or detonating an explosive, or stealing, or traveling to a foreign country without a passport. The argument that worthless drugs ought to be sold to cancer patients because they sometimes make the patient feel better is misleading, and even dangerous. After all, a bath and a shampoo might make a patient feel better, but they will not cure his cancer.

What is meant by "the treatment of choice"?

The phrase "treatment of choice" is not to be confused with the phrase "freedom of choice," which is trumpeted by people who want the government to permit the sale of safe, but worthless drugs. The treatment of choice means: that treatment most likely, given the nature of the cancer, to produce a cure. In other words, the doctor will select the treatment that produces the best rate of cure for a particular cancer. Example: the treatment of choice for cancer of the stomach is normally surgery; for cancer of the vocal cords (when the tumor is small), radiotherapy; for leukemia, chemotherapy.

What is the "Medical Freedom of Choice" bill?

Introduced by Representative Steven Symms of Idaho, the bill proposes to drop the word effective from the law that requires a drug to be both safe and effective before it can be sold to the public. If the bill passes, a drug need not in the future be proved effective, but only safe. Supporters of the bill argue that people ought to be free to choose their own medicine – as long as it is safe.

Opponents of the bill contend that its passage will invite the kind of quackery that bedeviled this country at the turn of the century, when thousands of patent medicines were advertised as cures for everything from coughs to cancer. If the bill is passed, say its critics, all the protections now enjoyed by the public will be removed, as counters are flooded with worthless potions, elixirs, tonics, nostrums, and balms. Worst of all, according to the critics, will be the misleading advertising that is bound to accompany these worthless drugs. Cancer patients, it is feared, will be led to avoid uncomfortable treatments and to seek easy ones. The easy path, however, does not often lead to cure.

6 The Future

Among all forms of mistake, prophecy is the most gratuitous.
George Eliot, *Middlemarch*

Newspapers and magazines, television and radio frequently report prophecies about cure-alls for cancer – prophecies that are not only unjustified but also misleading. When dying patients are led to believe that a cure for cancer is near, they plague their last days with anxiety: another month, another week of life may usher in the long-awaited cure – or so they think. Similarly, their families suffer agonies of indecision: should they or should they not remove a dying spouse, or parent or child, from curative treatment and give him terminal care when a cure may be forthcoming – or so they hope. The reverse – the prediction that a cure will never be found – is, of course, no better. Such cynical forecasts merely cause people to complain that costly research is a quest for the miraculous, and hence the unattainable. They forget Pascal's instruction: "It is not possible to have a reasonable belief against miracles."

In this chapter there are no prophecies – only descriptions of current research and new forms of treatment. If these descriptions make the future seem uncertain but promising, then they have presented the future as it is. Research in science and medicine will progress in ways that cannot be foretold. Even prevention, which can guarantee a future largely free of cancer, is unpredictable, since no one can know whether people and their governments will choose to limit the use of cancer-causing agents. Only one thing is certain: the future need not be left to chance. Through research and prevention, people can – if they will – shape the future much as they want it to be.

THE FUTURE OF RESEARCH

Why are scientists taking so long to discover a cure for cancer?

Scientists in cancer research are like mechanics entrusted with a miniature machine they do not understand. This machine – a living cell – is more complex than the most sophisticated computer. Some of its parts serve functions that have not yet been discovered; other parts are probably too small to be seen, even with the most powerful microscope. All of the parts are closely related, so the smallest fault may cause enormous damage. When such a machine goes wrong, no one knows how or why. Hence no one can repair it.

Sometimes, by chance, a mechanic may fix a broken machine by tampering with its parts. In much the same way, a scientist in cancer research may one day learn to fix or kill a cancerous cell by tampering, for example, with its genes. But just as the mechanic's job would be easier if he knew how the parts in the machine worked, so the scientist's job would be easier if he knew how the genes in a cell behaved. For this reason, it is essential that biologists explore, through basic research, the mysteries of normal cells.

What is the difference between applied and basic research?

Applied (or practical) research is the attempt to acquire knowledge that can be used to solve a particular problem. Basic (or theoretical) research is the attempt to acquire knowledge for its own sake. In applied research, scientists seek to address a specific problem – for example, the need to eradicate boll weevils from cotton fields. In basic research, they seek to explore the mysteries of life, for the same reason that most people explore the world – to satisfy their consuming curiosity about themselves and their environment.

For most scientists, the difference between applied and basic research is artificial. The results obtained in one area are usually applicable in the other. Experiments in basic research provide the information without which applied research cannot proceed.

Isn't basic research often worthless?

Some people, including a few scientists and doctors, think so. They argue that it is wasteful for thousands of dollars to be spent for experiments on the mating behavior of moths or the function of a chemical in the human body. But since people cannot predict how future knowledge may be used, they cannot know in advance that a particular experiment is worthless. Some of the unlikeliest experiments have led to the greatest improvements in medicine.

Few doctors in the 1930's, for example, could have foreseen much practical value in Wendell Stanley's research on the tobacco mosaic virus – a scourge of the tobacco plant. In particular, Stanley's achievement in crystallizing the virus must have seemed trifling at best. But since a crystallized virus contains no impurities and can therefore be accurately tested, this apparent trifle initiated experiments that eventually enabled Dr. Jonas Salk to develop a vaccine against polio.

Which has contributed more to the control of cancer: applied or basic research?

It is impossible to say, since research of both types has contributed to every advance in prevention and treatment.

Consider the history of chemotherapy. As a result of applied research, scientists have developed nearly fifty different cancer drugs. As a result of basic research, scientists have charted the life cycle of cells. Consequently, doctors are able to administer chemotherapy at times when cancerous cells are most susceptible to injury and death. Basic research, in short, has complemented applied research, with the result that doctors can now prolong – and sometimes save – the lives of patients who were once regarded as incurable.

How is basic research currently related to cancer research?

At present, scientists are trying to explain how a cell performs its numerous activities. They must identify, for example, the specific functions served by each of the thousands of genes in the cell nucleus. They must discover how the mitochondria, which produce energy, move about within the cell. And they must learn the nature and purpose of the cell membrane, the cell plasma, and the chemical parts that make up the cytoplasm and nucleus.

The more scientists learn about normal cells, the sooner they will discover how cancerous cells differ from normal cells and how such differences occur. In other words, they will discover why cancerous cells multiply without restraint and how they invade various parts of the body.

What are the current theories about cancer?

The major theories are hardly more numerous than the fingers on one hand. And every theory may be correct, since the problem of why cells become cancerous may have numerous solutions.

ABNORMALITIES IN THE CELL NUCLEUS

Theory A cell may become cancerous when a change (mutation) occurs in one of its genes. Genes have different functions: some make proteins, some control cell reproduction, some direct the activities of their fellows. A mutation in any one of these genes may cause a cell to die, to sicken, or to become cancerous.

Theory Hidden in a cell may be foreign genetic material – viruses. The viruses may be newly acquired or may be descendants of ancient viruses that have been passed on from generation to generation for perhaps thousands or even millions of years. Presumably, these viruses remain silent unless disturbed by X-rays or chemicals. In that event, they may become active, causing the cells they inhabit to become cancerous.

ABNORMALITIES IN THE CYTOPLASM

Theory The behavior of genes may be controlled by the cytoplasm. which is the cellular material that surrounds the nucleus. Since the genes govern cell division, cancer may occur if the cytoplasm misdirects the genes.

According to this theory, the genes in a cancerous cell misbehave because of changes in the cytoplasm – not because of changes in the genes. If this theory is true, cancerous changes in a cell may be reversible, since defects in the cytoplasm are more easily corrected than defects in the genes. Evidence in support of this theory is derived from (i) research in which cancerous cells have been made to behave like normal cells; and (ii) a landmark experiment with frogs. In this experiment, scientists tried to determine which part of a cancerous cell was responsible for the cancer: the nucleus or the cytoplasm. So they extracted the nucleus from each of two cells – from a cancerous frog *cell* and from a healthy frog *egg* (that is, from the single female germ cell that develops, after fertilization, into a tadpole). Then they transplanted the nucleus from the cancerous cell into the egg. If the nucleus was responsible for the cancer, they reasoned, the tadpole that developed from the egg would be abnormal. But the tadpole appeared to be healthy, although it was short-lived. The scientists had to conclude that a cell may become cancerous because of changes not in the nucleus, but in the cytoplasm.

Theory When damaged by X-rays or chemicals, the power plants in the cytoplasm of a cell (the mitochondria) may stop producing energy. This change in the behavior of the mitochondria may cause a cell to become cancerous.

Scientists who reject this theory point out that many cancerous tumors do, in fact, use the mitochondria to produce energy. Proponents of the theory argue that damage to the mitochondria may account for some cancers, but not for others.

ABNORMALITIES IN THE CELL MEMBRANE
Theory Cancerous cells may spread from a tumor (metastasize) to distant parts of the body because of some element in the cell membrane. In order to test this theory, scientists are looking for differences between the membranes of normal and cancerous cells, and also between the membranes of cancerous cells that metastasize easily and cancerous cells that do not.

OTHER
Theory Supposedly present in all the organs of the body are immature (undifferentiated) cells – cells that have not matured, for example, into skin, or kidney, or bone. Scientists propose that these cells have failed to mature for one of two reasons: (i) because the cells have been damaged; or (ii) because the body keeps in reserve undeveloped cells (called stem cells) that mature, in time of injury, and thus help the body to heal. If X-rays or chemicals provoke a damaged cell into dividing, or a stem cell into dividing prematurely, a cancerous tumor may form.

Theory Cancerous changes in a cell may be caused by proteins (antibodies) that "attack" the cell's genes. These proteins, it is argued, are produced by the body in order to keep dead cells from becoming toxic. But since dead cells are similar to cells that are still alive, the proteins may accidentally attack a living cell and damage some of its genes. If the genes that are damaged control cell division, cancer may result.

How are scientists trying to control cancer?

By exploring at least five different means to control the causes of cancer and to treat the disease effectively when it does occur. In particular, scientists are seeking:

1 To inhibit the action of cancer-causing agents. When exposed to cancer-causing chemicals, viruses, or X-rays, some people get cancer and some do not. If scientists can learn why some people are unaffected, perhaps they can provide protection to the others. Already scientists know, in a few instances, how to use one chemical to counteract the damaging effects of a second chemical. Through further research, they may find other ways to make cancer-causing agents safe.

2 To make the body resistant to cancer. Scientists are looking for vaccines or chemicals to stimulate the body's natural defenses – that is, its immune system – so that the body will destroy cancerous cells before they can start to form tumors.

3 To achieve earlier detection of cancer. Scientists who study patterns of disease in large populations (epidemiologists) are learning to predict which people have a high risk of developing cancer. Such factors as family history, exposure to carcinogens, or blood types can be used to identify people who are susceptible to particular cancers. Once these people have been warned, annual diagnostic tests may help them to discover cancer early, while it can still be cured. Because existing diagnostic tests are often costly, uncomfortable, and even inaccurate (see pp. 35–37), scientists are trying to develop better tests – in particular, chemical tests, like the one that detects, from the presence of a certain hormone in the blood, cancer of the placenta (choriocarcinoma).

4 To cure cells that have become cancerous. By altering the hormones, chemicals, or genetic material of cancerous cells, scientists may be able to correct the cancer-causing defect and make the cells normal again.

5 To develop new means of treating cancerous growths. When surgery, radiotherapy, and chemotherapy are combined in new ways, cancers that were once incurable can sometimes be cured. But a great many doctors and scientists think that significant advances in treatment will be made only when the body's immune system can be made to cooperate in a cure. For example, after a major growth has been surgically

removed, the body must be made to destroy any cancerous cells that remain.

How do scientists keep up with current research?

By subscribing to scientific journals, by attending seminars and meetings, and by visiting laboratories around the world to observe the work of other scientists.

Although it is conceivable that experiments may be needlessly duplicated, that potentially fruitful collaborations may fail to take place, and that differences in standards of measurement may cause one scientist's work to be unintelligible to another, international organizations are promoting cooperation among scientists from many countries.

The World Health Organization, for example, supports an International Agency for Research on Cancer. And the International Union Against Cancer has helped organize an International Scientist-to-Scientist Information Exchange Program. This program assists small groups working on similar projects in different countries to exchange news about their work.

In the United States, the National Cancer Institute maintains an International Cancer Research Data Bank that has a computer service for retrieving summaries of published papers on cancer research, descriptions of current research projects, and information about the newest methods for treating cancer. With terminals in five hundred locations within the United States and additional terminals in nine foreign countries, this computer is available for use by many thousands of scientists.

None of these services, however, can promote communication unless research groups agree to speak the same scientific language. If a group in Japan, for example, tests a cancer drug on one strain of melanoma cells, while a group in Russia tests the same drug – or another one – on a different strain of melanoma cells, their findings may not be comparable. For this reason, scientists have established standard strains of cancer cells to be used as the standard measure of reference in laboratories throughout the world. For example, during a conference in Geneva in September, 1974, they agreed that L1210 leukemia cells would be a standard strain. Scientists who wish to cooperate in this agreement can receive samples of these cells, along with standard reference drugs, from the National Cancer Institute in Bethesda, Maryland. In addition, scientists engaged in cancer research can consult the International Classifications of Diseases for Oncology – a text now in its eighth edition – for standard terms by which to classify cancerous tumors.

Note: Most scientists throughout the world are trained to speak and write in English, so that scientific seminars and papers can be understood by research groups in all countries.

How long will it take to cure cancer?

When the United States Congress passed the National Cancer Act in 1971, politicians, and even a few scientists, promised a cure or a vaccine for cancer within five years. Now James Watson, winner of the Nobel prize for his work on the structure of genes, estimates that it may be twenty-five to fifty years before scientists know what molecular changes take place when a cell becomes cancerous. To cure or prevent the disease will probably take much longer.

Understandably, people feel cheated. Promises have been made and not fulfilled. Critics of the National Cancer Act are demanding that the government reduce its support for cancer research. If scientists cannot proceed with reasonable speed, argue the critics, perhaps they should not proceed at all.

But science cannot choose the speed at which it advances; nor does it yield predictable results. In 1846, for example, the distinguished doctor Henry Bence Jones was asked to analyze some "animal matter" found in the urine of a patient with cancer of the bone (multiple myeloma). Jones identified the matter as a protein, but was unable to determine its source. For more than 100 years, no one could explain the Bence-Jones protein, as that animal matter came to be called. Even when the protein was finally identified as a product of the immune system, the identification had no particular significance for cancer research. But it did promote scientific knowledge of the body's immune system and thus enabled doctors to perform organ transplants and to understand the nature of respiratory infections and allergies. By a remarkably crooked path, a question in cancer research – the Bence-Jones inquiry – has led to answers in several other fields of medicine. Perhaps one day the path will lead back to cancer, if immunotherapy can be made to serve effectively as a cancer treatment.

Science may seem to be slow; but in all fairness, it is likely to discover a cure before people engage in prevention. As Sir Richard Doll, Regius Professor of Medicine at Oxford University, has remarked: "If prevention of cancer requires a change in smoking habits, drinking habits, eating habits, exposure to sunlight and sexual relations – it may be such change won't be universally adopted tomorrow. It may prove in the long run easier to control the incidence of cancer by controlling the basic mechanism in the cell." Before growing impatient with science, people should perhaps grow impatient with themselves.

How much money for research is enough?

By the end of the 1970s, the United States will have spent approximately $7 billion on cancer research. The rest of the world will have spent at least another billion, and perhaps much more. But despite this expenditure of money, two-thirds of all cancer patients will still die from the disease.

Many people want an accounting: an accurate description of what has been learned from basic research; a full report of recent advances in the diagnosis and treatment of cancer; a list of the causes of cancer and the ways in which these causes are being controlled. Such an accounting is right and necessary. People should know what science has accomplished, lest they expect too much – or too little – from their doctors and their governments. But no account, however satisfactory or disappointing, can determine public policy. A balance sheet of results is no measure of the value of research.

Science proceeds by leaps of imagination that cannot be purchased for a fixed price. Billions of dollars may be spent on modest advances that one day, quite by accident, spark an important idea. Were the billions wasted or well spent? Would the idea have happened in any case? Maybe yes, maybe no. The point is: science cannot be judged as a cost-effective enterprise.

Affluent societies must consider that research is an investment in the future. The greater the number of scientists they support, the greater the likelihood that a cure will be found. But the cure will be costly. If cancer were simply a matter of money, scientific research would not be worthwhile. But since it is rather a matter of life, extravagant expenditures for research may be not only tolerable, but even desirable.

THE FUTURE OF TREATMENT

What is the future of surgery, radiotherapy, and chemotherapy?

In surgery, techniques are well advanced, so great improvements are unlikely. But some new techniques are under study: for example, freezing tumors with liquid nitrogen (cryosurgery), and burning them with laser beams or with a "jet-cutter" – an instrument that exposes tissue to scorching heat produced by ionized gas. Surgery in the future, moreover, will profit from advances in a variety of support services. Improvements in plastic surgery, for example, will enable doctors to reconstruct badly deformed faces and limbs. In addition new procedures for transplanting organs, and more effective antibiotics will greatly increase a patient's chances for recovery.

In radiotherapy, great improvements may be possible with neutrons or pions (tiny atomic particles). In particular, pions (which are also called pi mesons) may enable doctors to concentrate radioactive energy in a tumor so that normal tissue suffers little damage. Pions may also be effective against cancer in volumes far smaller than those needed with X-rays, which are now used in most radiotherapy. But pions are remarkably expensive to produce; and existing accelerators cannot create pion beams of sufficient intensity to destroy large tumors. At the Los Alamos Meson Physics Facility in New Mexico, scientists are trying to overcome these difficulties.

In chemotherapy, there is always the possibility that new drugs or new combinations of drugs will produce new cures. During the past decade, for example, cancer of the testicle and childhood leukemia have become curable because of improvements in chemotherapy. In recent laboratory experiments, it has been shown that if cells from a patient's tumor are grown in a laboratory dish and treated with drugs, doctors can discover which drugs are best suited for treating the patient's cancer. At present, though, such a procedure is too costly and complex for use in most hospitals.

Finally, surgery, radiotherapy, and chemotherapy may be combined imaginatively to cure cancers that are now regarded as incurable.

What new treatments are being devised?

One treatment currently being studied is *hyperthermia* – the application of heat to patients with cancerous tumors. Heat may be applied to the area of the tumor with a high-frequency electric current; or the patient may be anaesthetized, wrapped in blankets or a space suit, and subjected to temperatures ranging from 108°F to 110°F. Because cancerous cells are destroyed by levels of heat that are relatively harmless to normal cells, hyperthermia can shrink a tumor. But this treatment has never produced a cure, since it cannot destroy every cancerous cell in the body. Moreover, if it causes a tumor to shrink too rapidly, as sometimes happens, the patient can die from the flood of poisons that are suddenly released by the dead cancerous cells.

At a recent meeting, cancer specialists described a new treatment in which a radioactive substance was combined with a protein (an antibody) that has a magnet-like attraction for the patient's tumor. When the protein reaches the tumor, the radioactive substance destroys the cancerous cells. Since the protein may be able to reach small tumors hidden in the far recesses of the body, this treatment may prove useful for widespread cancer (metastasis).

Of all the new treatments under investigation, possibly the most promising is *immunotherapy*, a form of treatment in which the body's immune system is activated to help cure the patient.

What is the immune system?

The immune system defends the body against foreign intruders. A few of these intruders – like transplanted organs – are friendly; but most – like viruses and bacteria – are harmful. Every intruder bears on its surface a fingerprint (a chemical) known as an antigen. This antigen identifies the intruder and warns the body of potential harm. When the body senses the presence of an antigen, it prepares to launch an attack.

In one type of attack, white blood cells from the thymus gland (T-cells) touch the intruder and make an imprint of its antigen. The T-cells then mature and multiply into an army of killers programmed to find the intruder and destroy it.

In another type of attack, white blood cells from the bone marrow (B-cells) touch the intruder and, in response to its antigen, form antibodies that render the intruder harmless.

Once an intruder is destroyed or disarmed, the scavenger cells of the body – the macrophages – clear away the debris. Meanwhile, the body retains a memory of the intruder's fingerprint, or antigen, so that any future invasion by the same intruder can be quickly and efficiently crushed. It is this memory of particular antigens that creates in the body an immunity against specific diseases. A vaccine can also create an immunity, by exposing the body to small amounts of an antigen. In so doing, the vaccine creates in the body a "memory" of an intruder that has not yet staged an invasion.

Why is the immune system important in cancer research?

Scientists have shown that many cancer patients have deficient immune systems. Cancer patients, for example, accept transplanted grafts of skin much more easily than healthy people. Perhaps they do so because their immune systems have been weakened by radiotherapy and chemotherapy – or by the cancer-causing agents that originally induced their cancers. But the very fact that cancer-causing agents do weaken the body's immune system is curious. Scientists wonder why these agents suppress the immune system. They wonder, too, why people with suppressed or deficient immune systems run ten times the normal risk of developing cancer, and why cancer patients whose immune systems are severely suppressed respond to radiotherapy and chemotherapy less readily than those whose systems are still somewhat active.

The immune system, clearly, is related to cancer. But how? No one knows for sure, although scientists think that a strong immune system may act as a natural – if sometimes inadequate – defense against cancerous changes in the body.

How does the immune system react to cancerous cells?

The most familiar theory is the "immune surveillance theory," which states that in healthy people cancerous cells arise with surprising frequency, but a vigilant immune system keeps the cells from doing harm. Before a cancerous cell has time to divide and grow into a lethal tumor, the body's white blood cells destroy it and bear it away.

If the immune surveillance theory is right, then a cancerous tumor results when the immune system fails to recognize the enemy. But not all scientists agree. Some theorize that a single cancerous cell cannot possibly provoke the immune system into reacting. Instead, it may take hundreds or perhaps even thousands of cells to raise an alarm. But, by then, the alarm is fruitless: the cancerous tumor is too large or too powerful to be destroyed by the body's own defenses.

A third theory holds that the immune system tries to establish an immunity against every intruder that invades the body. But an immunity – that is, a memory of the intruder (see pp. 237–238) – can be established only if the system encounters and destroys an intruder in large quantities. What, then, of intruders that do not occur in large quantities? The immune system may first enhance or encourage them to multiply; then, when the intruders have multiplied sufficiently, it may destroy them and all their offspring – thereby establishing immunity. Such behavior, of course, has its dangers. If the immune system enhances the growth of especially murderous intruders (for example, cancerous cells), it may find itself overwhelmed by the intruders before it can kill them.

Still another possibility is that cancerous cells cannot be destroyed by the immune system, perhaps because the cells secrete a substance – a "Blocking Factor" – that protects them from harm.

Unfortunately, scientists have no idea which of these theories comes closest to the truth. The immune system is complex; knowledge of its behavior is incomplete. As always in cancer research, the lesson is plain: the body must be better known before cancer can be understood.

Can stress and/or mental depression cause cancer?

Perhaps, especially if the immune system is meant to guard against cancerous cells in the body. Stress, whether mental or physical, increases the activity of the adrenal gland, which in turn suppresses the immune system. Similarly, mental depression, by producing hormonal and chemical changes that are not well understood, can also suppress the immune system. Should cancerous cells arise in the body while the immune system is suppressed and off guard, a cancerous tumor may form – a tumor that has, in a sense, been "caused" by stress or mental depression.

How may the immune system be used to control cancer?

If cancerous cells, like foreign intruders, bear fingerprints (antigens), the immune system may, like a good detective, be able to track them down or perhaps even destroy them. Consider how this work may be done.

1 Prevention (*immunoprophylaxis*). Vaccines may be developed to strengthen the immune system, so that the body will kill a cancerous cell as soon as it appears – or better yet, as soon as a normal cell behaves suspiciously, whether or not the cell has become cancerous. Other types of vaccines may enable the body to neutralize a cancer-causing chemical or virus.

2 Detection. Particular kinds of cancerous cells may be found to have special fingerprints – that is, tumor-associated antigens. Doctors may learn how to test for these antigens and so detect a cancer early, before a perceptible tumor has formed. Two such antigens are chorioembryonic antigen (CEA), which is sometimes found in patients with cancer of the colon, and alphafetoprotein, which is often found in patients with cancer of the testicle. Unfortunately, neither antigen has enabled doctors to detect an early cancer in these organs.

3 Treatment (*immunotherapy*). A means may be found to stimulate the immune systems of cancer patients, so that their bodies destroy any cancerous cells left behind after surgery, radiotherapy, or chemo-therapy. Few, if any, doctors expect that immunotherapy alone will ever be sufficient to cure a patient with advanced cancer. But when a primary tumor has been removed or treated with X-rays or drugs, the immune system may then be persuaded to eradicate surviving cancerous cells and small secondary tumors.

Many doctors, in fact, suspect that the only patients who are cured are those whose immune systems reinforce their therapies. It is likely, for example, that surgery and radiotherapy usually fail to destroy some cancerous cells that have traveled far from the site of the primary tumor. Even drugs, which circulate throughout the body, can easily miss cancerous cells hidden in the brain or in other drug-resistant tissue. Thus, patients who have been cured of their cancers are probably those who were able to help cure themselves. Immunotherapy may one day assure that all patients have this ability.

Is there likely to be a vaccine against cancer?

A vaccine creates immunity by enabling the body to recognize a potential intruder's fingerprints – that is, its antigen (see pp. 237–238). Antigens are found on the surfaces of (i) all cancer-causing viruses; (ii) some cancer-causing chemicals; (iii) most cancerous cells. So a vaccine against cancer-causing agents – or even against cancer itself –

is theoretically possible. But a cure-all vaccine (one that is effective against all agents or all cancers) will be difficult for scientists to develop.

A vaccine against cancer-causing agents, for example, would have to immunize the body against hundreds or perhaps thousands of agents, each with a different fingerprint. In all probability, there is an easier way to control cancer-causing chemicals: namely, by identifying and banning those chemicals that cause cancer in a high percentage of the people exposed to them. Cancer-causing viruses are another matter. If it can be proved, for example, that leukemia or Burkitt's lymphoma is associated with a particular virus, a vaccine against that virus might be an efficient means of controlling the cancer. But such a vaccine would immunize the body against only one cancer – or, more precisely, against only one cause of one cancer. No small achievement, but no cure-all either.

For a vaccine to be effective against all cancers, it will most likely have to immunize the body not against cancer-causing agents, but rather against cancerous cells. These cells, however, may have as many different fingerprints as do cancer-causing agents. Perhaps more. In experiments with animals, for example, scientists have found that cancers caused by a virus always bear the same fingerprints; but cancers caused by a chemical do not. Unless all cancerous cells have some fingerprint in common, scientists may find it impossible to develop a vaccine against them.

Of course, even if a vaccine is developed, it must be proven safe. Doctors could not take the chance of vaccinating millions of infants against a disease like childhood leukemia only to discover twenty, thirty, or forty years later that the vaccine causes leukemia, or another cancer, in adults. Since a great deal of time can elapse between exposure to a cancer-causing agent and the appearance of cancer in the body, any proposed vaccine will have to undergo many years of tests before it can be certified as safe.

What kinds of immunotherapy are there?

Any attempt to restore the immune system to its normal strength (*immunorestoration*) or to endow it with more than normal strength is a form of immunotherapy. Since the immune system is usually suppressed by a cancerous growth, surgery to remove such a growth is, strictly speaking, a form of immunorestoration. Similarly, since the immune system is suppressed by X-rays and cancer drugs, a short interruption in a program of radiotherapy or chemotherapy may serve as a form of immunorestoration, if it enables the system to recover its strength. But when doctors speak of immunorestoration or immunotherapy, they generally refer to procedures still being developed in laboratory experiments with animals and in field tests with humans. These procedures are passive immunotherapy and active immunotherapy.

What is passive immunotherapy?

Passive immunotherapy requires two people: Person A, who has cancer; and Person B, who is injected with some of A's cancerous cells. Because A's cells are utterly foreign to B, B's immune system attacks them. As a result of this attack, B becomes immune to A's cancer. Parts of B's immune system – his blood serum or his white blood cells – may then be injected into A's body. There, it is hoped, they will again attack A's cancer, and kill it.

Passive immunotherapy, then, is the practice of treating a cancer patient with substances obtained from the immune system of another person.

In experiments with animals, passive immunotherapy has been used to kill cancerous cells. But in human beings, the therapy has not been successful, because blood serum and white blood cells from another person are usually rejected by the cancer patient's body.

What is active immunotherapy?

In active immunotherapy, the cancer patient is injected with a foreign substance – one that provokes his immune system to launch an attack. It is hoped that during this attack, the immune system will destroy not only the foreign substance, but also the patient's cancer.

Because most of the substances that can provoke the immune system are toxic, even lethal, research in active immunotherapy is more often conducted on laboratory animals than on human beings. The most widely studied substance in both animals and humans is BCG – a vaccine composed of weakened live bacteria. Commonly used in Europe to immunize people against tuberculosis, BCG has proved effective against some cancers in animals when the BCG is administered in large amounts.

But in humans, its effect on a tumor is generally unpredictable. Although good results have been obtained in some patients with cancer of the skin (melanoma) or with acute myelocytic leukemia, BCG is known to cause some serious side effects, including death. Hence scientists have begun to experiment with bacteria other than those contained in BCG, as well as with parts of bacteria – for example, their membranes or cytoplasm. Preliminary results suggest that some of these parts may be less toxic than BCG and also more effective in suppressing the growth of tumors.

Of course, BCG and similar substances give the immune system no specific information about the fingerprint (antigen) of the tumor it is meant to destroy. Thus, they excite a "nonspecific" response. An immune system excited by *nonspecific immunotherapy* is not unlike a plane strafing a broad area of forest. No doubt the plane will kill some prey. But it would certainly kill many more if the pilot could sight his target and take aim. For this reason, some scientists are experimenting with another form of active immunotherapy – namely, *specific immunotherapy*, which would enable the immune system to take specific aim against a particular cancer. In one experiment with specific immunotherapy, scientists obtained some antigen from a patient's tumor, united that antigen with another, more powerful antigen, and then injected the patient with the new "double-barreled" antigen. In another experiment, scientists removed part of a patient's tumor, extracted the nuclei from the tumorous cells (that is, enucleated them), and injected the patient with the enucleated cellular material. In each case, the injected substance provoked the patient's immune system to attack his own cancer; but no cures have yet been produced. Only further study will reveal how, why, and – most important – when such procedures can be safely and effectively used for the treatment of patients with cancer.

What is Coley's toxin?

Coley's toxin, a mildly poisonous mixture of bacterial substances, was developed at the turn of the century by Dr. William Coley as a remedy for cancer. Coley had observed that cancer is sometimes cured in a patient who contracts a serious infection like cholera – if, of course, the patient survives the infection. Most do not. So in October 1891, Coley attempted to cure a cancer patient by infecting him with a less serious type of infection – an acute fever-producing skin disease called erysipelas. Coley's patient survived and was cured; but the treatment was too harsh for most others. So Coley developed a milder treatment – the toxin.

In general, Coley's toxin proved worthless; but there were nevertheless reports that it had produced some cures. Coley believed that his remedy could work by creating a fever to burn away cancerous cells. And in part he may have been right: scientists now know that cancerous cells often die from levels of heat that are relatively harmless to normal cells. But if Coley's toxin in fact produced cures, it probably did so by provoking in patients an immune response. The toxin, in short, was most likely an early – and not very effective – form of active immunotherapy.

What are the limitations of immunotherapy?

Doctors estimate that the body's immune system, when strengthened by immunotherapy, may be able to kill between 1 and 10 million cancerous cells. But the smallest detectable tumor contains at least 1 billion cells. Thus, unless study of the immune system enables doctors to design new forms of immunotherapy – forms not yet even imagined – immunotherapy will serve only to supplement, not to replace, treatment with surgery, X-rays, and drugs.

What are the side effects of immunotherapy?

Any substance that provokes an immune response may cause asthmatic attacks. In addition, BCG has been known to cause malaise, muscle pain, fever, acute infection, and hepatitis. But the primary danger of immunotherapy is that patients may become resistant to treatment, may entirely lose their immune response to cancer, and may die from a recurrence of the disease.

Has immunotherapy ever produced any cures?

Although information from field tests is inconclusive, immunotherapy appears to have had some effect in a few individuals. In patients with cancer of the skin (melanoma), for example, immunotherapy may prevent the cancer from recurring after surgery. In adults with acute myelocytic leukemia, it may delay the inevitable recurrence of the disease. And in patients with early cancer of the lung, it may help to prolong life. But aside from several reports that BCG can eradicate small cancers of the skin, immunotherapy has produced no cures.

Most field tests, of course, have been conducted on patients who are terminally ill – patients, in other words, who were unlikely to be cured by immunotherapy or any other means. It may seem, then, that immunotherapy has not been given a fair chance to prove itself, especially since scientists doubt that the immune system, at its best, can destroy more than a few million cancerous cells. But human life comes before research. Doctors have quite properly been unwilling to test immunotherapy on patients with early cancer – except when they have had good reason to believe not merely that immunotherapy will cure the patient as efficiently as other treatments, but rather that it will cure him *more* efficiently. Not until extensive field tests with the terminally ill suggest that immunotherapy may be the treatment of choice (see p. 225) for particular cancers, will immunotherapy be given its "fair chance."

What is the future of immunotherapy?

Because the immune system is barely understood by scientists and doctors, immunotherapy proceeds by trial and error. Doctors must try a particular form of immunotherapy, estimate roughly whether the therapy produces an immune response in the patient, and conclude whether the therapy has or has not been effective in controlling the cancer. Of course, by its very nature, trial and error involves numerous mistakes – many more mistakes than the average cancer patient can afford. Thus, until immunotherapy becomes more sophisticated, it must be reserved, with few exceptions, for patients who are terminally ill and therefore willing to risk a treatment that may have unpredictable results.

The research that will improve immunotherapy will have to address a variety of questions. For example: Do human cancers have special fingerprints (tumor-related antigens)? Is there a "Blocking Factor" that protects some cancers from the immune system? Does immunotherapy kill cancerous cells, or does it merely keep them from dividing? Is there a right dose and a right time for using immunotherapy? Can the immune system destroy cancerous cells when drugs cannot reach them – for example, when they are hidden in the brain? Are all substances that provoke an immune response useful in controlling cancer?

So long as these questions remain unanswered, immunotherapy will be only a promising child: a prodigy without discipline or direction. But many scientists believe that the child may mature into the most effective and versatile of treatments. On the strength of this belief, scientists continue to explore the nature and potential of the immune system.

Conclusion

Better is the end of a thing than the beginning thereof.

Ecclesiastes 7:8

The origins of a book are not unlike the sources of a mountain stream. Innumerable rivulets, drawn by gravity, coalesce, one after another, and with increasing momentum run downhill to form a single river of water. In much the same way, innumerable events, phrases, impressions, and memories coalesce over time to form the idea for a book. Even a book like this one, which reveals so little of its authors, originated in personal experience: an afternoon of browsing through Dillon's University Bookshop, across the street from University College, London; months of reading in ancient textbooks on medicine; a conversation with a surgeon during a drive from Los Angeles to Yosemite National Park; a death in the family; a nagging suspicion that medical terminology may be only a cloak to disguise how little doctors really know about mind and body.

Perhaps this book would never have happened if Dillon's, that most wonderful of bookstores, did not shelve books on the history of medicine near books on modern medical practice. An innocent search for information on medieval cautery and ligature so easily led, one day in fall 1976, to a disappointing, even an indignant, search for information on cancer. Though cancer books for the non-specialist abounded, they were mostly superficial. The nature of the disease, its symptoms, and its treatment seemed hardly to be addressed. Instead, prevention and cure were described in statements that were unduly optimistic and often poorly written. Surely a different kind of book was needed.

A few blocks from Dillon's is the Wellcome Library, with its vast collection of books on medicine from all periods of history. In one alcove of the library are most of the books on cancer. What they show is that until quite recently very little was known about the disease. (It is only in the last twenty-five years that research in cell biology has begun to reveal the complexity of the human cell.) What ancient doctors practiced, modern doctors still practice, though with greater skill and subtlety. Both old theories and new caution against imprudent treatment, lest the disease spread. One ancient writer specifically warns against treating a tumor of the Egyptian god Xensu (probably a tropical ulcer) because "something arises therein as though wind were in it, causing irritation. The tumor calls with a loud voice to thee, 'It is a tumor of the god Xensu. Do thou nothing there against.'"

"To do nothing," comes an echo, "is often better than cutting a tumor and spreading it throughout the body." The words were spoken by a surgeon in 1960, somewhere between Los Angeles and Yosemite National Park. "I have known doctors to operate on black moles that they thought were benign," he explained. "But they were melanomas. And the patient died in a matter of weeks." That thought – of a doctor causing a cancer to spread because of his failure to recognize the difference between a benign and a malignant tumor – lingers yet.

And so too does the memory of a gentle man who, in 1965, at the age of fifty-nine, died in Philadelphia. A heavy smoker, a plumber, he worked during World War II at Cramp's shipyard among the asbestos. By the time his cancer was discovered, it had already spread to his brain; within weeks it had crippled him. When his doctor was asked whether an early diagnosis could have saved his life, the reply was: "Even if we had discovered the cancer in his lung two years ago, the only advantage that I can see is that you would have known two years earlier that he was going to die." The doctor, who had been consulted only when it was far too late for him to be of use, was saying what had been said 3,500 years ago: that some tumors are best left alone.

But what of those tumors that are best treated? How should they be treated? Is the treatment painful? How often does it work? What if it doesn't work? In the course of writing this book, the authors pursued these questions, and many other clinical problems, with Dr. A. Robert Kagan, Chief, Department of Radiation Therapy, Southern California Permanente Medical Group, and his colleague Dr. Harvey A. Gilbert. With David M. Prescott, Professor of Molecular, Cellular, and Developmental Biology at the University of Colorado, Boulder, they pursued theoretical issues: What are cells? How do they function? What causes them to go awry? Is there any way to correct the mechanism of a misguided cell? For David Prescott, these questions were familiar. Because he teaches a course every spring in the biology of cancer, he is often approached by students when cancer strikes their families. "They have no one else to ask, no place to go for information," he explains. "So they come to me."

This book is a place to go for information. For facts. But fact and opinion are often difficult to separate. If cancer can be likened to an insurrection, then the clinical doctors are soldiers in the field, who think that the insurrection can be put down by attacking the law-breakers with chemical warfare, radiation, and knives. The scientists, by contrast, are theorists in the laboratory, who think that cancer can be eradicated by discovering what initially causes the lawbreaker (the misguided cell) to misbehave. Since both camps have their strengths, both camps must be fairly represented. Whether this book makes a fair representation remains to be judged.

Whether it makes a clear representation – in a graceful style that neither obscures nor falsifies – also remains to be judged. It was the authors' intention to honor the precept, according to John: in the beginning was the word. The word created the world. And to some degree it still does. Every day, through language, people fashion the world in their own image, or at least in their own language. How people speak – their choice of words, grammar, cadences – reveals the way they view their lives. What they say reflects what they are. In their language can be read their education and occupations, their experience and prejudices, their state of mind and attitude toward others. The language in this book is no different. If read with discernment, it should reveal a concern for the ear, as well as the eye; a desire to be understood rather than to be technical. It should reveal a bias for short sentences and an avoidance of lines choked with syllables; a preference for simple words and a limited use of polysyllabic ones. In the questions the authors ask are to be found their interests, in the answers their anxieties. If an ease of language cloaks their rough labor, then they have successfully disguised the caustic tools of polish.

Doubt, of course, remains: perhaps more polish might have yielded greater ease. But just as a craftsman may spoil his work by failing to perfect it, so too may he spoil it by never having done with it. He makes an adjustment here, a correction there; he alters this and changes that. Endlessly, until the work slowly and imperceptibly loses its form. Lest the authors of this book be guilty of not knowing that

> That which is crooked cannot be made straight:
> and that which is wanting cannot be numbered

they end.

GLOSSARY

Adjuvant treatment
  Drugs or X-rays administered
  before or after surgery as a
  precautionary measure. Doctors
  use adjuvant treatment when
  they are uncertain if a cancer
  has spread beyond the site of
  the original tumor.

Ames test
  A test to identify chemicals that
  alter the genetic structure of
  cells. Chemicals that do so
  are usually cancer-causing.

Anaesthesia
  Total or partial loss of
  sensation (especially, pain)
  and/or consciousness. An
  anaesthetic is a substance that
  produces anaesthesia. An
  anaesthesiologist is a doctor,
  and an *anaesthetist* a nurse,
  who administers an anaesthetic.

Analgesic
  A remedy that relieves or
  removes pain.

Antibiotic
  A drug – for example, penicillin
  – that is used to treat diseases
  caused by bacteria. Antibiotics
  are not effective against
  diseases caused by viruses.

Antibody
  A protein produced by the
  body's immune system in
  response to an intruder.
  Antibodies serve to render
  intruders harmless.

Antigen
  A protein that serves to identify
  intruders that have invaded the
  body. Antigens provoke the
  immune system to form
  antibodies.

Bacteria
  Single-celled organisms formed
  in the shape of rods, spheres,
  and spirals. Some bacteria are
  helpful to the body. Others
  cause disease – for example,
  tuberculosis.

Benign
  Favorable, gracious, kindly.
  Benign tumors are abnormal
  growths that are almost always
  enclosed in a fibrous capsule
  and do not spread to other parts
  of the body.

Biopsy
  A surgical procedure in which
  a doctor removes tissue from a
  tumor and examines it under a
  microscope.

Blood count
  A count of the number of white
  blood cells, red blood cells, and
  platelets in a sample of blood
  withdrawn from a patient's
  body. Abnormalities in the
  blood count may indicate
  infection, anemia, or danger of
  hemorrhaging.

Cachexia
  A general weakening of the
  body.

Carcinogen
  A cancer-causing chemical.

Carcinoma
  A cancer that originates in
  lining tissue – that is, the tissue
  that makes up the skin or lines

the intestine, kidney, mouth, uterus, lung, and other organs.

Catheter

A slender tube that can be passed into a blood vessel or through a canal (like the urethra, which leads to the bladder). Catheters are used to introduce fluids into the body (for example, blood) or to withdraw fluids (for example, urine).

Cell

The smallest unit of life. All living tissue is composed of cells.

Chemotherapy

Treatment in which a doctor destroys cancerous cells with drugs.

Clinical investigations

Investigations in which doctors test a new drug or treatment on human patients. Also called *clinical tests* and *field tests*.

Cobalt

A radioactive substance, used in radiotherapy. Cobalt produces gamma rays, a form of radiation very much like X-rays.

Co-carcinogen

A chemical that is not in itself cancer-causing, but that can somehow provoke another chemical to cause cancer.

Colostomy

An opening for feces constructed in the abdominal wall of a patient whose rectum has been removed.

Contagious

Communicable. A *contagious disease* is one that can be passed from one person to another.

Cure

The elimination of disease, so that a patient recovers his health. Since cancer may appear to be cured when it is not, doctors talk about cancer cures in terms of years: "a five year cure," "a six year cure," "a ten year cure."

Cyst

A small, benign sac filled with fluid or diseased matter.

Cytology

A form of examination in which cells are examined for the presence of cancer. The cells are taken from urine, from sputum, from smears of the nose, mouth, lungs, or cervix, or from washings of the stomach.

Cytoplasm

The soupy material that surrounds the nucleus of a cell.

Dehydration

Loss of fluid.

Diagnosis

A medical identification of a patient's disease.

Dialysis

The use of a kidney machine to remove impurities from a patient's blood.

Differentiated cells

Mature cells that perform a specific function in the body – – for example, blood cells, bone cells, or skin cells.

Edema

A swelling caused by the accumulation of fluid in the body's tissues.

Environment
    The air, earth, food, and water
    that comprise the community
    people live and work in.
Epidemiology
    The study of how and why
    diseases spread in large
    populations. An *epidemiologist*
    is a scientist or doctor who
    specializes in epidemiology.
Euthanasia
    Mercy killing.
Gene
    A unit of heredity. Genes reside
    in the nucleus of a cell.
Germ cell
    An egg cell or a sperm cell.
    When fertilized by a sperm cell,
    an egg cell begins to divide in
    order to form a baby.
Hemorrhage
    Heavy, uncontrolled bleeding.
Heredity
    The transmission from parent to
    child of characteristics (for
    example, hair color) that are
    determined by the genes.
Hormone
    A chemical produced by a gland.
    The hormone estrogen, for
    example, is produced by the
    ovaries; testosterone, by the
    testicles.
Hospice
    A hospital specially equipped
    for the care of dying patients.
Immune system
    The body's line of defense
    against disease.
Immunity
    Protection against a specific
    disease. The body normally
    creates immunity by forming
    antibodies against bacteria and

viruses that cause disease.
Immunotherapy
    Treatment that stimulates the
    body's immune system to
    destroy cancerous cells.
Impotence
    Inability to engage in sexual
    intercourse. In men, impotence
    usually means the inability to
    experience an erection.
Laryngectomy
    Surgical removal of the vocal
    cords or the voicebox (the
    larynx).
Leukemia
    A cancer that originates in the
    blood-forming tissue of the bone
    marrow or the lymph nodes.
Lymphatic system
    A drainage system that cleanses
    the fluid between cells and
    deposits the wastes from that
    fluid into the body's blood
    system. *Lymph* is the fluid that
    flows through the lymphatic
    vessels.
Lymphoma
    A cancer that originates in the
    body's lymphatic tissue – that is,
    the lymph nodes or the lymph
    tissue of such organs as the
    stomach, small intestine, and
    bone.
Lymph nodes
    Tiny glands that act as way
    stations in the body's lymphatic
    system. Fluids in the lymphatic
    vessels pass through the lymph
    nodes to be cleansed of
    impurities.
Macrophages
    Scavenger cells that bear away
    dead cells and other debris in
    the body.

Malignant
Harmful, hateful, cancerous.
Cancerous tumors are abnormal
growths that have the ability to
spread to other parts of the
body.

Mammography
X-ray examination of the
breast. A mammogram can
detect breast tumors while they
are still too small to be felt.

Mastectomy
Surgical removal of the breast.

Metabolism
The process by which the body's
cells convert food to energy.

Metastasis
The spreading of cancerous
cells from the site of the
original tumor to distant parts
of the body.

Metastatic pathway
The path traveled by cancerous
cells when they spread from a
tumor to distant parts of the
body.

Mucous membranes
The lining tissue of such organs
as the mouth and the intestine.
By producing juices
(secretions), the mucous
membranes keep these organs
moist.

Mutation
A change in the structure of a
gene.

Nucleus
The heart of the cell. The
nucleus contains the genes.

Oncology
The branch of medicine that
studies tumors. An *oncologist* is
a doctor who specializes in
oncology.

Palliation
Relief from the pain of disease.

Pap smear
A simple and painless test used
to detect cancer of the cervix
before a tumor can be seen or
felt.

Pathology
The branch of medicine that
studies disease. A *pathologist* –
a doctor who specializes in
pathology – examines cells
under a microscope in order to
discover evidence of disease.

Placebo
A harmless ineffective
substance, like a sugar pill,
given to a patient instead of a
drug.

Polyp
A small tumor that is usually
benign. Polyps often occur in
the mouth, bladder, or intestine.

Preclinical tests
Laboratory tests of a new drug
or treatment. Preclinical tests
must show that a drug or
treatment is safe and effective
before tests on human beings
are allowed.

Primary tumor
The original, or the first,
cancerous tumor to have
developed in a patient's body.

Prognosis
A medical prediction of how a
patient's disease may progress
and how likely the patient is to
recover.

Prosthetic device
An artificial device used to
replace a part of the body that
has been removed. Artificial
legs and false teeth are both

prosthetic devices.

Protein
A chemical containing, among other things, carbon, hydrogen, nitrogen, and oxygen.

Radiation
The energy produced from radioactive substances, or from machines that emit X-rays.

Radioactive isotope
A molecule that emits radiation.

Radiotherapy
Treatment in which a doctor destroys cancerous cells with X-rays.

Sarcoma
A cancer that originates in connective tissue and muscle – for example, bone and cartilage.

Secondary tumor
A tumor that develops in a distant part of the body as a result of cancerous cells having traveled beyond the site of the original tumor.

Staging operation
A series of biopsies on various organs and lymph nodes throughout the body. Doctors perform staging operations in order to determine how far a cancer has spread.

Surgery
Treatment in which a doctor removes cancerous tissue from the body by operating.

Symptomatic treatment
Treatment that seeks to relieve a patient's symptoms, rather than to cure his disease.

Therapeutic
Curative or healing.

Tissue
A collection of different cells organized to perform a specific function.

Tumor
An abnormal swelling or enlargement that serves no useful purpose in the body.

Undifferentiated cells
Immature cells that are incapable of performing their proper function in the body. An undifferentiated white blood cell, for example, cannot fight infection.

Urostomy
An opening for urine constructed in the abdominal wall of a patient whose bladder has been removed.

Vaccine
A substance injected into the body to create an immunity against a specific disease.

Virus
A small bit of genetic material encased in a coating of protein. Viruses, because they are parasites, can divide and multiply only when they feed on a living cell.

White blood cells
Cells that help the body to fight infection. White blood cells are produced in the bone marrow and the lymph nodes.

Xerography
X-ray examination of the breast. A xerogram is similar to a mammogram; but the xerogram uses more radiation and produces clearer pictures.

X-rays
Highly active, invisible beams of energy.

CANCER CENTERS

ARGENTINA
Buenos Aires
INSTITUTO DE ONCOLOGIA "ANGEL H.
  ROFFO"
"Angel H. Roff" Institute of Oncology
Avenida San Martin 5481
Buenos Aires, Argentina
Tel. 50-7100 53-0014 50-9128

AUSTRALIA
Melbourne
CANCER INSTITUTE (PETER
  MACCALLUM CLINIC)
481 Little Lonsdale Street
Melbourne, Victoria 3000, Australia
Tel. 602 1333

BELGIUM
Brussels
INSTITUT JULES BORDET
1 rue Héger Bordet
1000 Brussels, Belgium
Tel. 02/538 00 00
Louvain
CANCER INSTITUTE
Cliniques Universitaires (St-Raphaël)
Capucienenvoer 35
B-3000 Louvain, Belgium
Tel. (016) 22 84 21
CENTRUM VOOR GEZWELZIEKTEN
Louvain Cancer Center
Kapucijnenvoer 35
3000 Louvain, Belgium

BRAZIL
Rio de Janeiro
INSTITUTO NACIONAL DE CÂNCER
Brazilian National Cancer Institute
Praça Cruz Vermelha 23-ZC 86
20000 Rio de Janeiro, Brazil
Tel. (021) 222 7595
São Paulo
INST. CENTRAL-HOSP. A.C. CAMARGO –
  FUND. A. PRUDENTE

Central Inst. – A.C. Camargo Hosp. –
  A. Prudente Found.
Rua Prof. Antonio Prudente, 211
Postal Box 5271
01509 São Paulo, Brazil
Tel. 278. 8811

BULGARIA
Sofia
BULGARIAN ONCOLOGICAL RESEARCH
  INSTITUTE
Plovdivsko pole str. 6
1156 Sofia, Bulgaria
Tel. 72 05 45 and 72 06 54

CANADA
Edmonton
ALBERTA PROVINCIAL CANCER
  HOSPITALS BOARD
11560 University Avenue
Edmonton, Alberta, Canada
Tel. (403) 433-9461
Regina
ALLAN BLAIR MEMORIAL CLINIC
1555 Pasqua Street
Regina, Saskatchewan S4T 4L8,
Canada
Tel. (306) 527-9651
SASKATCHEWAN CANCER COMMISSION
4003 Dewdney Avenue
Regina, Saskatchewan S4T 4L8,
Canada
Tel. (306) 523-8288
Saskatoon
SASKATOON CANCER CLINIC
University Hospital, Saskatoon,
Saskatchewan S7N 0W8, Canada
Tel. (306) 343-9565
Toronto
ONTARIO CANCER INSTITUTE INC.
  PRINCESS MARGARET HOSPITAL
500 Sherbourne Street
Toronto, Ontario M4X 1K9, Canada
Tel. (416) 924-0671

Vancouver
BRITISH COLUMBIA CANCER INSTITUTE
2656 Heather Street
Vancouver, British Columbia V5Z-3J3,
Canada
Tel. (604) 874-9321
Winnipeg
MANITOBA CANCER TREATMENT AND
 RESEARCH FOUNDATION
700 Bannatyne Avenue
Winnipeg, Manitoba R3E 0V9, Canada
Tel. (204) 786-4731

CHILE
Santiago de Chile
INST. NACIONAL DEL RADIUM
 "DR. C. P. CORREA"
"Dr. C. P. Correa" National Radium
Institute
Zanartu No 1000, Casilla No 6677
Correo No 4, Santiago de Chile, Chile
Tel. 376008

CHINA
Peking
CHINESE ACADEMY OF MEDICAL
 SCIENCES – CANCER INSTITUTE
2 Ya Pao Lu, Chao Yang District
Peking, China
Tel. 55-6566

COLOMBIA
Bogotá
INSTITUTO NACIONAL DE CANCEROLOGÍA
Colombian National Cancer Institute
Calle la 9-85
Bogotá, Colombia
Tel. 46 60 19

CUBA
Havana
INSTITUTO DE ONCOLOGÍA Y
 RADIOBIOLOGÍA
Cuban Institute of Oncology and
 Radiobiology
29 and F Street
Havana 4, Cuba
Tel. 32-7531

CZECHOSLOVAKIA
Bratislava
ONKOLOGICKÝ ÚSTAV PRE SLOVENSKO
Slovakia Oncological Institute
Heydukova ulica č 10, 881 02
Bratislava, Czechoslovakia
Tel. 537 11, 575 41, 2, 3
Brno
ONKOLOGICKÝ ÚSTAV V BRNE
Brno Oncological Institute
Zlutý kopec 7
Brno, Czechoslovakia
Tel. 310
Prague
RADIOTHERAPEUTICKÁ KLINIKA
Prague Radiotherapy Institute
Na Truhlářce 100
18000 Prague 8, Czechoslovakia
Tel. 843945-7

DENMARK
Copenhagen
FINSEN INSTITUTE
Strandboulevarden 49
2100 Copenhagen, Denmark
Tel. 01-260850

EGYPT
Cairo
CAIRO UNIVERSITY CANCER INSTITUTE
Kasr El Aini Street, Cairo, Egypt
Tel. 843661; 842329

FRANCE
Angers
CENTRE PAUL PAPIN
Paul Papin Cancer Center
2 rue Moll
49036 Angers – Cédex, France
Tel. 883746
Bordeaux
FONDATION BERGONIÉ, CENTRE
 RÉGIONAL ANTICANCÉREUX
Bergonié Foundation Regional
 Cancer Center
180 rue de Saint-Genès
33076 Bordeaux Cédex, France
Tel. (56) 911325

Caen
CENTRE RÉGIONAL FRANÇOIS BACLESSE
François Baclesse Regional Cancer
  Center
Route de Lion sur Mer
14018 Caen Cédex, France
Tel. (31) 81 14 34

Dijon
CENTRE GEORGE – FRANÇOIS LECLERC
George – François Leclerc
  Anti-Cancer Center
1 Professor Marion Street
21034 Dijon Cédex, France
Tel. (80) 30 96 04

Lille
CENTRE OSCAR LAMBRET
Oscar Lambret Center
1 rue Frédéric Combemale
B. P. 3569, 59020 Lille Cédex, France
Tel. (20) 57 12 00

Lyon
CENTRE LÉON – BÉRARD
Léon Bérard Center
28 rue Laënnec
69373 Lyon Cédex 2, France
Tel. 16-78 74-08-36

Marseille
INSTITUT J. PAOLI – I. CALMETTES
J. Paoli – I. Calmettes Institute
232 Bd. de Sainte-Marguerite
13273 Marseilles Cédex 2, France
Tel. (91) 75 90 86

Montpellier
CENTRE REGIONAL DE LUTTE CONTRE
  LE CANCER
Montpellier Regional Cancer Center
Cliniques Saint Eloi
34059 Montpellier Cédex, France
Tel. (67) 63 28 73

Nantes
CENTRE ANTICANCÉREUX DE NANTES
Nantes Cancer Center
Quai Moncousu, 44035 Nantes Cédex,
  France
Tel. (40) 73 41 82

Nice
CENTRE ANTOINE LACASSAGNE
Antoine Lacassagne Center
36 Voie – Romaine
06054 Nice Cédex, France
Tel. (93) 80 54 23

Paris
FONDATION CURIE – INSTITUT DU
  RADIUM – SECTION MED & HOSP.
Curie Foundation – Radium Inst. –
  Med. & Hosp. Section
26 rue d'Ulm
75231 Paris Cédex 05, France
Tel. 6332360

Reims
INSTITUT JEAN-GODINOT
Jean-Godinot Institute
45 rue Cognacq Jay, B.P. 171
51056 Reims Cédex, France
Tel. (26) 06 05 04

Rennes
CENTRE RÉGIONAL DE LUTTE CONTRE
  LE CANCER DE RENNES
Rennes Regional Cancer Center
Pontachaillon
35000 Rennes, France
Tel. 59 16 04

Rouen
CENTRE HENRI-BECQUEREL
Henri-Becquerel Center
1 rue d'Amiens
76038 Rouen Cédex, France
Tel. 98 20 27

Saint-Cloud
CENTRE RENÉ HUGUENIN
René Huguenin Anti-Cancer Center
5 rue Gaston Latouche
92211 Saint-Cloud, France
Tel. 602-38-58

Strasbourg
CENTRE PAUL STRAUSS
Paul Strauss Regional Cancer Center
3 rue de la Poste de l'Hôpital
67085 Strasbourg Cédex, France
Tel. (88) 36 30 20

Toulouse
CENTRE CLAUDIUS REGAUD
Claudius Regaud Center
11 rue Piquemil
31300 Toulouse, France
Tel. (61) 42 94 27

Vandoeuvre
CENTRE ALEXIS VAUTRIN
Alexis Vautrin Center
R.N. 74, Brabois
54500 Vandoeuvre les Nancy, France
Tel. 55 81 66

Villejuif
INSTITUT GUSTAVE-ROUSSY
Gustave-Roussy Institute
16 bis avenue Paul-Vaillant Couturier
94800 Villejuif, France
Tel. 726 49-09

GERMANY
Berlin-Buch
ZENTRALINSTITUT FÜR
   KREBSFORSCHUNG
Central Institute for Cancer Research
Lindenberger Weg 80
1115 Berlin-Buch, Germany
   (Dem. Rep.)
Tel. 56 98 51

Essen
INNERE KLINIK (TUMORFORSCHUNG)
Essen Univ. Cancer Res. Center –
   Clinical Oncology Dept.
55 Hufelandstrasse
43 Essen 1, Germany (Fed. Rep.)
Tel. 0201/79911/2001

GREECE
Athens
HELLENIC ANTICANCER INSTITUTE
171 Alexandras Avenue
Athens 603, Greece
Tel. (21) 642 1201

Piraeus
METAXAS MEMORIAL CANCER
   HOSPITAL
51 Botassi Street
Piraeus 30, Greece

Thessaloniki
THEAGENION MEDICAL INSTITUTE
2 Serron Street
Thessaloniki, Greece
Tel. (031) 832 311

GUATEMALA
Guatemala City
INSTITUTO DE CANCEROLOGIA
Guatemala Cancerology Institute
6a. Av. 6-58 zona 11
Guatemala City, Guatemala
Tel. 40-3-32 43-8-41

HUNGARY
Budapest
ORSZÁGOS ONKOLÓGIAI INTÉZET
Hungarian National Institute of
   Oncology
Ráth Gy. U. 7/9
1525 Budapest PF. 21 XII Hungary
Tel. 354-350

INDIA
Ahmedabad
GUJARET CANCER
   AND RESEARCH INSTITUTE
New Civil Hospital Campus
Asarwa, Ahmedabad 380 016, India
Tel. 66084, 66085-86

Bombay
TATA MEMORIAL CENTRE
Ernest Borges Marg
Parel, Bombay 400 012, India
Tel. 448341/441431

Hyderabad
M.N.J. CANCER HOSPITAL AND
   RADIUM INSTITUTE
11-4-720/1 Red Hills
Hyderabad 50004, India
Tel. 38421/32623

Madras
CANCER INSTITUTE (W.I.A.)
Canal Bank Road
Adyar, Madras 600020, India
Tel. 412714/412185/412926

IRAN
Tehran
TAJ PAHLAVI CANCER INSTITUTE
University of Tehran
P.O. Box 14/1154
Tehran, Iran
Tel. 920005

IRELAND
Dublin
SAINT ANNE'S CITY HOSPITAL FOR
  DISEASES OF THE SKIN AND CANCER
Northbrook Road
Dublin, 6, Ireland
Tel. 01-976778
ST. LUKE'S HOSP RADIOTHERAPY
  AND CLINICAL ONCOLÓGY CENTRE
"Oakland," Highfield Road
Rathgar, Dublin 6, Ireland
Tel. 01-974552

ITALY
Cagliari
OSPEDALE ONCOLOGICO
Cagliari Oncological Hospital
Via Jenner
Cagliari, Italy
Tel. 070-28 09 66

Milan
ISTITUTO NAZIONALE PER LO STUDIO
  E LA CURA DEI TUMORI
National Cancer Institute
Via G. Venezian 1
20133 Milan, Italy
Tel. 02-2390; 02-2366342

Naples
FOND. SEN PASCALE – IST. PER LO
  STUDIO E CURA DEI TUMORI
Sen. Pascale Found. Tumor Res. and
  Treatment Inst.
Cappella dei Cangiani Via M.
  Semmola
80131 Naples, Italy
Tel. 465466 255100 252465 252062 46To

Rome
REGINA ELENA INSTITUTE
Viale Regina Elena 291
00100 Rome, Italy

Turin
ISTITUTO DI ONCOLOGIA DI TORINO
Turin Oncological Institute
31 via Cavour
10123 Turin, Italy
Tel. 882666

JAPAN
Chiba
CHIBA UNIV. INST. OF PULMONARY
  CANCER RESEARCH
Inohana, 1-8-1
Chiba, Japan
Tel. 0472 (22) 7171
Nagoya
AICHI CANCER CENTER
81-1159 Kanokoden, Tashiro-Cho,
  Chikusa-Ku
Nagoya 464, Japan
Tel. (052) (762) 6111
Tokyo
KOKURITSU GAN CENTER
National Cancer Center
5-1-1 Tsukiji
Chuo-ku, 104 Tokyo, Japan
Tel. (03) 542-2511
TOKYO UNIV. INSTITUTE OF MEDICAL
  SCIENCE
P.O. Takanawa
Tokyo, Japan
Tel. Tokyo 443-8111
ZAIDANHOJIN GANNKENKYUKAI
Japanese Foundation for Cancer
  Research
Kami-Ikebukuro 1-37-1, Toshima-ku
Tokyo 170, Japan
Tel. (03) 918-0111

KOREA
Seoul
YONSEI CANCER CENTER
P.O. 1010
Seoul, Korea (Rep.)
Tel. Yonsei University Medical College

MEXICO
Mexico City
HOSPITAL DE ONCOLOGÍA, C.M.N.
C.M.N. Oncological Hospital
Av. Cuauhtémoc 330
Mexico 7, D.F., Mexico
Tel. 771-05-25
INSTITUTO NACIONAL DE
  CANCEROLOGÍA
National Cancer Institute

Av. Niños Héroes 151
Mexico City 7, Mexico
Tel. 578-60-51

NETHERLANDS
Amsterdam
NEDERLANDS KANKERINST. – A. VAN
  LEEUWENHOEK ZIEKENHUIS
Netherlands Cancer Inst. – A. van
  Leeuwenhoek Hospital
Sarphatistraat 108
Amsterdam, Netherlands
Tel. (0)20-253712
Groningen
UNIVERSITAIR KANKER CENTRUM
Groningen University Cancer Center
Academisch Ziekenhuis
Oostersingel 59
Groningen, Netherlands
Tel. 050-139123, app. 2317

NORWAY
Oslo
NORWEGIAN RADIUM HOSPITAL &
  NORSK HYDROS INST. FOR CANCER
  RESEARCH
Montebello
Oslo 3, Norway
Tel. 55 40 80

PERU
Lima
INSTITUTO NACIONAL DE
  ENFERMEDADES NEOPLÁSICAS
Peruvian National Neoplastic Disease
  Institute
Avenida Alfonso Ugarte 825
Lima, Peru
Tel 23-6979

POLAND
Gliwice
INSTYTUT ONKOLOGII GLIWICE
Gliwice Institute of Oncology
Wybrzeze Armi Czerwonej 15
44-100 Gliwice, Poland
Tel. 91-10-63

Cracow
INSTYTUT ONKOLOGII
Kraków Institute of Oncology
Garncarska 11
31-115 Cracow, Poland
Tel. 266-80
Poznan
WOJEWÓDZKI ZESPÓŻ SPECJALISTYCZNY
  CHERÓB PŻC I GRUŹLICY
Regional Chest Diseases Control
  Center
Szamarzewskiege 62, 60 569 Poznan
  Poland
Tel. 425-73 404-91
Warsaw
INSTYTUT ONKOLOGII IM M.
  SKOLODOWSKIEJ-CURIE
M. Sklodowska-Curie Memorial
  Institute of Oncology
15 Wawelska St.
02-034 Warsaw, Poland
Tel. 22-12-76

PORTUGAL
Lisbon
PORTUGUESE INST. OF ONCOLOGY –
  FRANCISCO GENTIL
rua Prof. Lima Basto
Lisbon 4, Portugal
Tel. 76 3140/9

PUERTO RICO
San Juan
PUERTO RICO UNIV. COMPREHENSIVE
  CANCER CENTER
University of Puerto Rico
P.O. Box 5067
San Juan 00936, Puerto Rico
Tel. (809) 763-2443 or 767-9626

ROMANIA
Bucharest
INSTITUTUL ONCOLOGIC
Oncological Institute
11 Bd. 1 May
P.B. 5916 Bucharest, Romania
Tel. 50.20.30 and 50.31.48

Cluj
INSTITUTUL ONCOLOGIC CLIJ – NAPOCA
Cluj-Napoca Oncological Institute
Strada Republicii Nr. 34-36
3400 Cluj-Napoca, Romania
Tel. 23920

SOUTH AFRICA
Bloemfontein
O.F.S. INSTITUTE OF ISOTOPES AND
   RADIATION
National Hospital
Bloemfontein, South Africa
Tel. 7-0411 Ext. 523

SPAIN
Valencia
INSTITUTO VALENCIANO DE ONCOLOGIA
Valencia Oncology Institute
Calle Prof. Beltran Baguena 19
Valencia 9, Spain
Tel. 3-66-82-00

THAILAND
Bangkok
THAI NATIONAL CANCER INSTITUTE
Rama VI Road
Bangkok 4, Thailand
Tel. 2822126

TUNISIA
Tunis
SALAH AZAIZ INSTITUTE
Boulevard du 9 avril
Bab Saadoun
Tunis, Tunisia
Tel. 260 622

TURKEY
Ankara
ANKARA ONKOLOJI HASTAHANESI VE
   ENISTITÜSÜ
Ankara Oncology Hospital and
   Institute
Etimesgut, Ankara, Turkey
Tel. 110182, 181207, 116682 and 251T

UNITED KINGDOM
London
INSTITUTE OF CANCER RESEARCH
34 Sumner Place
London SW7 3NU, England
Tel. 01-584-9122
ROYAL MARSDEN HOSPITAL
Fulham Road
London SW3, England
Tel. 01-352 8171
Manchester
CHRISTIE HOSPITAL AND HOLT RADIUM
   INST. AND PATERSON LABS.
Withington, Manchester M20 9BX
   England
Tel. 061-445 8123

UNITED STATES OF AMERICA
Alabama
UNIVERSITY OF ALABAMA IN
   BIRMINGHAM COMPREHENSIVE
   CANCER CENTER
University Station
Birmingham, Alabama 35294, USA
Tel. (205) 934-5077
California
CANCER RESEARCH INSTITUTE
1282 Moffitt Hospital
University of California
San Francisco, California 94143, USA
Tel. (415) 666-2201
LOS ANGELES COUNTY UNIV. OF
   SOUTHERN CAL. COMP. CANCER
   CENTER
2025 Zonal Avenue
Los Angeles, California 90033, USA
Tel. (213) 226-2008
SOUTHERN CALIFORNIA CANCER CENTER
1414 South Hope Street
Los Angeles, California 90015, USA
Tel. (213) 748-2411
UCLA CANCER CENTER
924 Westwood Boulevard, Suite 650
Los Angeles, California 90024, USA
Tel. (213) 825-1532
Connecticut
YALE COMPREHENSIVE CANCER CENTER
Yale-New Haven Med. Center

333 Cedar Street
New Haven, Connecticut 06510, USA
Tel. (203) 436-1736

District of Columbia

VINCENT T. LOMBARDI CANCER
  RESEARCH CENTER
Georgetown Univ. Med. Center
3800 Reservoir Road, N.W.
Washington, D.C. 20007, USA
Tel. (202) 625-7118

Florida

FLORIDA COMPREHENSIVE CANCER
  CENTER
P.O. Box 520875, 1400 N.W. 10th Ave.
Miami, Florida, USA
Tel. (305) 547-6096

Kentucky

LOUISVILLE REGIONAL CANCER CENTER
Walnut and Preston Streets
Louisville, Kentucky 40201, USA
Tel. (502) 588-5245

Maryland

JOHNS HOPKINS UNIVERSITY
  ONCOLOGY CENTER
Johns Hopkins Hospital
332 Carnegie Building
Baltimore, Maryland 21205, USA
Tel. (301) 955-3300

Massachusetts

BOSTON UNIV. CANCER RESEARCH
  CENTER
Boston Univ. Med. Center
80 East Concord Street
Boston, Massachusetts 02118, USA
Tel. (617) 262-4200

NEW ENGLAND DEACONESS HOSP.
  CANCER RESEARCH INST
  & Shields Warren Radiation Lab.
135 Pilgrim Road
Boston, Massachusetts 02215, USA
Tel. (617) 734-7000

SIDNEY FARBER CANCER CENTER
35 Binney Street
Boston, Massachusetts 02115, USA
Tel. (617) 739-1100

Michigan

MICHIGAN CANCER FOUNDATION
110 East Warren Avenue

Detroit, Michigan 48201, USA
Tel. (313) 833-0710

Minnesota

MAYO COMPREHENSIVE CANCER CENTER
200 First Street, S.W.
Rochester, Minnesota 55901, USA
Tel. (507) 282-2511

New York

BETH ISRAEL MEDICAL CENTER
10 Nathan D. Perlman Place
New York, New York 10003, USA
Tel. (212) 673-3000

MEMORIAL SLOAN-KETTERING CANCER
  CENTER
1275 York Avenue
New York, New York 10021, USA
Tel. (212) 794-7000

ROSWELL PARK MEMORIAL INSTITUTE
666 Elm Street
Buffalo, New York 14263, USA
Tel. (716) 845-2300

North Carolina

DUKE COMPREHENSIVE CANCER CENTER
P.O. Box 3814, Duke Univ. Medical
  Center
Durham, North Carolina 27710, USA
Tel. (919) 684-2282

Pennsylvania

FOX CHASE CANCER CENTER
7701 Burholme Avenue
Philadelphia, Pennsylvania 19111,
  USA
Tel. (215) 342-1000

Texas

UNIV. OF TEXAS SYST. CANCER CENTER,
  M.D. ANDERSON HOSP. AND
  TUMOR INST.
Texas Medical Center
Houston, Texas 77025, USA
Tel. (713) 792-2121

Washington

FRED HUTCHINSON CANCER RESEARCH
  CENTER
1124 Columbia
Seattle, Washington 98104, USA
Tel. (206) 292-2912

Wisconsin

WISCONSIN CLINICAL CANCER CENTER

701C University Hospitals
1300 University Avenue
Madison, Wisconsin 53706, USA
Tel. (608) 263-2553

URUGUAY
Montevideo
INSTITUTO DE RADIOLOGÍA
Montevideo Institute of Radiology
Bulevar Artigas No. 1550
Montevideo, Uruguay
Tel. 798889

USSR
Alma-Ata
KAŽAHSKIJ NII ONKOLOGII I RADIOLOGII
Kazakhstan Cancer and Radiology
  Research Institute
91 Abai Avenue
480072 Alma-Ata, USSR
Tel. 671064
Ashchabad
TURKMENSKIJ NII ONKOLOGII
Turkmenistan Cancer Research
  Institute
53 Pervomajskaja
744012 Ashchabad, USSR
Tel. 54480
Baku
BAKU RES. INST. OF ROENTGENOLOGY,
  RADIOLOGY & ONCOLOGY
Block 3161
Bagdasar Avakyan Street
370102 Baku, USSR
Erevan
EREVAN INST. OF ROENTGENOLOGY &
  ONCOLOGY
8 Tumanyan Street
Erevan, USSR
Tel. 58-26-83 and 52-27-71
Frunze
KIRGHIZ RESEARCH INST. OF
  ONCOLOGY & RADIOLOGY
92, 50-year October Street
Frunze, USSR
Tel. 4-42-45
Kiev
KIEVSKIJ NII RENTGENO-

RADIOLOGIČESKIJ ONKOLOGIČESKIJ
Kiev Roentgen-Radiology and
  Cancer Research Institute
41 Lomonosov Street
252022 Kiev, USSR
Tel. 63-10-09
Kishinev
MOLDAVSKIJ NII ONKOLOGII
Moldavian Cancer Research Institute
30 Stepnaya Street
277025 Kishinev, USSR
Tel. Ministry of Health, Moldavian T
Leningrad
NII ONKOLOGII IM PROF. N.N. PETROVA
Prof. N. N. Petrov Research Institute
  of Oncology
68 Leningradskaya Street
Pesochny-2, Leningrad 188646, USSR
Tel. 44-90-06
Minsk
BIELORUSKIJ NII ONKOLOGII I
  MEDICINSKOJ RADIOLOGII
Byelorussian Cancer and Medical
  Radiology Research Institute
Lesnoe, Minsk, USSR
Tel. 699595
Moscow
ONKOLOGIČESKIJ INSTITUT IM P.A.
  GERCENA
P.A. Gersten Cancer Institute
Vtoroy Botkinsky projezd, 3
125284 Moscow, USSR
Tel. 253-29-09
ONKOLOGIČESKIJ NAUČNYJ CENTR
USSR Academy of Medical Sciences,
Cancer Research Center
Kashirskoye sh. 6
115478 Moscow, USSR
Tel. 111-83-71
Obninsk
INSTITUT MEDICINSKOJ RADIOLOGII
USSR Acad. of Med. Sciences Inst. of
  Med. Radiology
Koroleva 4
249020 Obninsk, USSR
Tel. 136-39-53
Rostov-on-Don
ROSTOVSKIJ NII ONKOLOGII

Rostov Cancer Research Institute
14 Linya Street
344037 Rostov-on-Don, USSR
Tel. 5-53-38
Tashkent
UZBEKSKIJ NII ONKOLOGII I RADIOLOGII
Uzbekistan Cancer and Radiology
  Research Institute
383 Chigatai Street
700000 Tashkent, USSR
Tel. 460512
Tbilisi
GRUSINSKIJ NII ONKOLOGII
Georgian Cancer Research Institute
21 Pavlov Street
Tbilisi, USSR
Tel. 371934
Vilnius
LITOVSKIJ NII ONKOLOGII
Lithuanian Cancer Research Institute
2 Polosko Street
232007 Vilnius, USSR
Tel. 29667

VENEZUELA
Caracas
HOSPITAL ONCOLÓGICO "PADRE
  MACHADO"
"Padre Machado" Oncological
  Hospital
Calle El Degredo
Los Castaños El Cementerio
Caracas DF Venezuela
Tel. 617749-618211-616092

VIETNAM
Ghia-Dinh
INSTITUT NATIONAL DU CANCER
Vietnam National Cancer Institute
3 Nguyên van Hoc
Ghia-Dinh, Vietnam
Tel. 23853
Ho Chi Minh City
INSTITUT DU CANCER DU VIET-NAM

Vietnam Cancer Institute
68 Doàn thi Diêm
Ho Chi Minh City 3, Vietnam
Tel. 24326

YUGOSLAVIA
Belgrade
INSTITUT "KSENOFON ŠAHOVIĆ"
"Ksenofon Šahović" Institute
Pasterova 14
11000 Belgrade, Yugoslavia
Tel. 685-059
Ljubljana
ONKOLOŠKI INSTITUT
Ljubljana Institute of Oncology
Zaloška cesta 2, p.p. 17
61105 Ljubljana, Yugoslavia
Tel. 323063, 316490
Novi Sad
NOVI SAD INST. ZA ONK. KLIN. BOLNICE
Novi Sad Inst. of Oncology and
  Clinical Hosp.
Branimira Ćosića 37
21000 Novi Sad, Yugoslavia
Tel. 021/21-174
Rijeka
ZAVOD ZA RADIOTERAPIJU I
  ONKOLOGIJU
Rijeka Institute of Radiotherapy and
  Oncology
Kidrićeva 44
51000 Rijeka, Yugoslavia
Tel. 22-065, 22-066
Zagreb
SREDIŠNJI INSTITUT ZA TUMORE I
  SLIČNE BOLESTI
Croatian Central Institute for Tumors
  and Allied Diseases
Ilica 197,41000 Zagreb, Yugoslavia
Tel. 572-111 or 573-216
ZAGREB UNIVERSITY ONCOLOGICAL
  SCHOOL
Šalata 3, 41000 Zagreb, Yugoslavia

SELECTED READING LIST

AGRAN, LARRY *The Cancer Connection: And What We Can Do About It.* Boston: Houghton Mifflin, 1977.

AMERICAN CANCER SOCIETY *Unproven Methods of Cancer Management.* New York: American Cancer Society, 1971. [Originally published in a shorter version as *Unproven Methods of Cancer Treatment.* New York: American Cancer Society, 1966]

BRODY, JANE E., with HOLLEB, ARTHUR I. *You Can Fight Cancer and Win.* New York: Quadrangle/New York Times Book Co., 1976/77; New York: McGraw-Hill (paperback), 1978.

BURN, IAN, and LL MEYRICK, ROGER *Understanding Cancer: A Guide for the Caring Professions.* London: Her Majesty's Stationery Office, 1977.

"Cashing In on Fear: The Selling of Cancer Insurance." *Consumer Reports,* 43:6 (June, 1978), 336–8.

CORBETT, THOMAS H. *Cancer and Chemicals.* Chicago: Nelson-Hall, 1977.

GLEMSER, BERNARD *Man Against Cancer.* New York: Funk & Wagnalls, 1969; London: Bodley Head, 1969.

GOODFIELD, JUNE *Cancer Under Siege.* London: Hutchinson, 1975. *The Siege of Cancer.* New York: Random House, 1975; New York: Dell (Laurel paperback), 1976. [American edition of *Cancer Under Siege*]

HARRIS, R[OBERT] J[OHN] C[ECIL] *Cancer: The Nature of the Problem.* Harmondsworth (England) and Baltimore: Penguin Books, 1962; 1964 rev. ed.; 1976 rev. ed. [Pelican Books, no. A549]

HINTON, JOHN *Dying* Harmondsworth (England) and Baltimore: Penguin Books, 1967; 1972 rev. ed. [Pelican Books, no. A866]

ISRAËL, LUCIEN *Conquering Cancer,* translated from the French by Joan Pinkham. New York: Random House, 1978. [French edition: *Le Cancer aujourd'hui.* Paris: Bernard Grasset (Editions Grasset & Fasquelle), 1976]

KÜBLER-ROSS, ELISABETH *On Death and Dying.* New York: Macmillan, 1969; London: Tavistock Publications, 1970. *Questions and Answers on*

Death and Dying. New York: Macmillan, 1974.

MCGRADY, PAT *The Savage Cell: A Report on Cancer and Cancer Research.* New York: Basic Books, 1964.

MAPLE, ERIC *Magic, Medicine & Quackery.* London: Robert Hale, 1968; South Brunswick, N.J.: A. S. Barnes, 1968.

PRESCOTT, DAVID M. *Cancer: The Misguided' Cell.* Indianapolis and New York: Pegasus, 1973.

SAUNDERS, CECILY Selected papers, available from St. Christopher's Hospice, 51–3 Lawrie Park Road, London SE26.

SHIMKIN, MICHAEL B. *Contrary to Nature.* Washington: U.S. Department of Health, Education, and Welfare, Public Health Service, National Institutes of Health, 1977. *Science and Cancer.* Bethesda, Maryland: U.S. Department of Health, Education, and Welfare, Public Health Service, National Cancer Institute, 1964; Bethesda, Maryland: U.S. National Cancer Institute, 1969 rev. ed.; Washington: U.S. Department of Health, Education, and Welfare, Public Health Service, National Institutes of Health, National Cancer Institute, 1973/74 rev. ed.

STODDARD, SANDOL *The Hospice Movement: A Better Way of Caring for the Dying.* Briarcliff Manor, N.Y.: Stein and Day, 1977/78.

THOMAS, LEWIS *The Lives of a Cell: Notes of a Biology Watcher.* New York: The Viking Press, 1974; New York: Bantam (paperback), 1975.

TWYCROSS, R. G. *The Dying Patient.* London: C[hristian] M[edical] F[ellowship] Publications, 1975.

WHELAN, ELIZABETH *Preventing Cancer.* New York: W. W. Norton, 1978.

INDEX